BLACK HAMMER

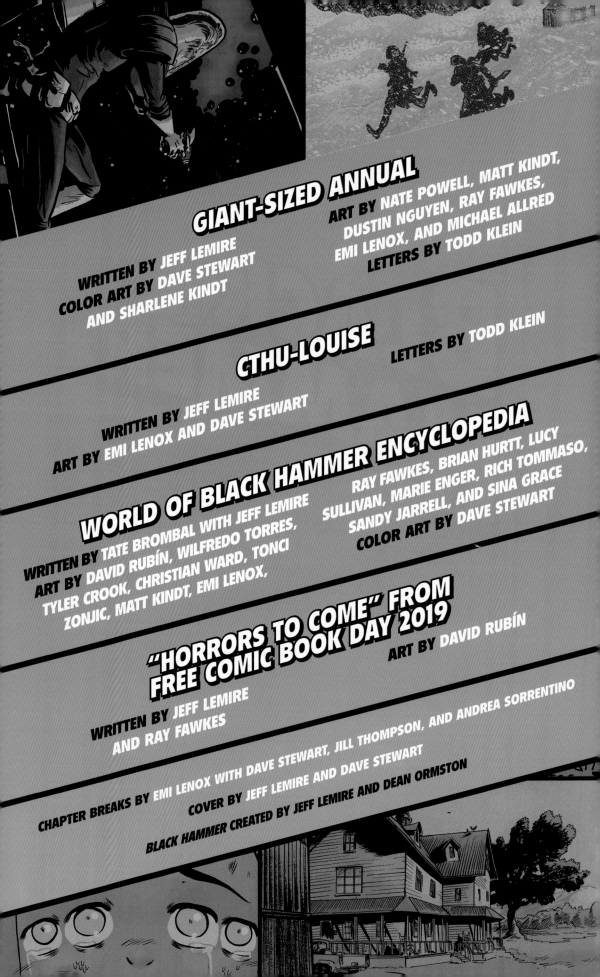

GIANT-SIZED ANNUAL

WRITTEN BY JEFF LEMIRE
COLOR ART BY DAVE STEWART
AND SHARLENE KINDT

ART BY NATE POWELL, MATT KINDT,
DUSTIN NGUYEN, RAY FAWKES,
EMI LENOX, AND MICHAEL ALLRED
LETTERS BY TODD KLEIN

CTHU-LOUISE

LETTERS BY TODD KLEIN

WRITTEN BY JEFF LEMIRE
ART BY EMI LENOX AND DAVE STEWART

WORLD OF BLACK HAMMER ENCYCLOPEDIA

WRITTEN BY TATE BROMBAL WITH JEFF LEMIRE
ART BY DAVID RUBÍN, WILFREDO TORRES,
TYLER CROOK, CHRISTIAN WARD, TONCI
ZONJIC, MATT KINDT, EMI LENOX,

RAY FAWKES, BRIAN HURTT, LUCY
SULLIVAN, MARIE ENGER, RICH TOMMASO,
SANDY JARRELL, AND SINA GRACE
COLOR ART BY DAVE STEWART

"HORRORS TO COME" FROM FREE COMIC BOOK DAY 2019

ART BY DAVID RUBÍN

WRITTEN BY JEFF LEMIRE
AND RAY FAWKES

CHAPTER BREAKS BY EMI LENOX WITH DAVE STEWART, JILL THOMPSON, AND ANDREA SORRENTINO

COVER BY JEFF LEMIRE AND DAVE STEWART

BLACK HAMMER CREATED BY JEFF LEMIRE AND DEAN ORMSTON

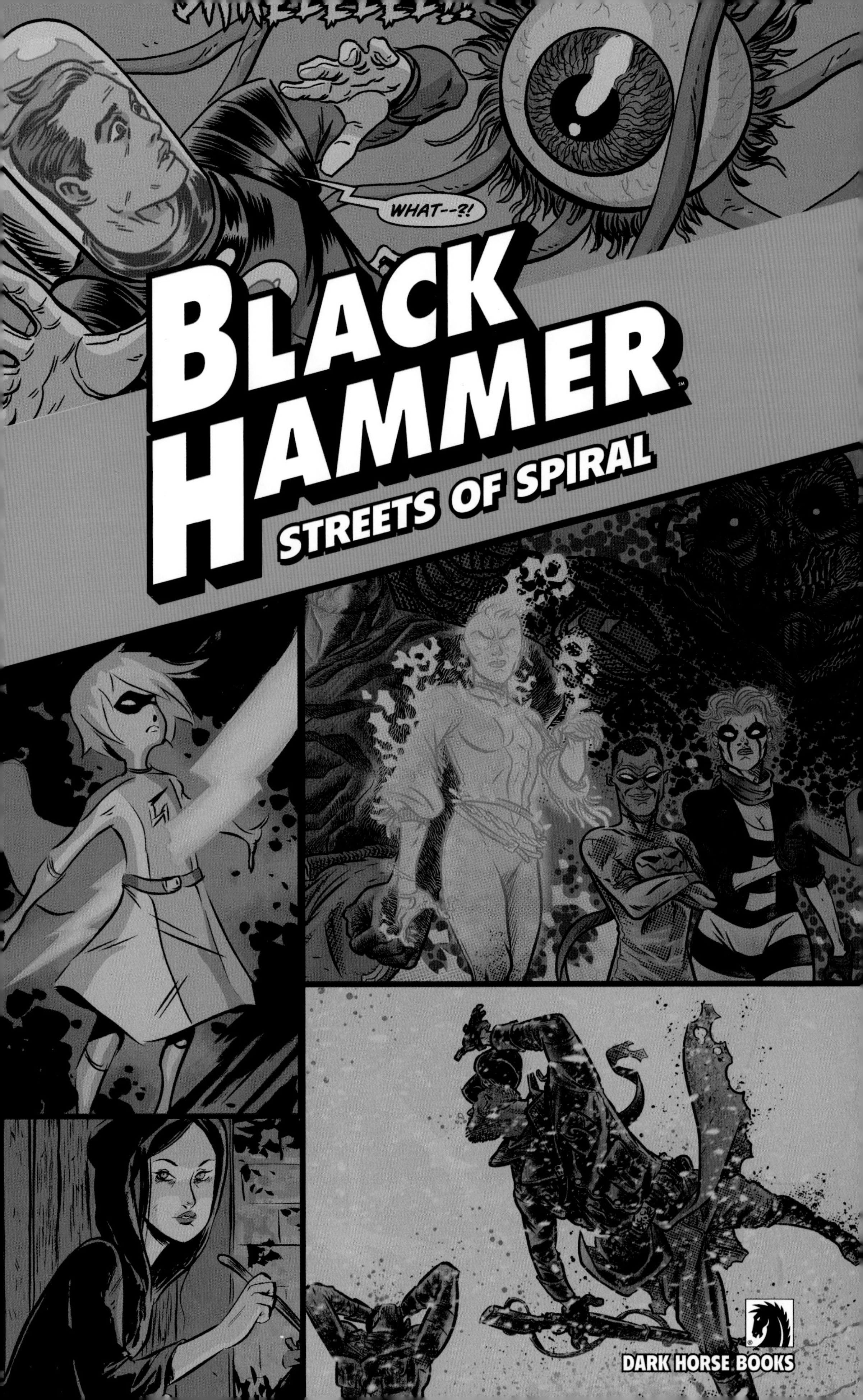
WHAT--?!
BLACK HAMMER
STREETS OF SPIRAL
DARK HORSE BOOKS

PRESIDENT AND PUBLISHER
MIKE RICHARDSON

EDITOR
DANIEL CHABON

ASSISTANT EDITORS
**CHUCK HOWITT,
BRETT ISRAEL, AND
CARDNER CLARK**

DESIGNER
ETHAN KIMBERLING

DIGITAL ART TECHNICIAN
JOSIE CHRISTENSEN

BLACK HAMMER: STREETS OF SPIRAL

Collects: *Black Hammer: Giant Sized Annual, Black Hammer: Cthu-Louise, World of Black Hammer Encyclopedia*,
and material from *Free Comic Book Day 2019*.

Library of Congress Cataloging-in-Publication Data

Names: Lemire, Jeff, writer. | Powell, Nate, artist. | Lenox, Emi, artist. |
  Rubin, David, 1977- artist.
Title: Black Hammer : streets of spiral / written by Jeff Lemire [and others]
  ; art by Nate Powell, Emi Lenox, David Rubin [and others].
Description: First edition. | Milwaukie, OR : Dark Horse Books, 2019. |
  "Black Hammer created by Jeff Lemire and Dean Ormston."
Identifiers: LCCN 2019018729 | ISBN 9781506709413 (pbk.)
Subjects: LCSH: Comic books, strips, etc.
Classification: LCC PN6728.B51926 L39 2019 | DDC 741.5/973--dc23
LC record available at https://lccn.loc.gov/2019018729

Published by
Dark Horse Books
A division of Dark Horse Comics LLC
10956 SE Main Street
Milwaukie, OR 97222

DarkHorse.com

To find a comics shop in your area, visit comicshoplocator.com

First edition: September 2019
978-1-50670-941-3

10 9 8 7 6 5 4 3 2 1
Printed in China

NEIL HANKERSON Executive Vice President TOM WEDDLE Chief Financial Officer RANDY STRADLEY Vice
President of Publishing NICK McWHORTER Chief Business Development Officer DALE LaFOUNTAIN Chief
Information Officer MATT PARKINSON Vice President of Marketing CARA NIECE Vice President of Production
and Scheduling MARK BERNARDI Vice President of Book Trade and Digital Sales KEN LIZZI General Counsel
DAVE MARSHALL Editor in Chief DAVEY ESTRADA Editorial Director CHRIS WARNER Senior Books Editor CARY
GRAZZINI Director of Specialty Projects LIA RIBACCHI Art Director VANESSA TODD-HOLMES Director of Print
Purchasing MATT DRYER Director of Digital Art and Prepress MICHAEL GOMBOS Senior Director of Licensed
Publications KARI YADRO Director of Custom Programs KARI TORSON Director of International Licensing SEAN
BRICE Director of Trade Sales

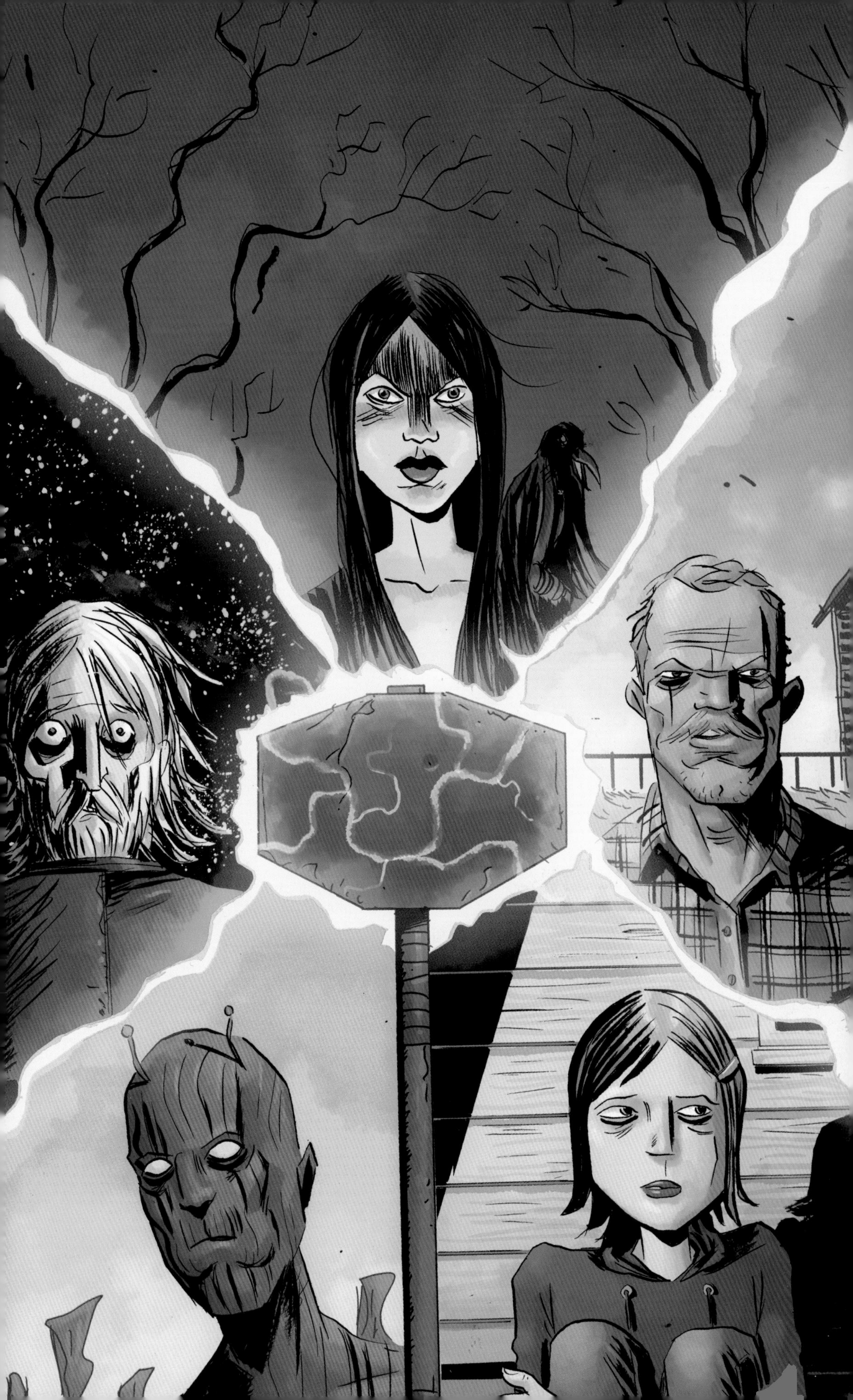

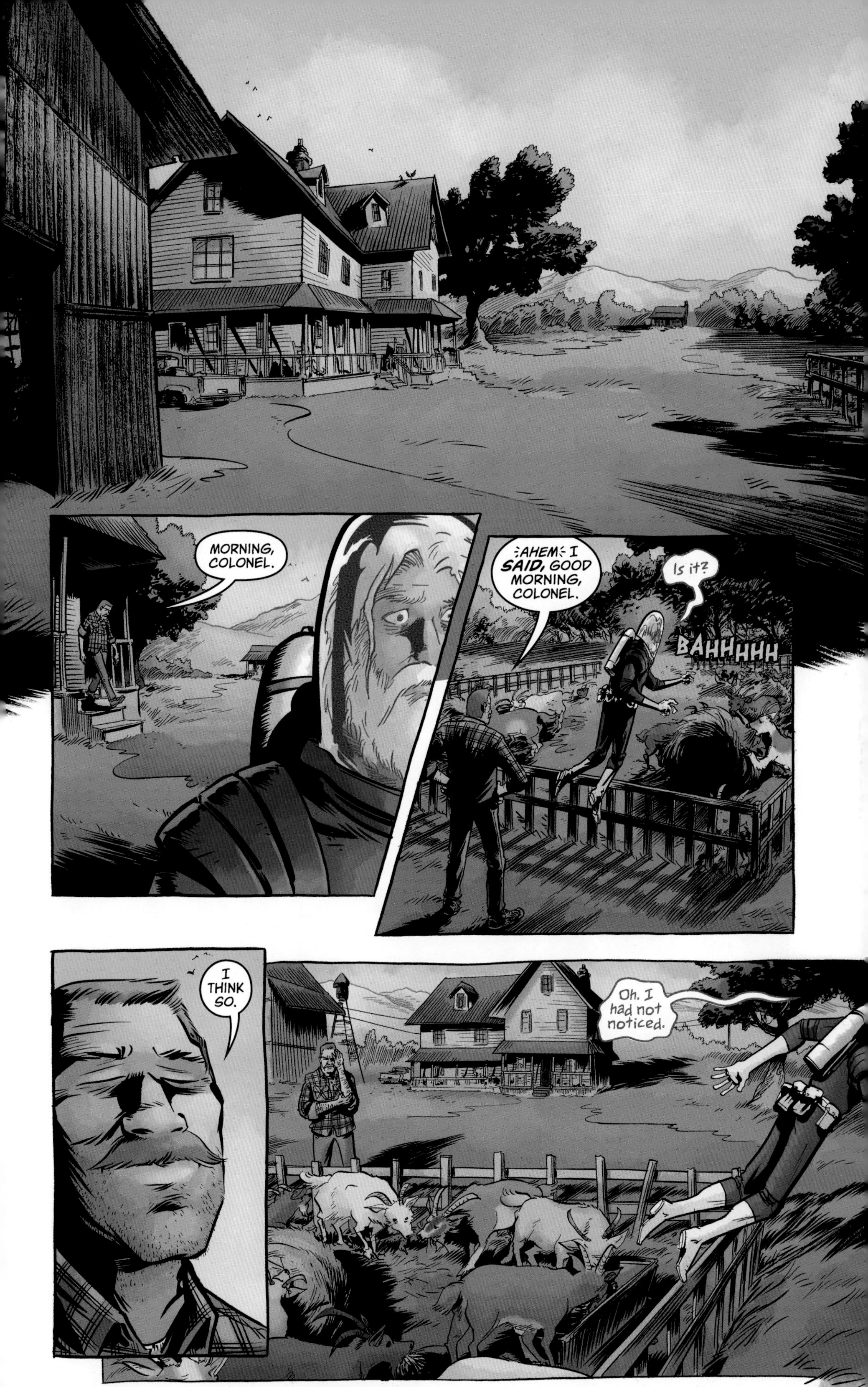
MORNING, COLONEL.
AHEM I SAID, GOOD MORNING, COLONEL.
Is it?
BAHHHHH
I THINK SO.
Oh. I had not noticed.

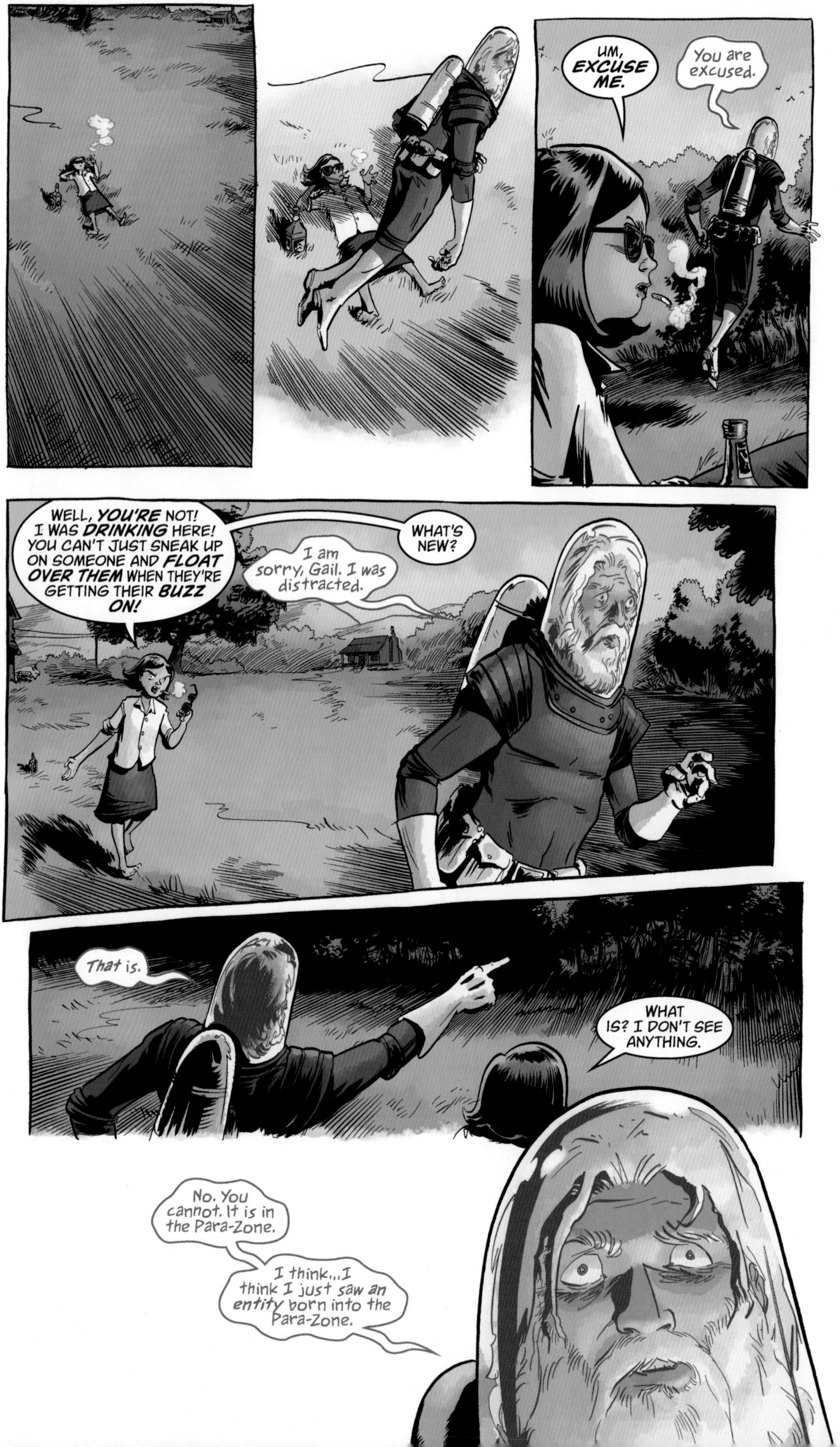
UM, EXCUSE ME.
You are excused.
WELL, YOU'RE NOT! I WAS DRINKING HERE! YOU CAN'T JUST SNEAK UP ON SOMEONE AND FLOAT OVER THEM WHEN THEY'RE GETTING THEIR BUZZ ON!
WHAT'S NEW?
I am sorry, Gail. I was distracted.
That is.
WHAT IS? I DON'T SEE ANYTHING.
No. You cannot. It is in the Para-Zone.
I think...I think I just saw an entity born into the Para-Zone.

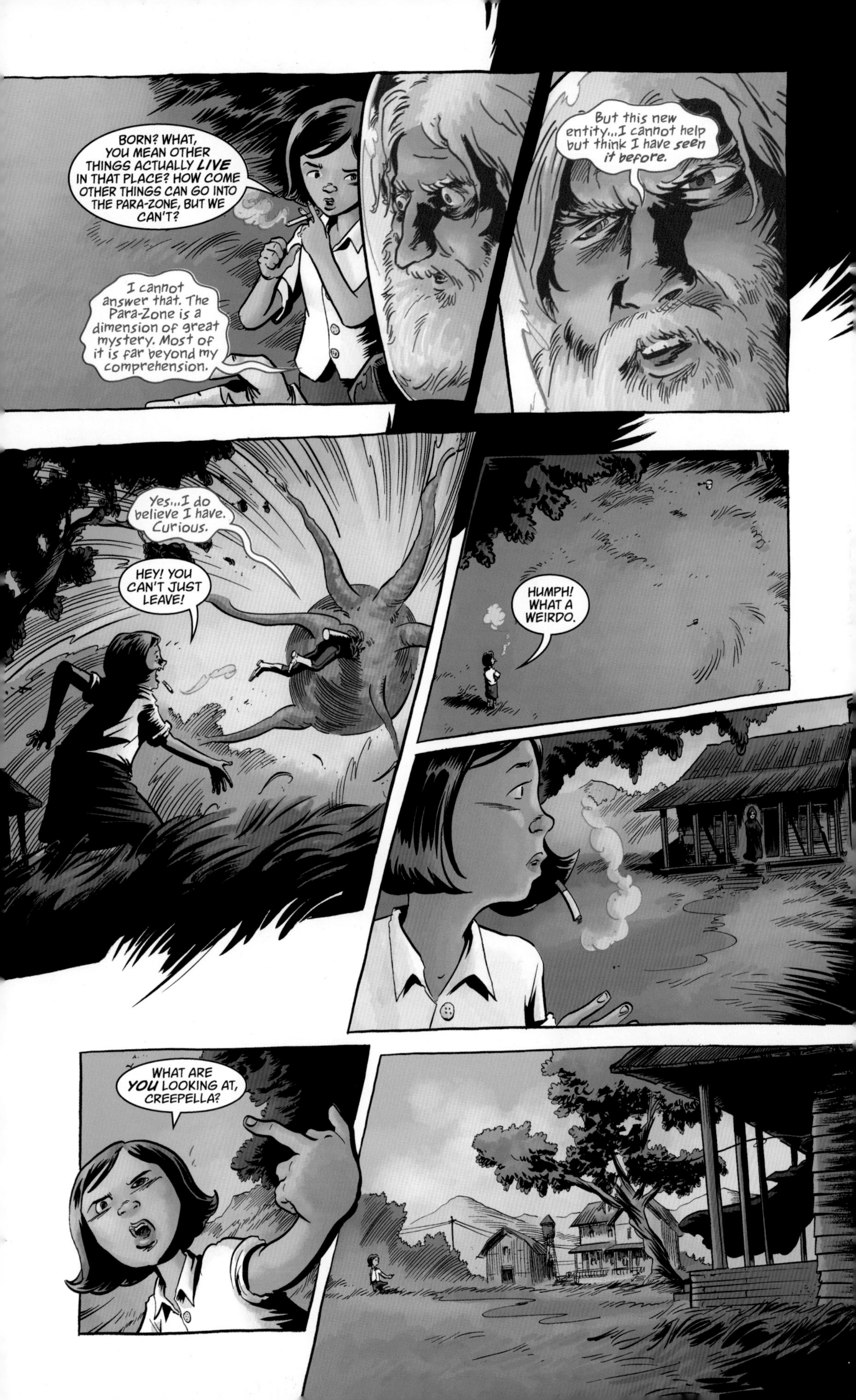
BORN? WHAT, YOU MEAN OTHER THINGS ACTUALLY LIVE IN THAT PLACE? HOW COME OTHER THINGS CAN GO INTO THE PARA-ZONE, BUT WE CAN'T?
I cannot answer that. The Para-Zone is a dimension of great mystery. Most of it is far beyond my comprehension.
But this new entity...I cannot help but think I have seen it before.
Yes...I do believe I have. Curious.
HEY! YOU CAN'T JUST LEAVE!
HUMPH! WHAT A WEIRDO.
WHAT ARE YOU LOOKING AT, CREEPELLA?

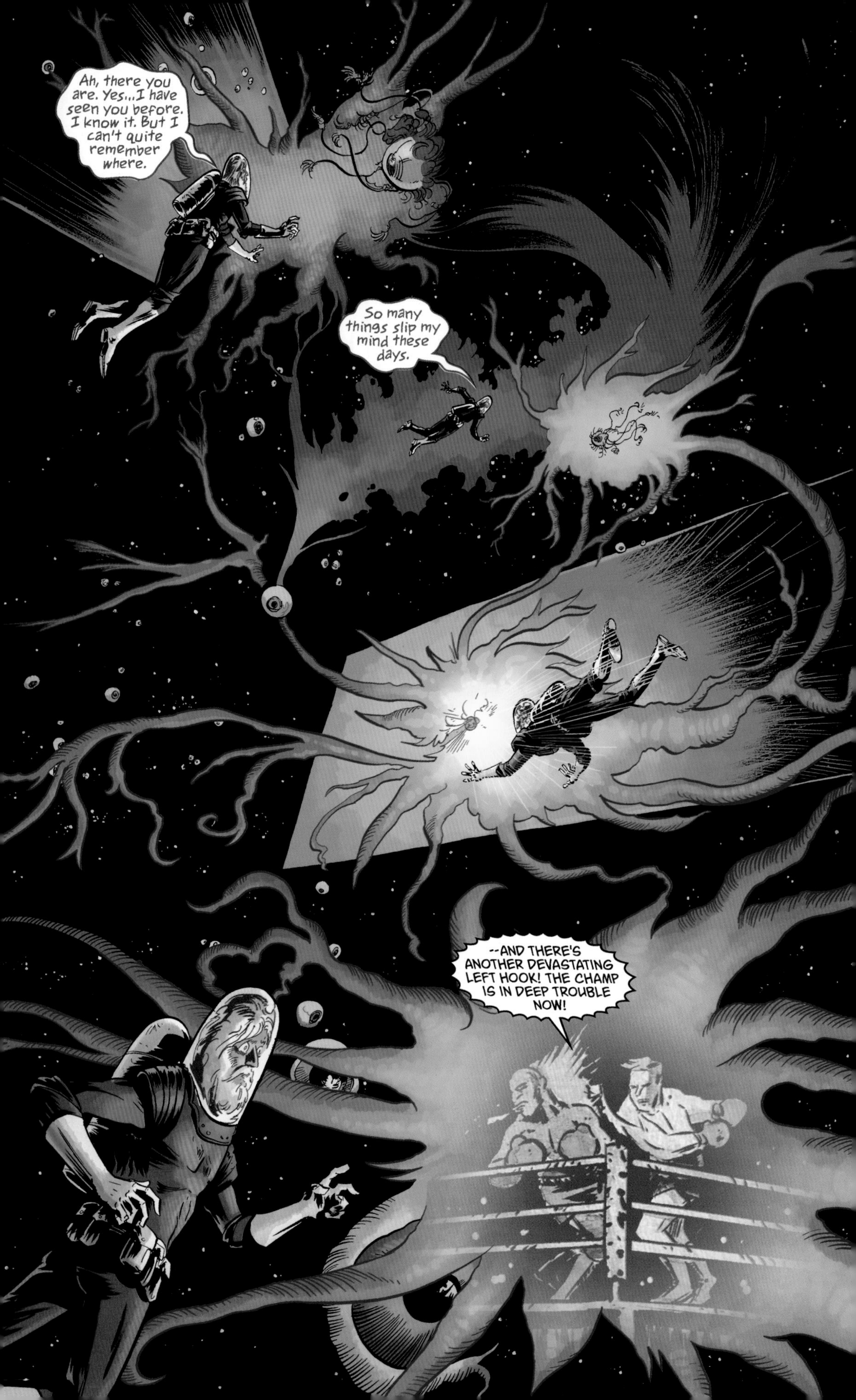
Ah, there you are. Yes...I have seen you before. I know it. But I can't quite remember where.
So many things slip my mind these days.
--AND THERE'S ANOTHER DEVASTATING LEFT HOOK! THE CHAMP IS IN DEEP TROUBLE NOW!

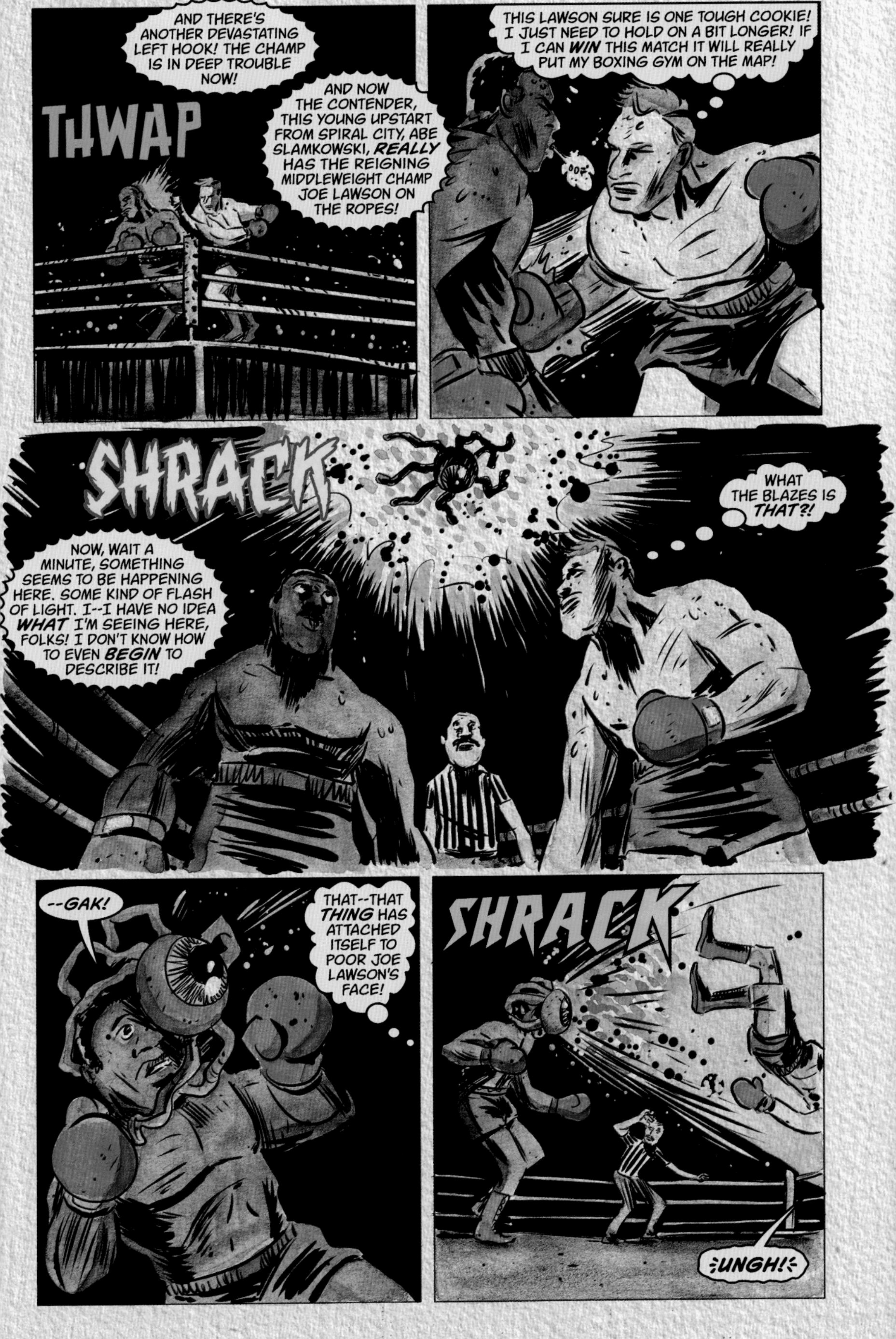
AND THERE'S ANOTHER DEVASTATING LEFT HOOK! THE CHAMP IS IN DEEP TROUBLE NOW!
THWAP
AND NOW THE CONTENDER, THIS YOUNG UPSTART FROM SPIRAL CITY, ABE SLAMKOWSKI, REALLY HAS THE REIGNING MIDDLEWEIGHT CHAMP JOE LAWSON ON THE ROPES!
THIS LAWSON SURE IS ONE TOUGH COOKIE! I JUST NEED TO HOLD ON A BIT LONGER! IF I CAN WIN THIS MATCH IT WILL REALLY PUT MY BOXING GYM ON THE MAP!
OOF
SHRACK
WHAT THE BLAZES IS THAT?!
NOW, WAIT A MINUTE, SOMETHING SEEMS TO BE HAPPENING HERE. SOME KIND OF FLASH OF LIGHT. I--I HAVE NO IDEA WHAT I'M SEEING HERE, FOLKS! I DON'T KNOW HOW TO EVEN BEGIN TO DESCRIBE IT!
--GAK!
THAT--THAT THING HAS ATTACHED ITSELF TO POOR JOE LAWSON'S FACE!
SHRACK
UNGH!

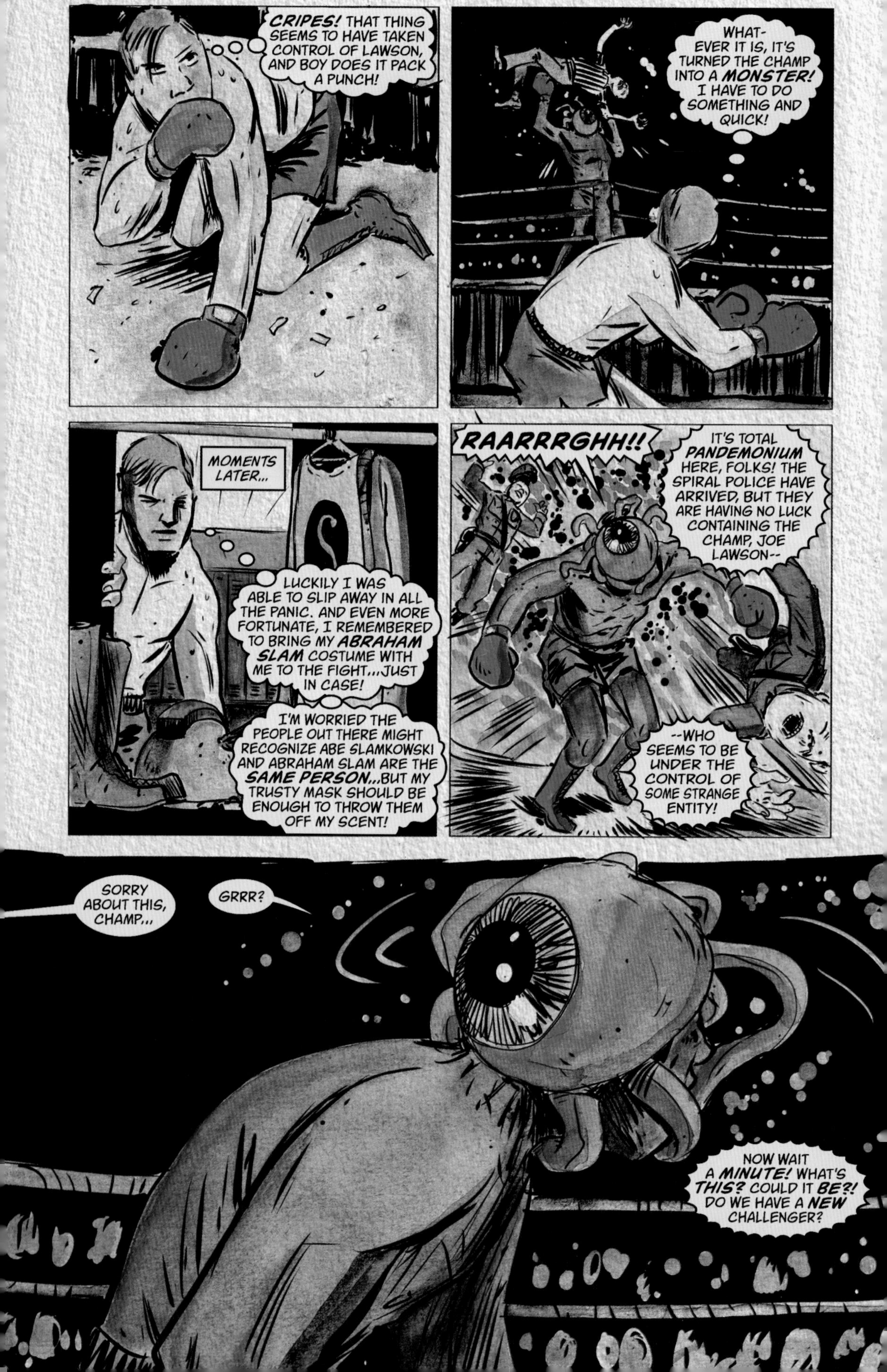
CRIPES! THAT THING SEEMS TO HAVE TAKEN CONTROL OF LAWSON, AND BOY DOES IT PACK A PUNCH!
WHAT-EVER IT IS, IT'S TURNED THE CHAMP INTO A MONSTER! I HAVE TO DO SOMETHING AND QUICK!
MOMENTS LATER...
LUCKILY I WAS ABLE TO SLIP AWAY IN ALL THE PANIC. AND EVEN MORE FORTUNATE, I REMEMBERED TO BRING MY ABRAHAM SLAM COSTUME WITH ME TO THE FIGHT...JUST IN CASE!
I'M WORRIED THE PEOPLE OUT THERE MIGHT RECOGNIZE ABE SLAMKOWSKI AND ABRAHAM SLAM ARE THE SAME PERSON...BUT MY TRUSTY MASK SHOULD BE ENOUGH TO THROW THEM OFF MY SCENT!
RAARRRGHH!!
IT'S TOTAL PANDEMONIUM HERE, FOLKS! THE SPIRAL POLICE HAVE ARRIVED, BUT THEY ARE HAVING NO LUCK CONTAINING THE CHAMP, JOE LAWSON--
--WHO SEEMS TO BE UNDER THE CONTROL OF SOME STRANGE ENTITY!
SORRY ABOUT THIS, CHAMP...
GRRR?
NOW WAIT A MINUTE! WHAT'S THIS? COULD IT BE?! DO WE HAVE A NEW CHALLENGER?

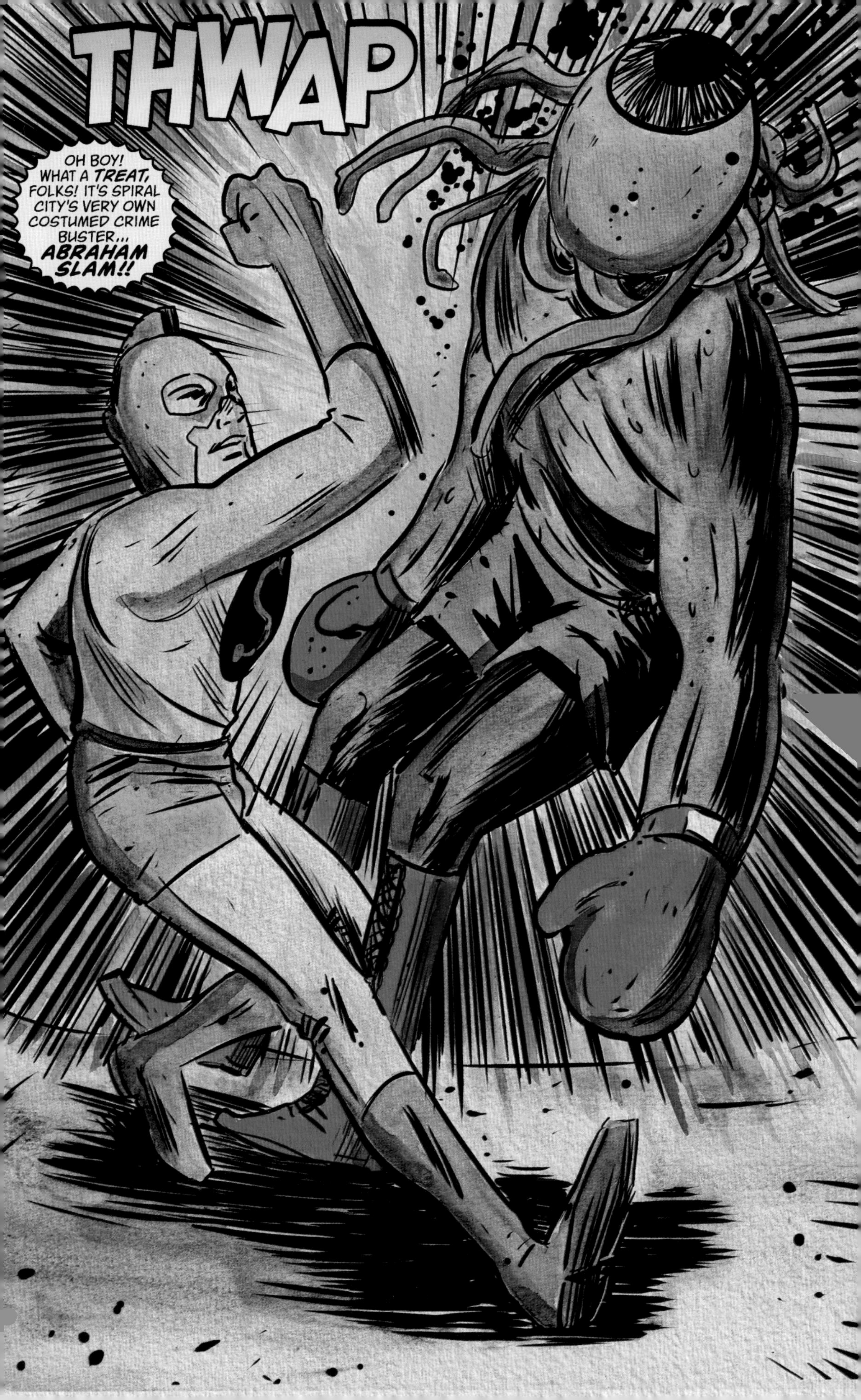
THWAP
OH BOY! WHAT A TREAT, FOLKS! IT'S SPIRAL CITY'S VERY OWN COSTUMED CRIME BUSTER... ABRAHAM SLAM!!

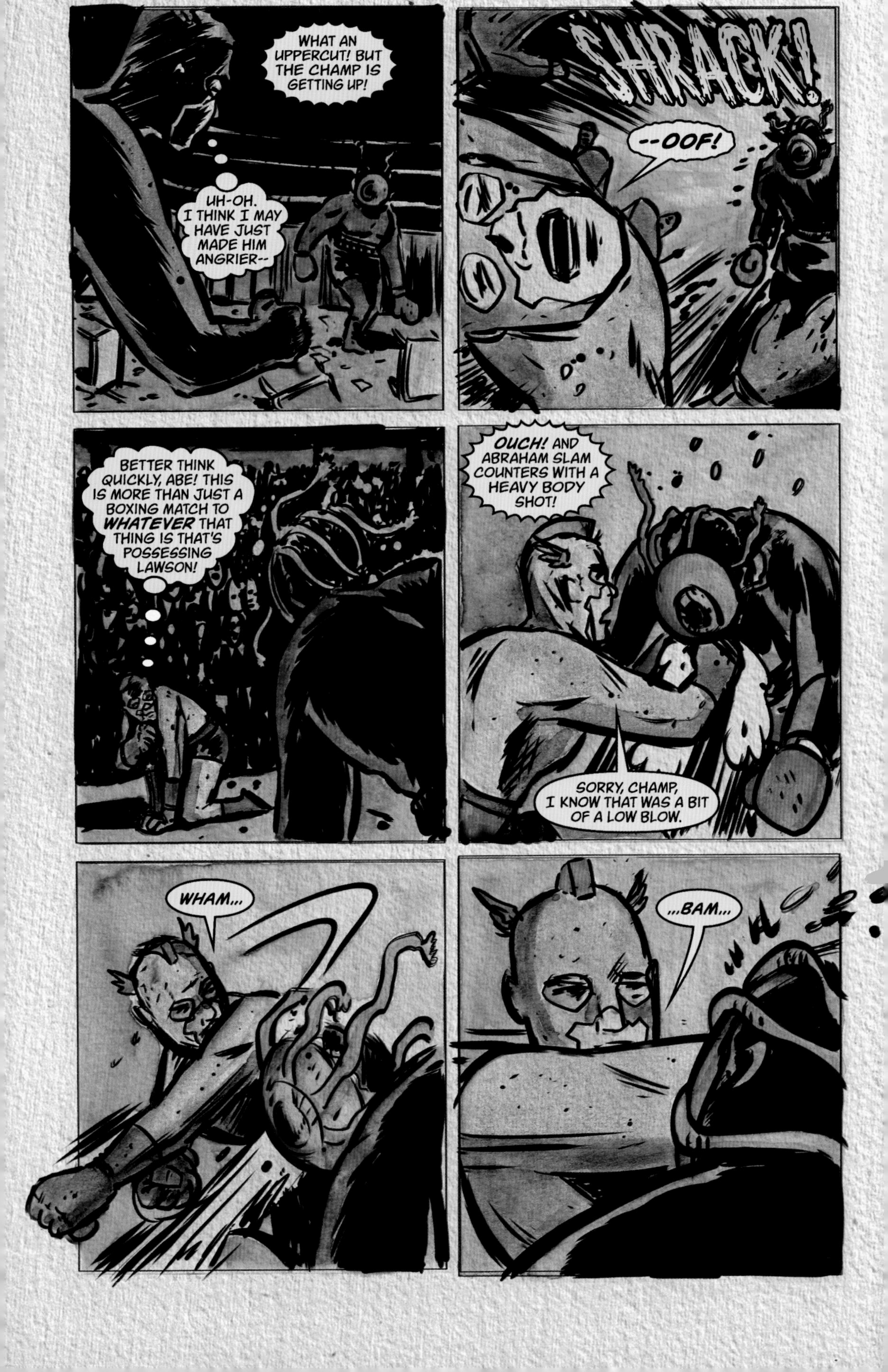
WHAT AN UPPERCUT! BUT THE CHAMP IS GETTING UP!
UH-OH. I THINK I MAY HAVE JUST MADE HIM ANGRIER--
SHRACK!
--OOF!
BETTER THINK QUICKLY, ABE! THIS IS MORE THAN JUST A BOXING MATCH TO WHATEVER THAT THING IS THAT'S POSSESSING LAWSON!
OUCH! AND ABRAHAM SLAM COUNTERS WITH A HEAVY BODY SHOT!
SORRY, CHAMP, I KNOW THAT WAS A BIT OF A LOW BLOW.
WHAM...
...BAM...

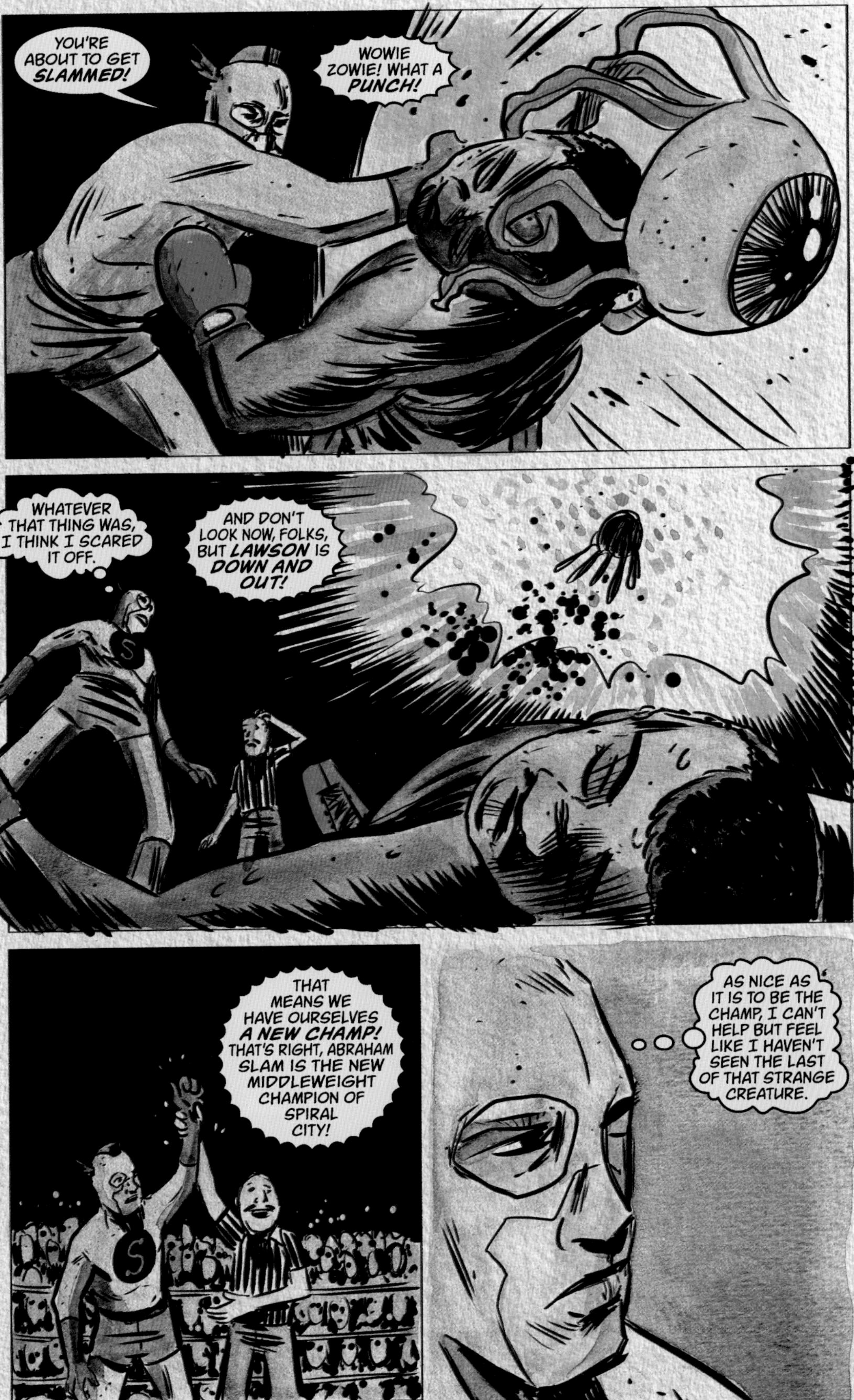
YOU'RE ABOUT TO GET SLAMMED!
WOWIE ZOWIE! WHAT A PUNCH!
WHATEVER THAT THING WAS, I THINK I SCARED IT OFF.
AND DON'T LOOK NOW, FOLKS, BUT LAWSON IS DOWN AND OUT!
THAT MEANS WE HAVE OURSELVES A NEW CHAMP! THAT'S RIGHT, ABRAHAM SLAM IS THE NEW MIDDLEWEIGHT CHAMPION OF SPIRAL CITY!
AS NICE AS IT IS TO BE THE CHAMP, I CAN'T HELP BUT FEEL LIKE I HAVEN'T SEEN THE LAST OF THAT STRANGE CREATURE.

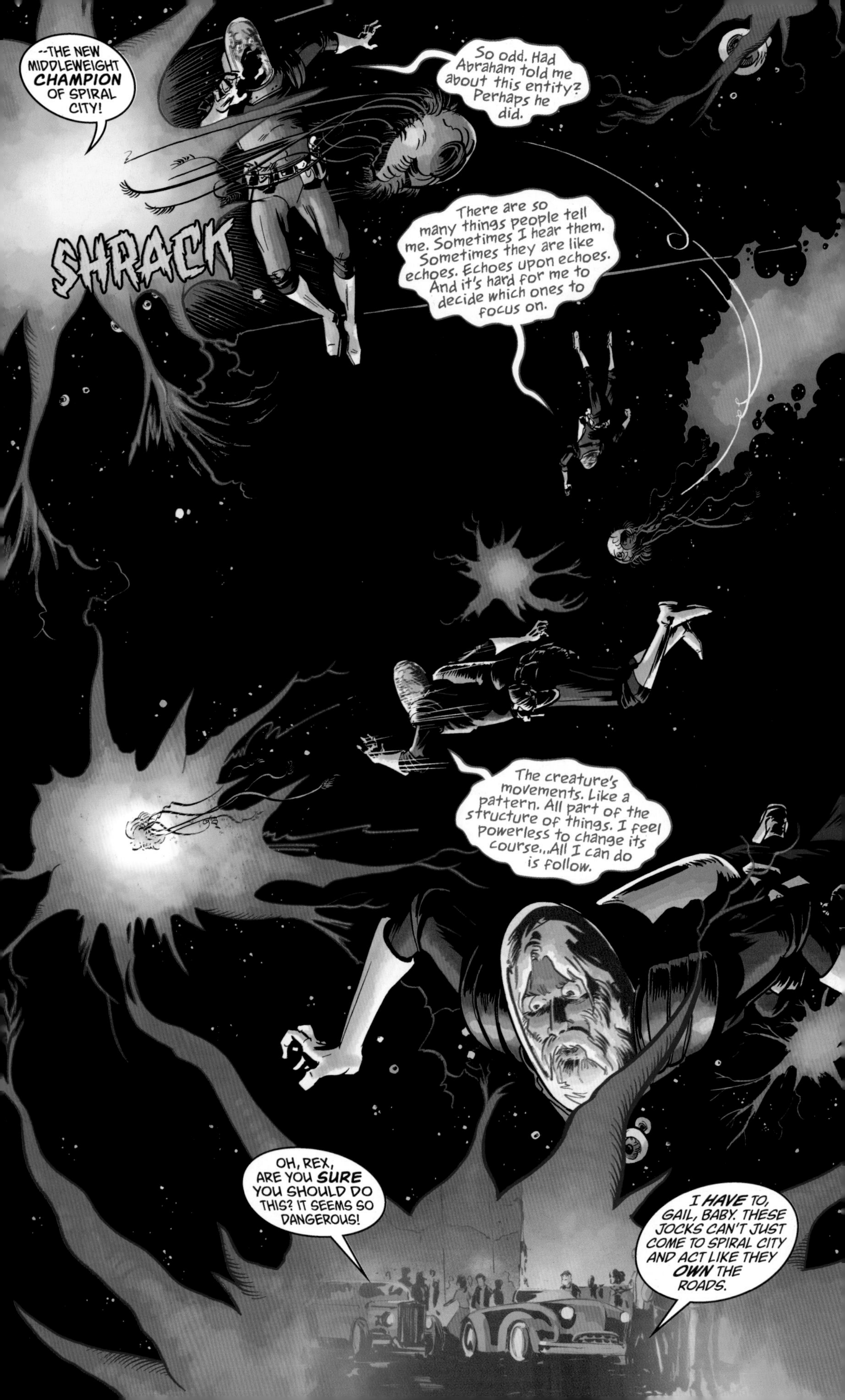
--THE NEW MIDDLEWEIGHT **CHAMPION** OF SPIRAL CITY!
So odd. Had Abraham told me about this entity? Perhaps he did.
SHRACK
There are so many things people tell me. Sometimes I hear them. Sometimes they are like echoes. Echoes upon echoes. And it's hard for me to decide which ones to focus on.
The creature's movements. Like a pattern. All part of the structure of things. I feel powerless to change its course...All I can do is follow.
OH, REX, ARE YOU **SURE** YOU SHOULD DO THIS? IT SEEMS SO DANGEROUS!
I ***HAVE*** TO, GAIL, BABY. THESE JOCKS CAN'T JUST COME TO SPIRAL CITY AND ACT LIKE THEY ***OWN*** THE ROADS.

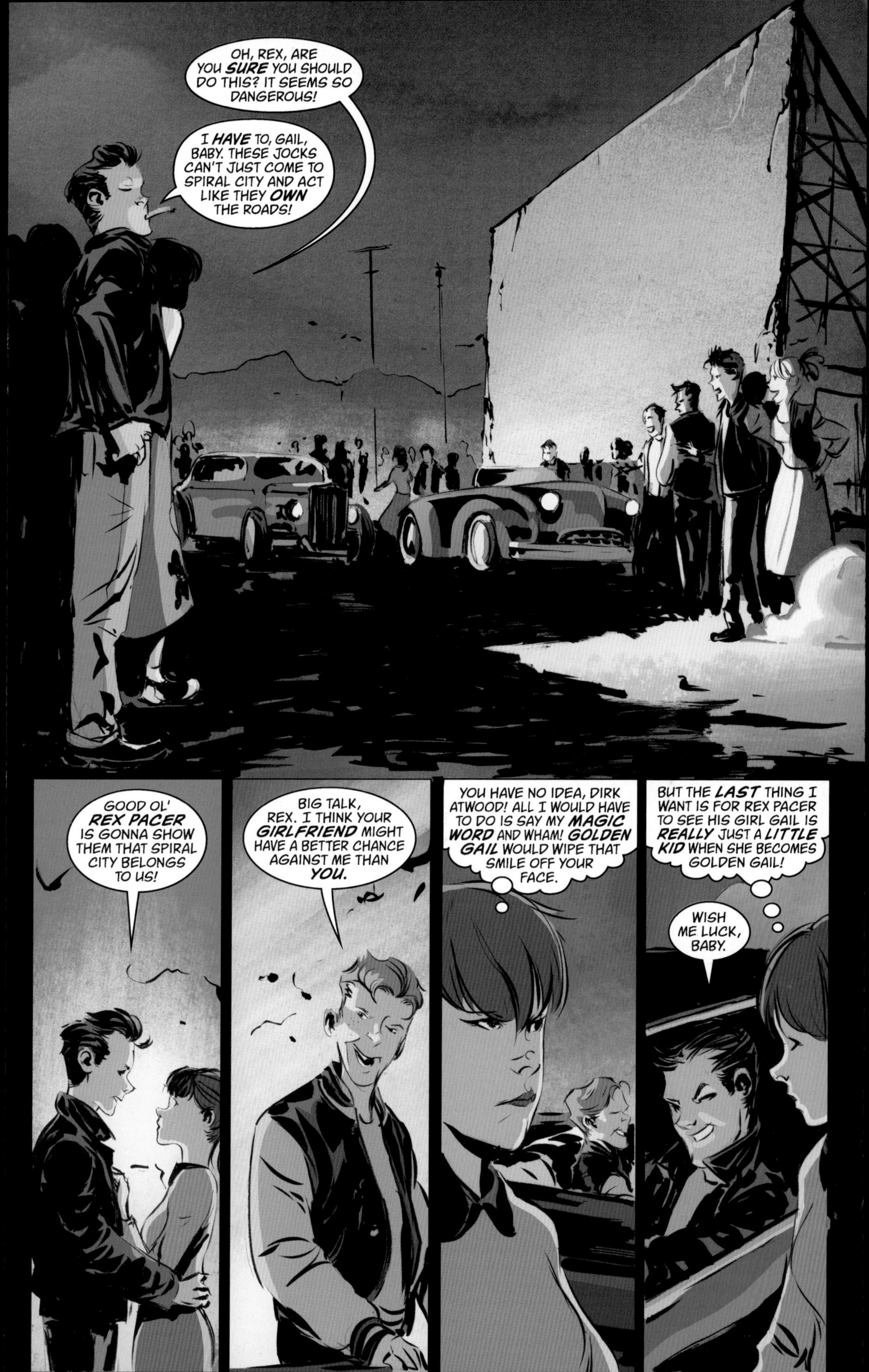
OH, REX, ARE YOU SURE YOU SHOULD DO THIS? IT SEEMS SO DANGEROUS!
I HAVE TO, GAIL, BABY. THESE JOCKS CAN'T JUST COME TO SPIRAL CITY AND ACT LIKE THEY OWN THE ROADS!
GOOD OL' REX PACER IS GONNA SHOW THEM THAT SPIRAL CITY BELONGS TO US!
BIG TALK, REX. I THINK YOUR GIRLFRIEND MIGHT HAVE A BETTER CHANCE AGAINST ME THAN YOU.
YOU HAVE NO IDEA, DIRK ATWOOD! ALL I WOULD HAVE TO DO IS SAY MY MAGIC WORD AND WHAM! GOLDEN GAIL WOULD WIPE THAT SMILE OFF YOUR FACE.
BUT THE LAST THING I WANT IS FOR REX PACER TO SEE HIS GIRL GAIL IS REALLY JUST A LITTLE KID WHEN SHE BECOMES GOLDEN GAIL!
WISH ME LUCK, BABY.

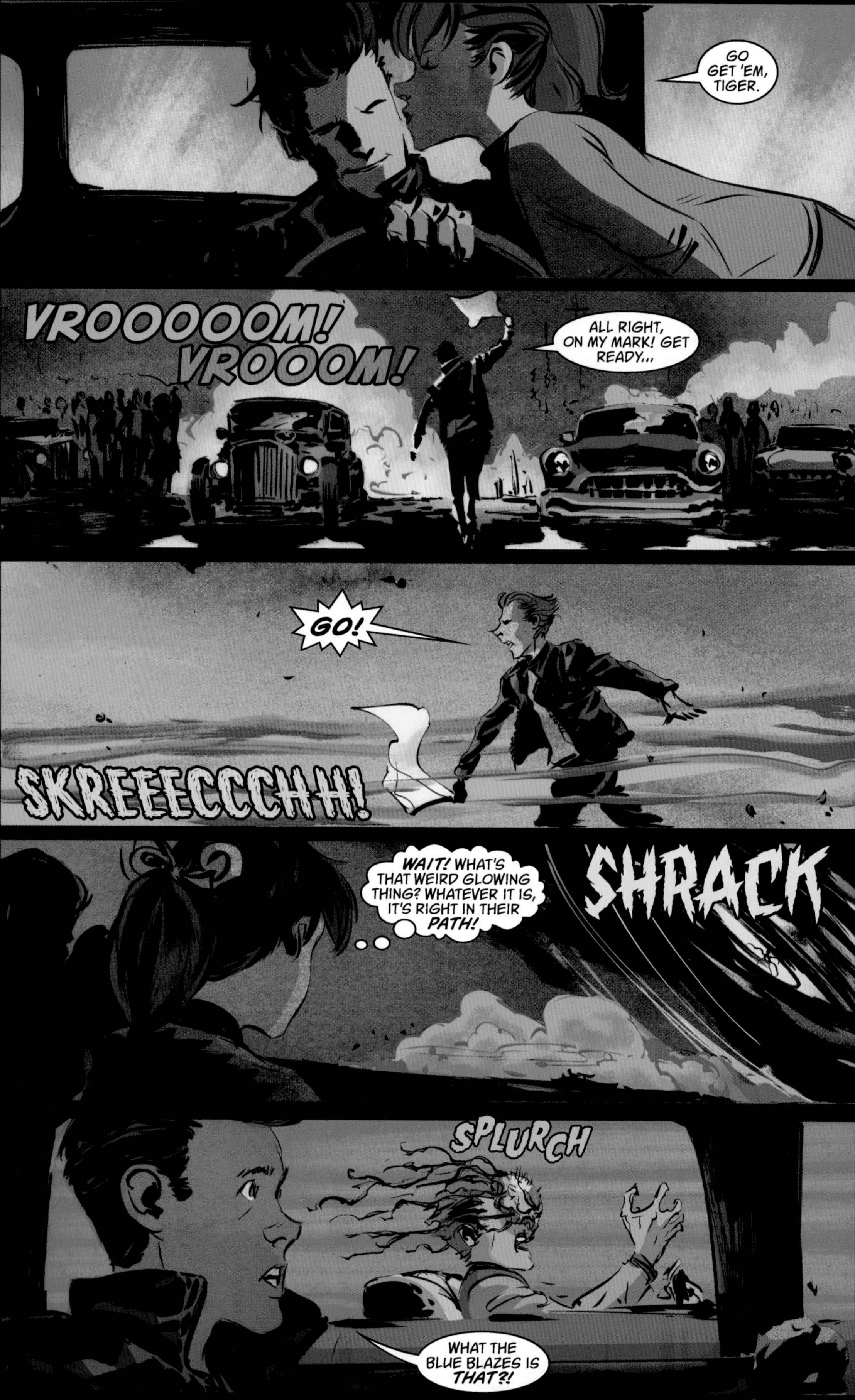

GO GET 'EM, TIGER.
VROOOOOM! VROOOM!
ALL RIGHT, ON MY MARK! GET READY...
GO!
SKREEEECCCHH!
WAIT! WHAT'S THAT WEIRD GLOWING THING? WHATEVER IT IS, IT'S RIGHT IN THEIR PATH!
SHRACK
SPLURCH
WHAT THE BLUE BLAZES IS THAT?!

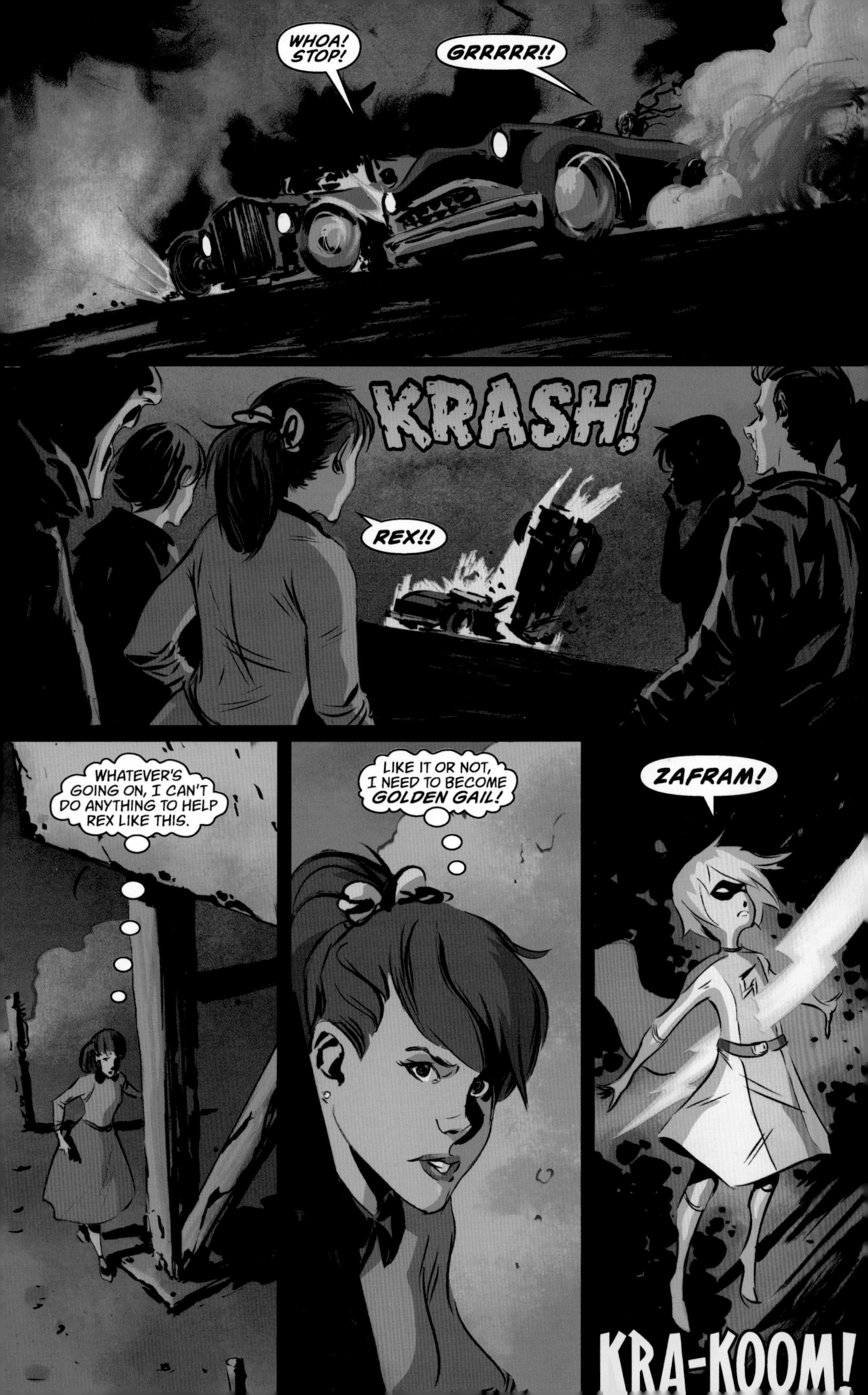
WHOA! STOP!
GRRRRR!!
KRASH!
REX!!
WHATEVER'S GOING ON, I CAN'T DO ANYTHING TO HELP REX LIKE THIS.
LIKE IT OR NOT, I NEED TO BECOME GOLDEN GAIL!
ZAFRAM!
KRA-KOOM!

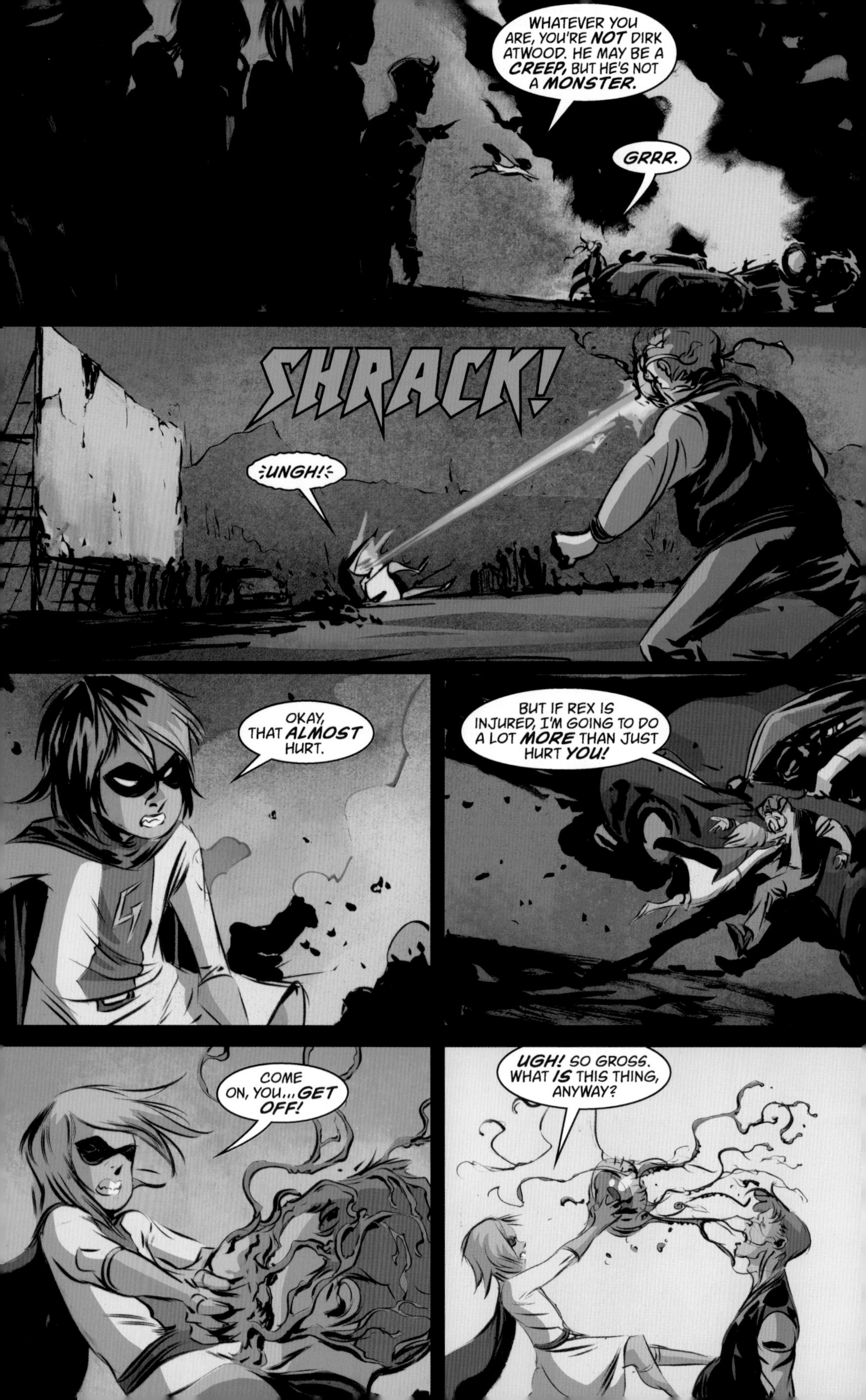
WHATEVER YOU ARE, YOU'RE NOT DIRK ATWOOD. HE MAY BE A CREEP, BUT HE'S NOT A MONSTER.
GRRR.
SHRACK!
UNGH!
OKAY, THAT ALMOST HURT.
BUT IF REX IS INJURED, I'M GOING TO DO A LOT MORE THAN JUST HURT YOU!
COME ON, YOU...GET OFF!
UGH! SO GROSS. WHAT IS THIS THING, ANYWAY?

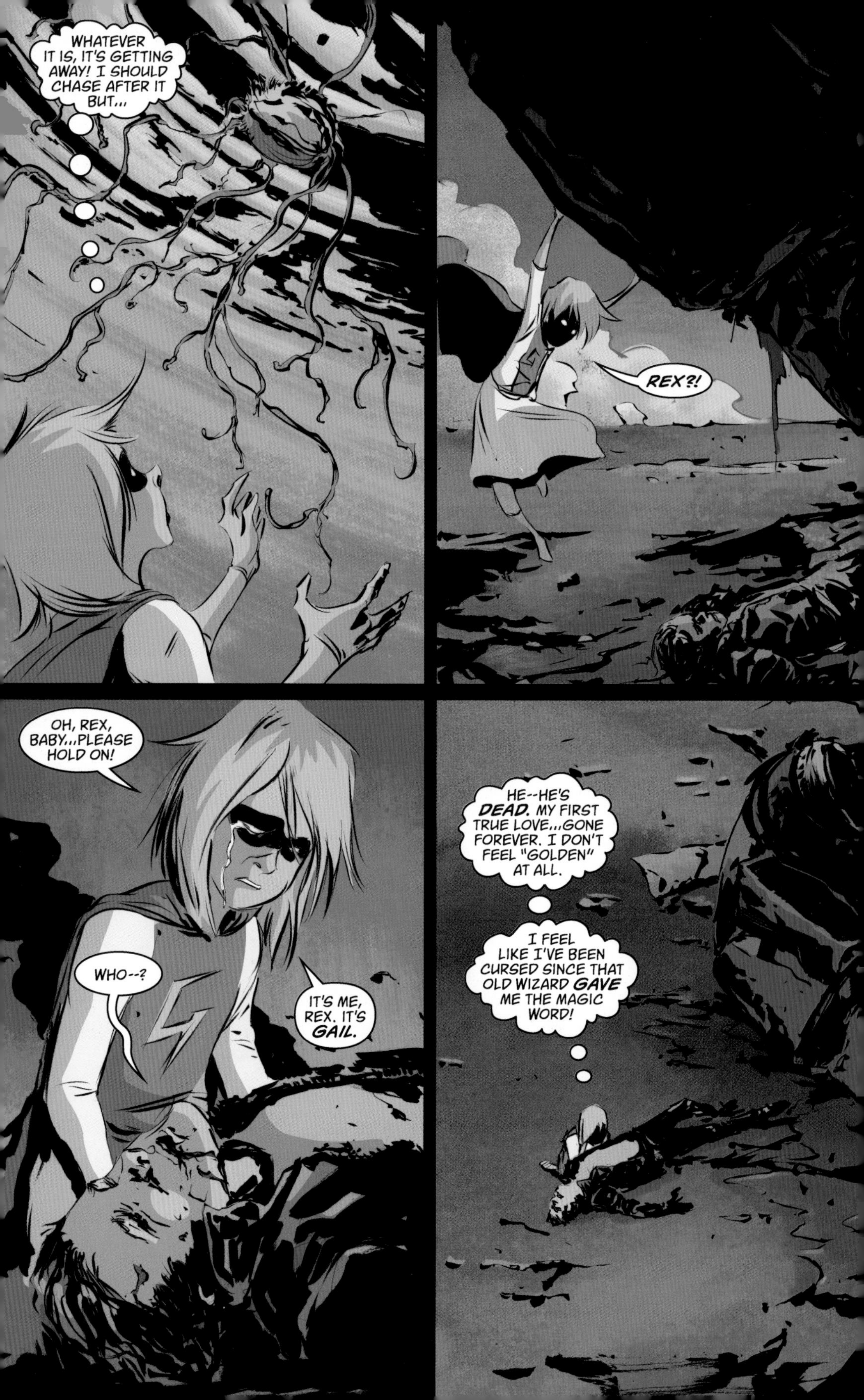
WHATEVER IT IS, IT'S GETTING AWAY! I SHOULD CHASE AFTER IT BUT...
REX?!
OH, REX, BABY...PLEASE HOLD ON!
WHO--?
IT'S ME, REX. IT'S GAIL.
HE--HE'S DEAD. MY FIRST TRUE LOVE...GONE FOREVER. I DON'T FEEL "GOLDEN" AT ALL.
I FEEL LIKE I'VE BEEN CURSED SINCE THAT OLD WIZARD GAVE ME THE MAGIC WORD!

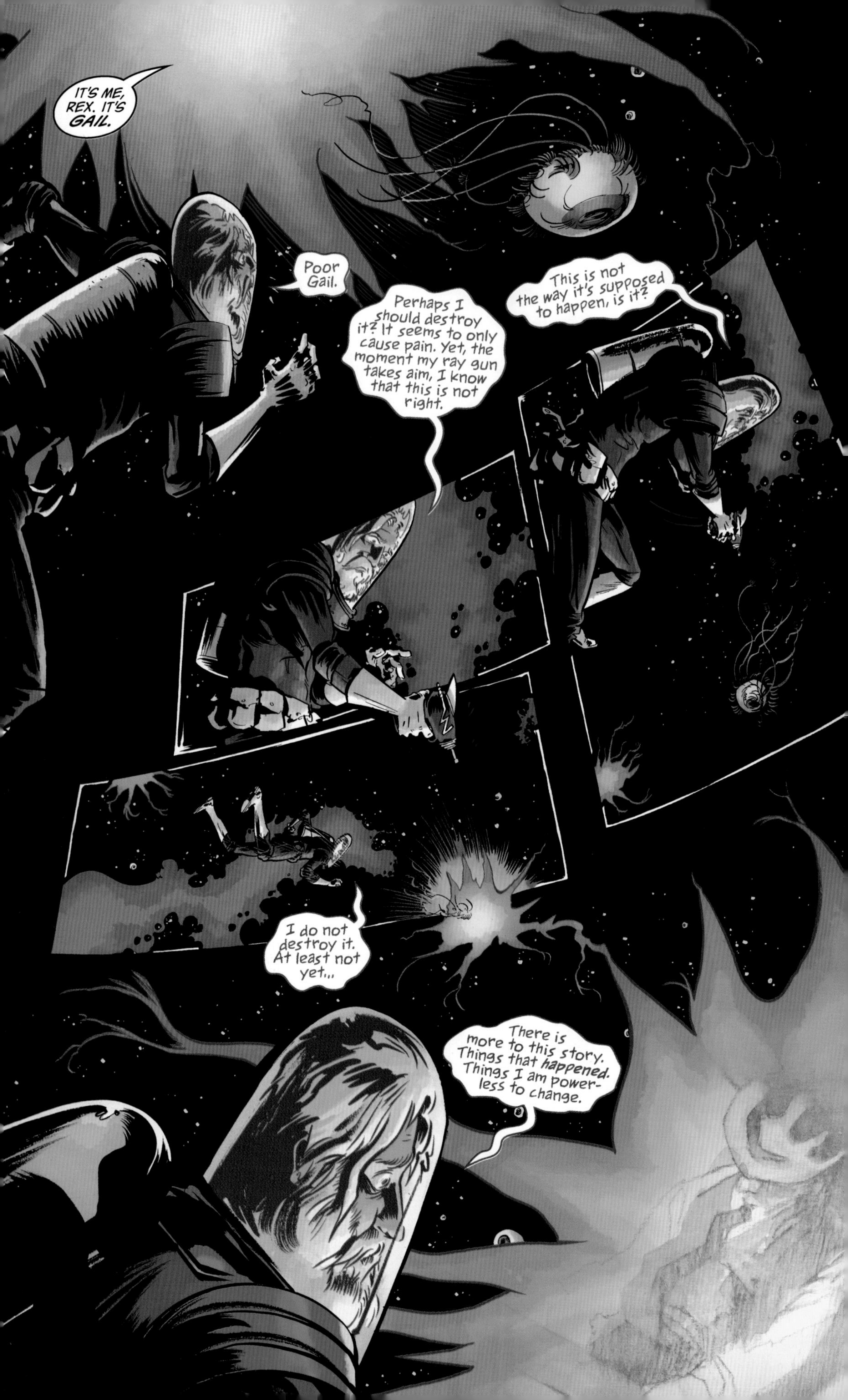
IT'S ME, REX. IT'S GAIL.
Poor Gail.
Perhaps I should destroy it? It seems to only cause pain. Yet, the moment my ray gun takes aim, I know that this is not right.
This is not the way it's supposed to happen, is it?
I do not destroy it. At least not yet...
There is more to this story. Things that happened. Things I am powerless to change.

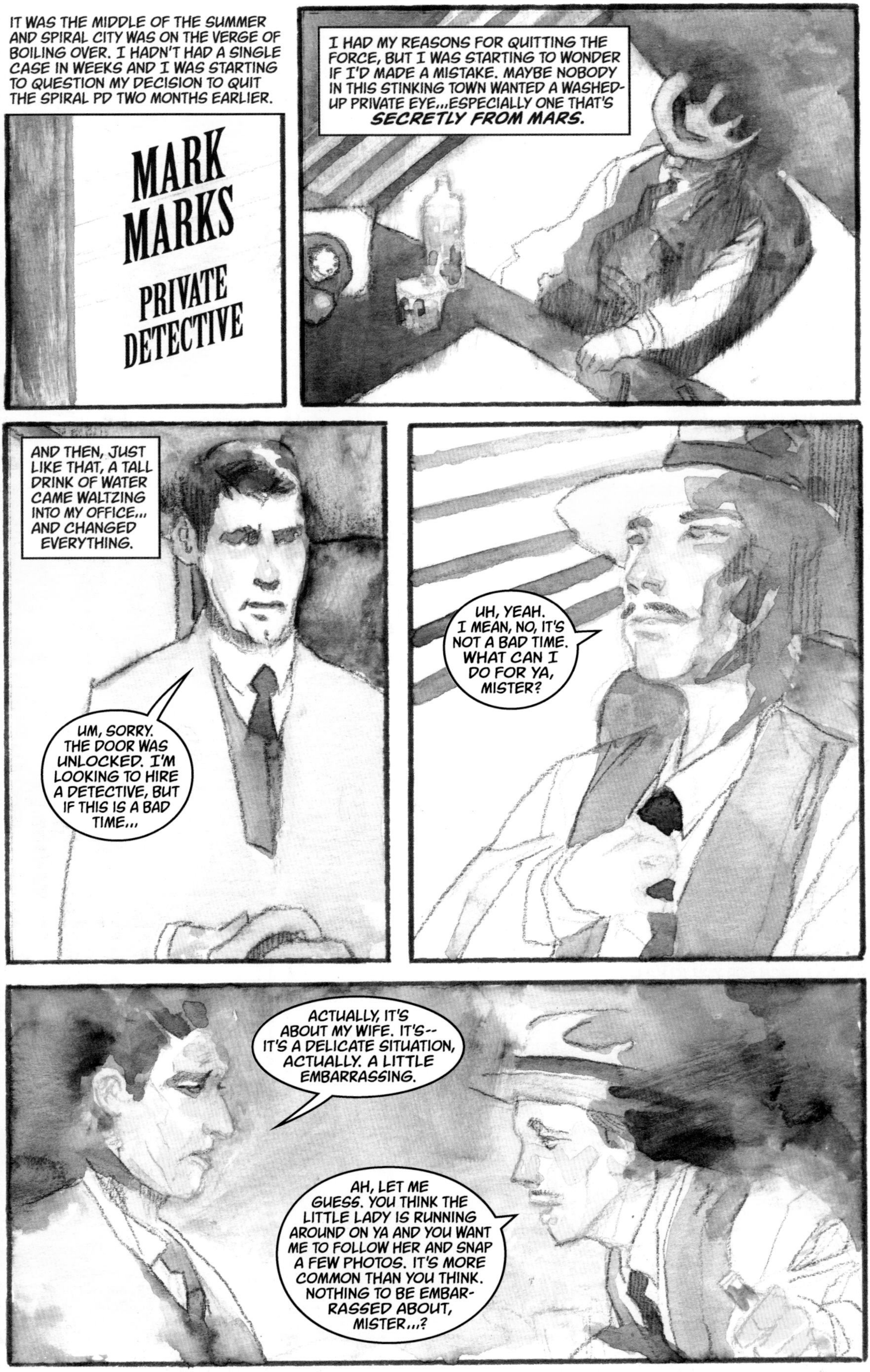
IT WAS THE MIDDLE OF THE SUMMER AND SPIRAL CITY WAS ON THE VERGE OF BOILING OVER. I HADN'T HAD A SINGLE CASE IN WEEKS AND I WAS STARTING TO QUESTION MY DECISION TO QUIT THE SPIRAL PD TWO MONTHS EARLIER.
MARK MARKS
PRIVATE DETECTIVE
I HAD MY REASONS FOR QUITTING THE FORCE, BUT I WAS STARTING TO WONDER IF I'D MADE A MISTAKE. MAYBE NOBODY IN THIS STINKING TOWN WANTED A WASHED-UP PRIVATE EYE...ESPECIALLY ONE THAT'S *SECRETLY FROM MARS.*
AND THEN, JUST LIKE THAT, A TALL DRINK OF WATER CAME WALTZING INTO MY OFFICE... AND CHANGED EVERYTHING.
UM, SORRY. THE DOOR WAS UNLOCKED. I'M LOOKING TO HIRE A DETECTIVE, BUT IF THIS IS A BAD TIME...
UH, YEAH. I MEAN, NO, IT'S NOT A BAD TIME. WHAT CAN I DO FOR YA, MISTER?
ACTUALLY, IT'S ABOUT MY WIFE. IT'S-- IT'S A DELICATE SITUATION, ACTUALLY. A LITTLE EMBARRASSING.
AH, LET ME GUESS. YOU THINK THE LITTLE LADY IS RUNNING AROUND ON YA AND YOU WANT ME TO FOLLOW HER AND SNAP A FEW PHOTOS. IT'S MORE COMMON THAN YOU THINK. NOTHING TO BE EMBARRASSED ABOUT, MISTER...?

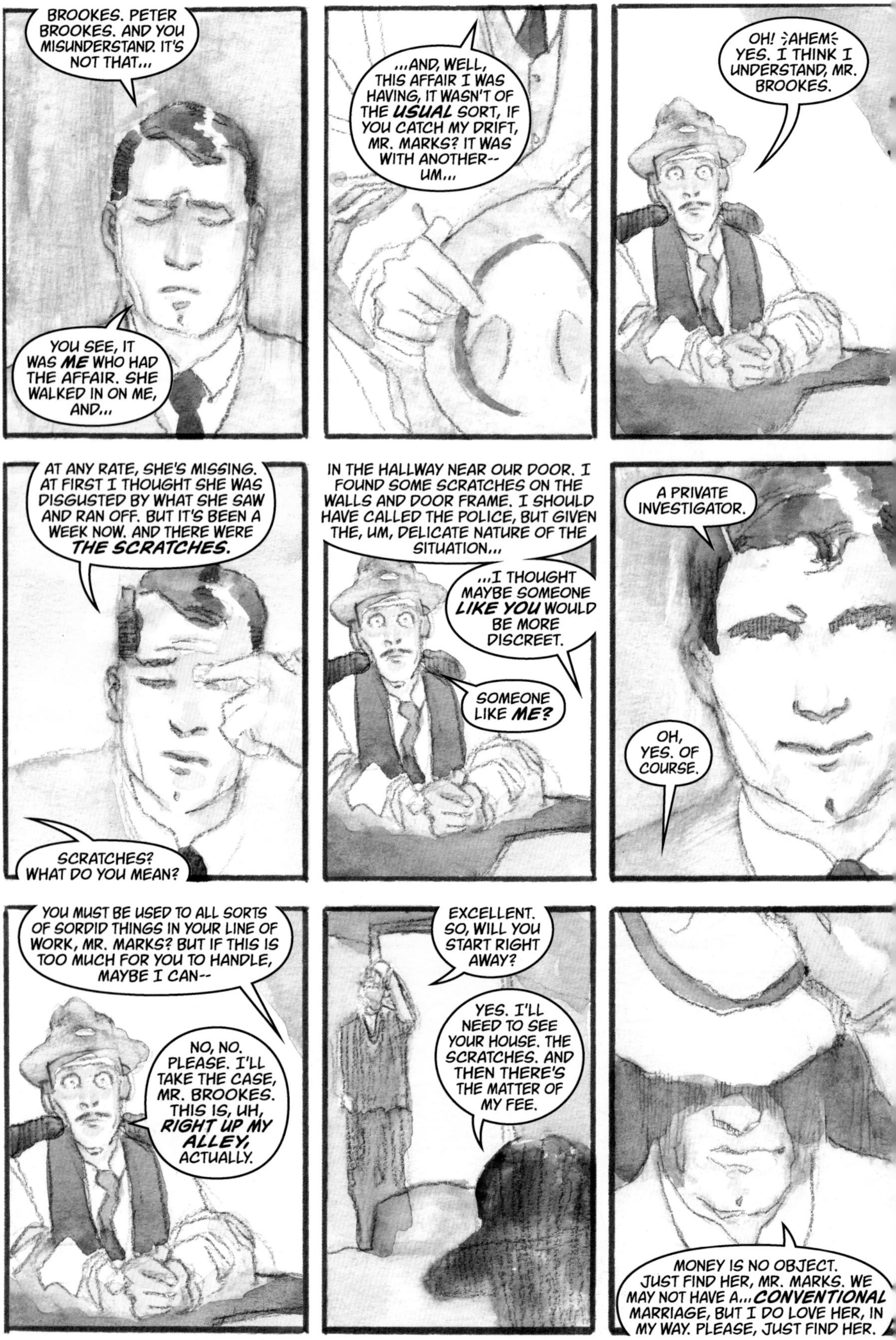
BROOKES. PETER BROOKES. AND YOU MISUNDERSTAND. IT'S NOT THAT...
YOU SEE, IT WAS ME WHO HAD THE AFFAIR. SHE WALKED IN ON ME, AND...
...AND, WELL, THIS AFFAIR I WAS HAVING, IT WASN'T OF THE USUAL SORT, IF YOU CATCH MY DRIFT, MR. MARKS? IT WAS WITH ANOTHER-- UM...
OH! AHEM YES. I THINK I UNDERSTAND, MR. BROOKES.
AT ANY RATE, SHE'S MISSING. AT FIRST I THOUGHT SHE WAS DISGUSTED BY WHAT SHE SAW AND RAN OFF. BUT IT'S BEEN A WEEK NOW. AND THERE WERE THE SCRATCHES.
SCRATCHES? WHAT DO YOU MEAN?
IN THE HALLWAY NEAR OUR DOOR. I FOUND SOME SCRATCHES ON THE WALLS AND DOOR FRAME. I SHOULD HAVE CALLED THE POLICE, BUT GIVEN THE, UM, DELICATE NATURE OF THE SITUATION...
...I THOUGHT MAYBE SOMEONE LIKE YOU WOULD BE MORE DISCREET.
SOMEONE LIKE ME?
A PRIVATE INVESTIGATOR.
OH, YES. OF COURSE.
YOU MUST BE USED TO ALL SORTS OF SORDID THINGS IN YOUR LINE OF WORK, MR. MARKS? BUT IF THIS IS TOO MUCH FOR YOU TO HANDLE, MAYBE I CAN--
NO, NO. PLEASE. I'LL TAKE THE CASE, MR. BROOKES. THIS IS, UH, RIGHT UP MY ALLEY, ACTUALLY.
EXCELLENT. SO, WILL YOU START RIGHT AWAY?
YES. I'LL NEED TO SEE YOUR HOUSE. THE SCRATCHES. AND THEN THERE'S THE MATTER OF MY FEE.
MONEY IS NO OBJECT. JUST FIND HER, MR. MARKS. WE MAY NOT HAVE A...CONVENTIONAL MARRIAGE, BUT I DO LOVE HER, IN MY WAY. PLEASE, JUST FIND HER.

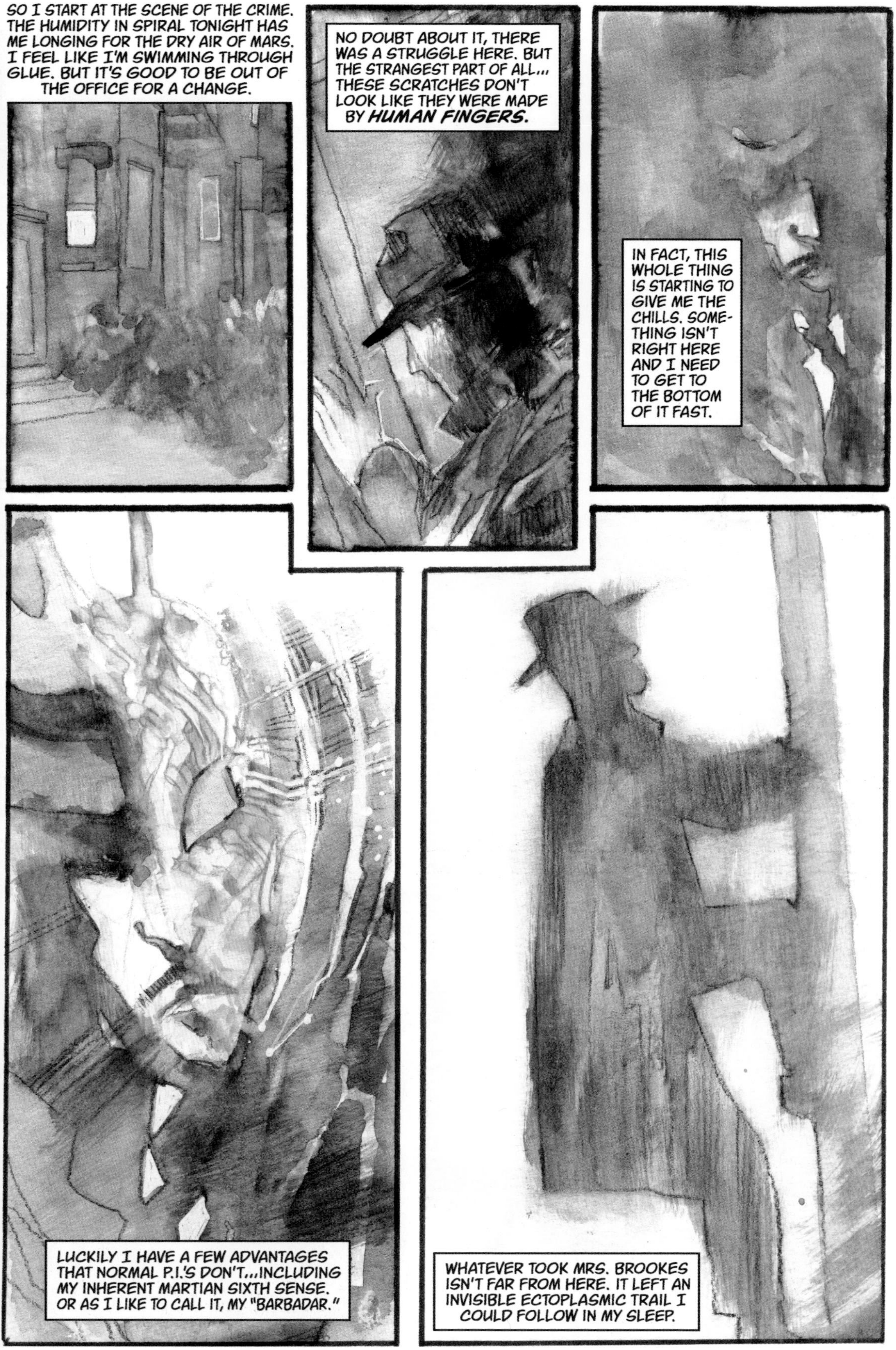
SO I START AT THE SCENE OF THE CRIME. THE HUMIDITY IN SPIRAL TONIGHT HAS ME LONGING FOR THE DRY AIR OF MARS. I FEEL LIKE I'M SWIMMING THROUGH GLUE. BUT IT'S GOOD TO BE OUT OF THE OFFICE FOR A CHANGE.
NO DOUBT ABOUT IT, THERE WAS A STRUGGLE HERE. BUT THE STRANGEST PART OF ALL... THESE SCRATCHES DON'T LOOK LIKE THEY WERE MADE BY HUMAN FINGERS.
IN FACT, THIS WHOLE THING IS STARTING TO GIVE ME THE CHILLS. SOMETHING ISN'T RIGHT HERE AND I NEED TO GET TO THE BOTTOM OF IT FAST.
LUCKILY I HAVE A FEW ADVANTAGES THAT NORMAL P.I.'S DON'T...INCLUDING MY INHERENT MARTIAN SIXTH SENSE. OR AS I LIKE TO CALL IT, MY "BARBADAR."
WHATEVER TOOK MRS. BROOKES ISN'T FAR FROM HERE. IT LEFT AN INVISIBLE ECTOPLASMIC TRAIL I COULD FOLLOW IN MY SLEEP.

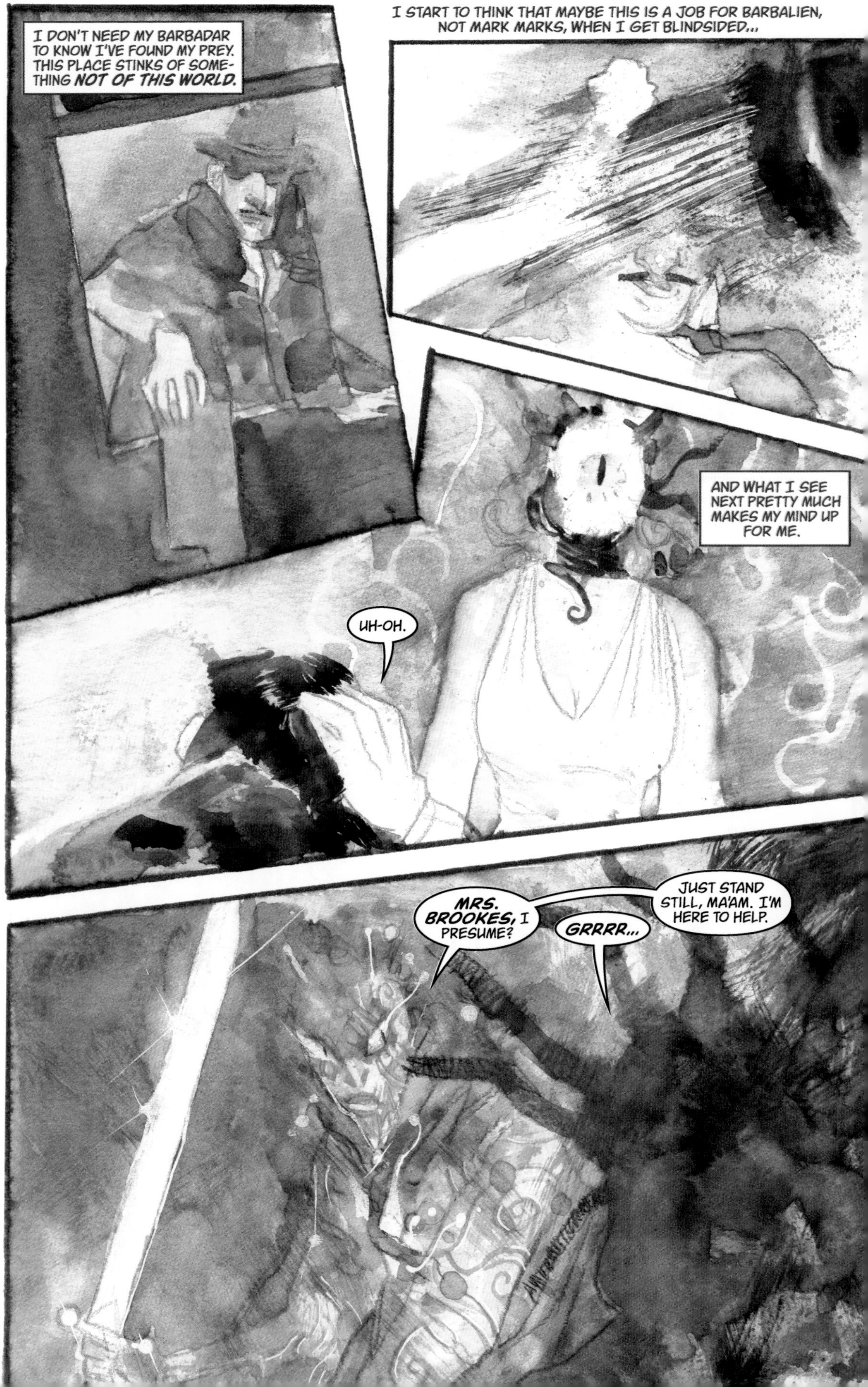
I DON'T NEED MY BARBADAR TO KNOW I'VE FOUND MY PREY. THIS PLACE STINKS OF SOMETHING NOT OF THIS WORLD.
I START TO THINK THAT MAYBE THIS IS A JOB FOR BARBALIEN, NOT MARK MARKS, WHEN I GET BLINDSIDED...
AND WHAT I SEE NEXT PRETTY MUCH MAKES MY MIND UP FOR ME.
UH-OH.
MRS. BROOKES, I PRESUME?
JUST STAND STILL, MA'AM. I'M HERE TO HELP.
GRRRR...

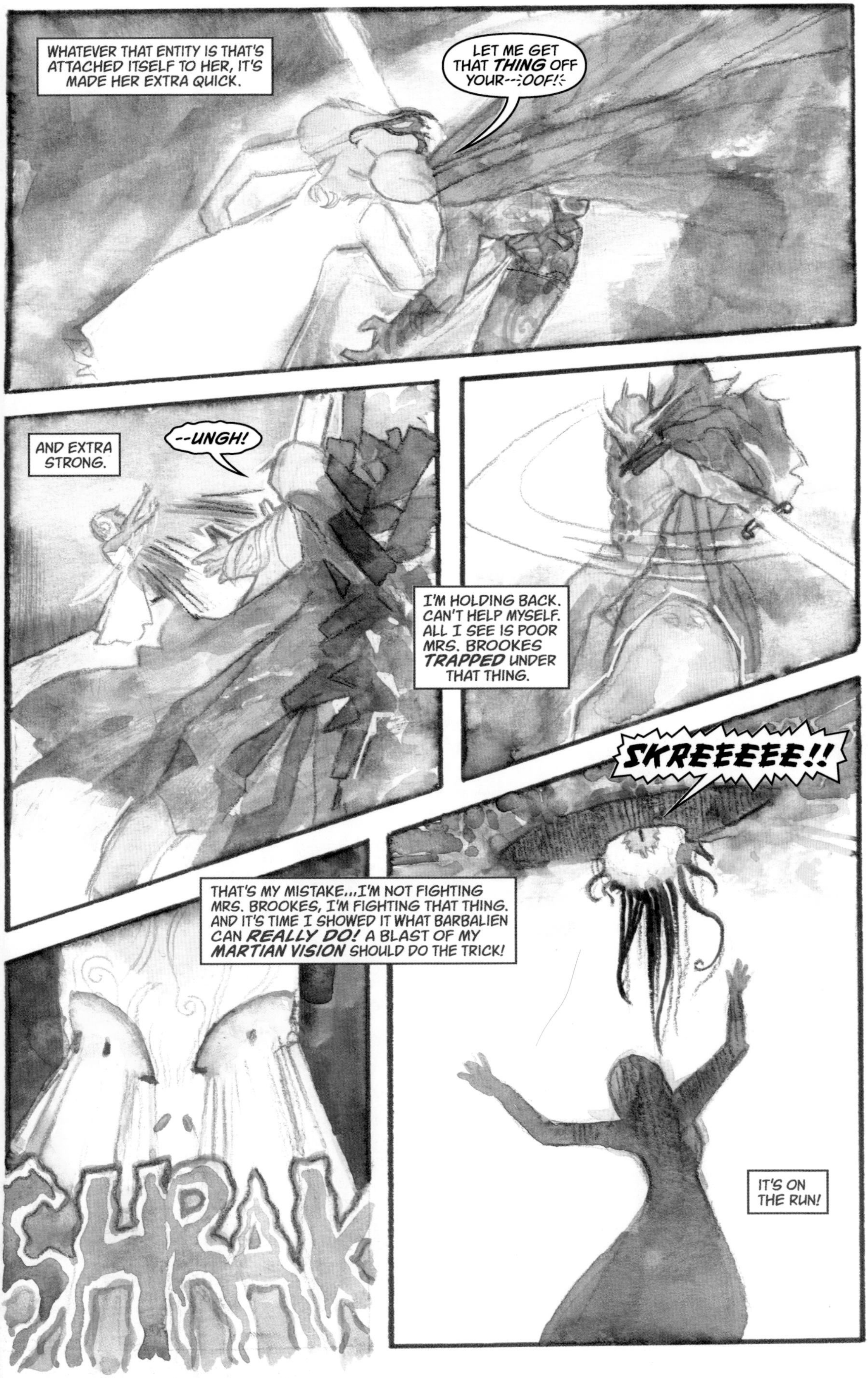
WHATEVER THAT ENTITY IS THAT'S ATTACHED ITSELF TO HER, IT'S MADE HER EXTRA QUICK.
LET ME GET THAT THING OFF YOUR-- OOF!
AND EXTRA STRONG.
--UNGH!
I'M HOLDING BACK. CAN'T HELP MYSELF. ALL I SEE IS POOR MRS. BROOKES TRAPPED UNDER THAT THING.
SKREEEEEE!!
THAT'S MY MISTAKE...I'M NOT FIGHTING MRS. BROOKES, I'M FIGHTING THAT THING. AND IT'S TIME I SHOWED IT WHAT BARBALIEN CAN REALLY DO! A BLAST OF MY MARTIAN VISION SHOULD DO THE TRICK!
SHRAK
IT'S ON THE RUN!

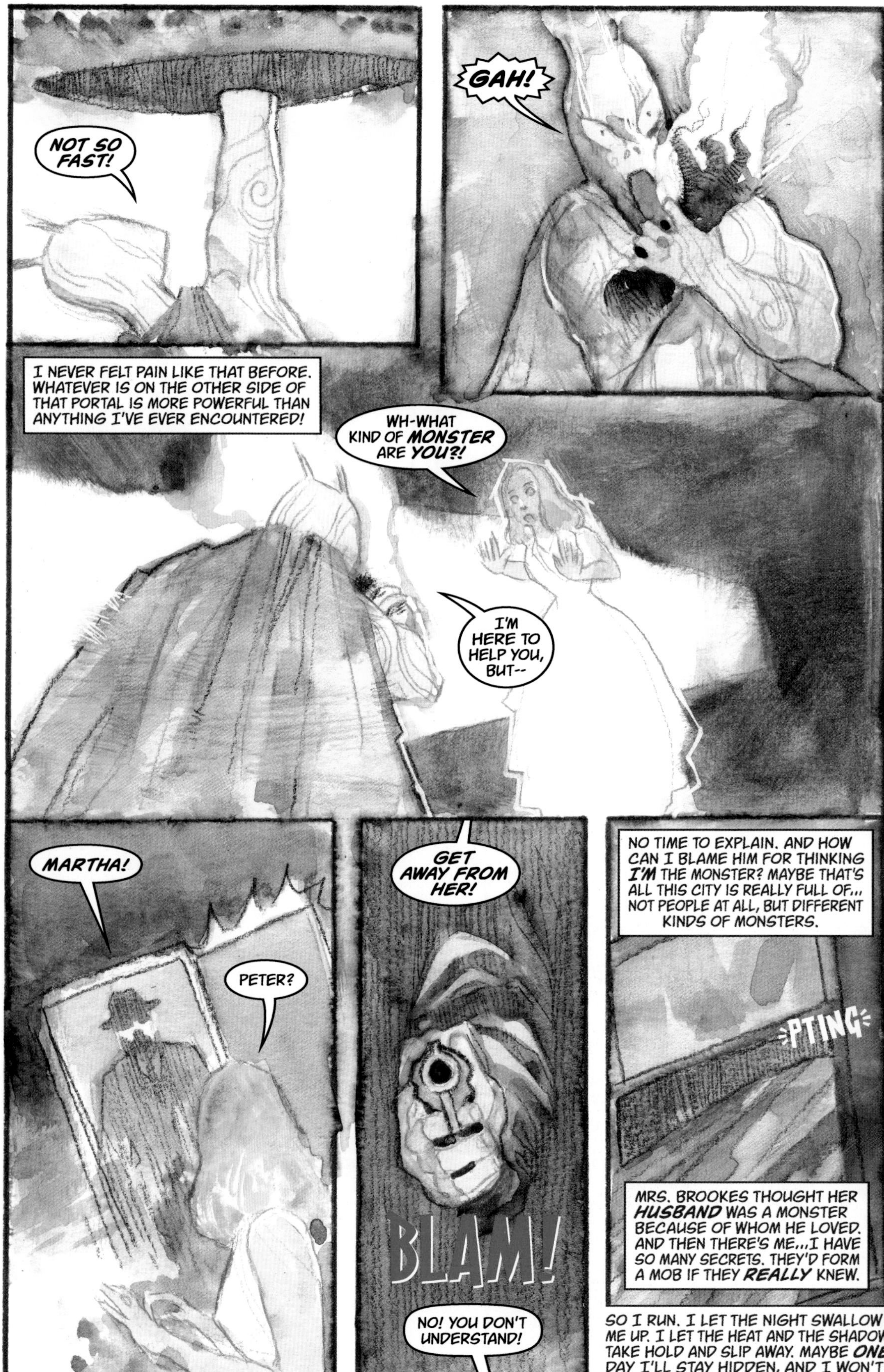
NOT SO FAST!
GAH!
I NEVER FELT PAIN LIKE THAT BEFORE. WHATEVER IS ON THE OTHER SIDE OF THAT PORTAL IS MORE POWERFUL THAN ANYTHING I'VE EVER ENCOUNTERED!
WH-WHAT KIND OF MONSTER ARE YOU?!
I'M HERE TO HELP YOU, BUT--
MARTHA!
PETER?
GET AWAY FROM HER!
BLAM!
NO! YOU DON'T UNDERSTAND!
NO TIME TO EXPLAIN. AND HOW CAN I BLAME HIM FOR THINKING I'M THE MONSTER? MAYBE THAT'S ALL THIS CITY IS REALLY FULL OF... NOT PEOPLE AT ALL, BUT DIFFERENT KINDS OF MONSTERS.
PTING
MRS. BROOKES THOUGHT HER HUSBAND WAS A MONSTER BECAUSE OF WHOM HE LOVED. AND THEN THERE'S ME...I HAVE SO MANY SECRETS. THEY'D FORM A MOB IF THEY REALLY KNEW.
SO I RUN. I LET THE NIGHT SWALLOW ME UP. I LET THE HEAT AND THE SHADOW TAKE HOLD AND SLIP AWAY. MAYBE ONE DAY I'LL STAY HIDDEN, AND I WON'T COME BACK AT ALL.

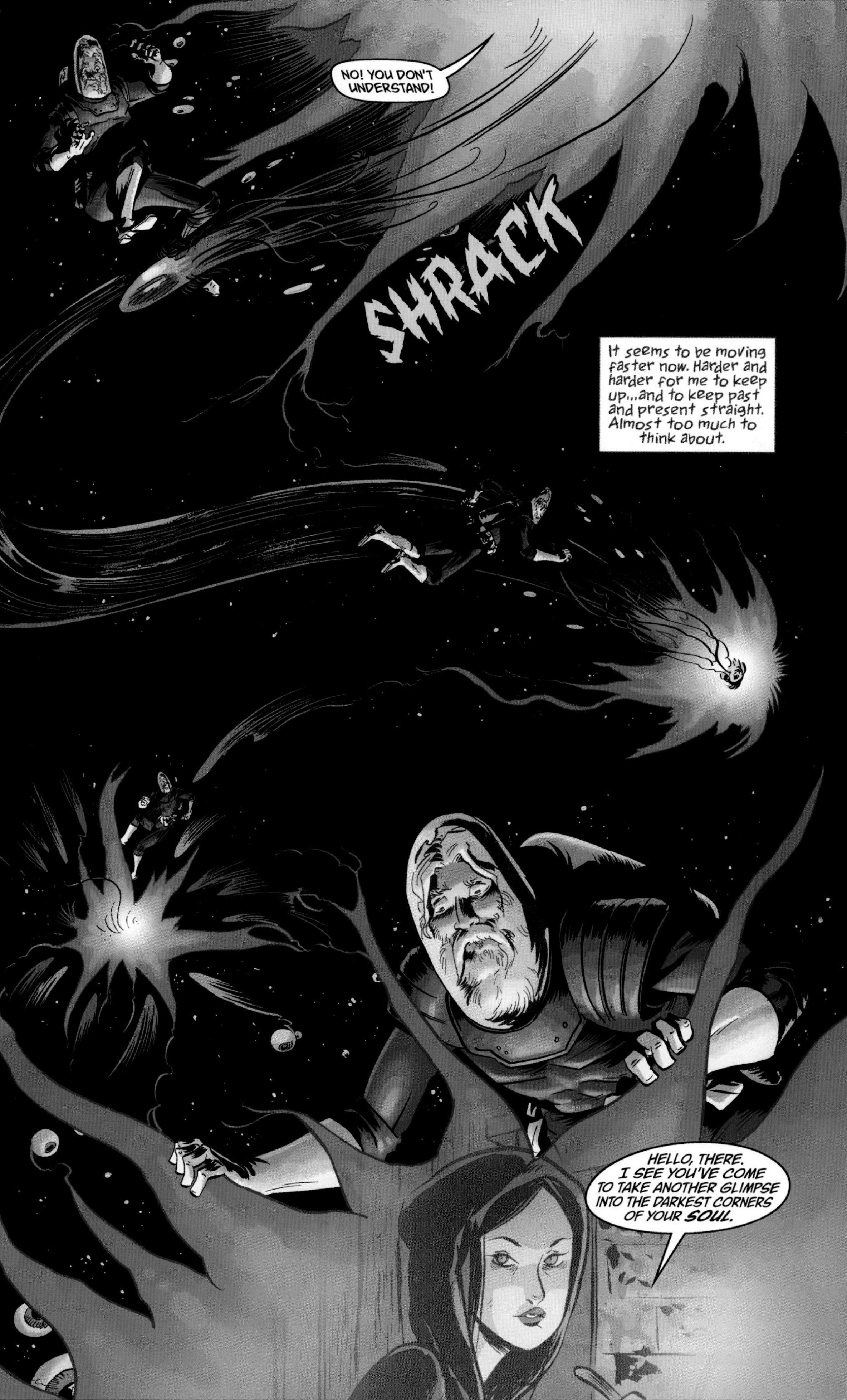

NO! YOU DON'T UNDERSTAND!
SHRACK
It seems to be moving faster now. Harder and harder for me to keep up...and to keep past and present straight. Almost too much to think about.
HELLO, THERE. I SEE YOU'VE COME TO TAKE ANOTHER GLIMPSE INTO THE DARKEST CORNERS OF YOUR SOUL.

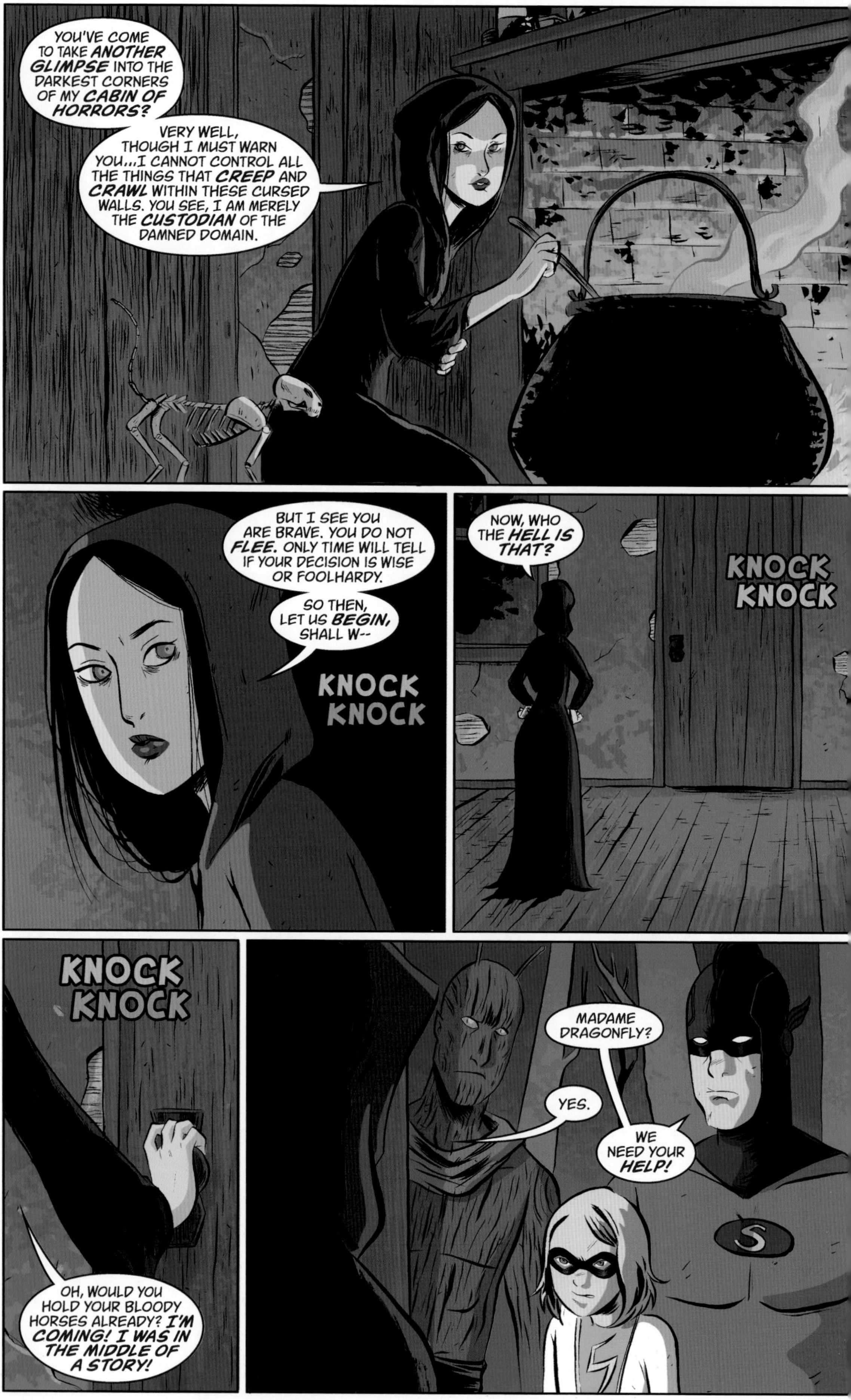
YOU'VE COME TO TAKE ANOTHER GLIMPSE INTO THE DARKEST CORNERS OF MY CABIN OF HORRORS?
VERY WELL, THOUGH I MUST WARN YOU...I CANNOT CONTROL ALL THE THINGS THAT CREEP AND CRAWL WITHIN THESE CURSED WALLS. YOU SEE, I AM MERELY THE CUSTODIAN OF THE DAMNED DOMAIN.
BUT I SEE YOU ARE BRAVE. YOU DO NOT FLEE. ONLY TIME WILL TELL IF YOUR DECISION IS WISE OR FOOLHARDY.
SO THEN, LET US BEGIN, SHALL W--
KNOCK KNOCK
NOW, WHO THE HELL IS THAT?
KNOCK KNOCK
KNOCK KNOCK
OH, WOULD YOU HOLD YOUR BLOODY HORSES ALREADY? I'M COMING! I WAS IN THE MIDDLE OF A STORY!
MADAME DRAGONFLY?
YES.
WE NEED YOUR HELP!

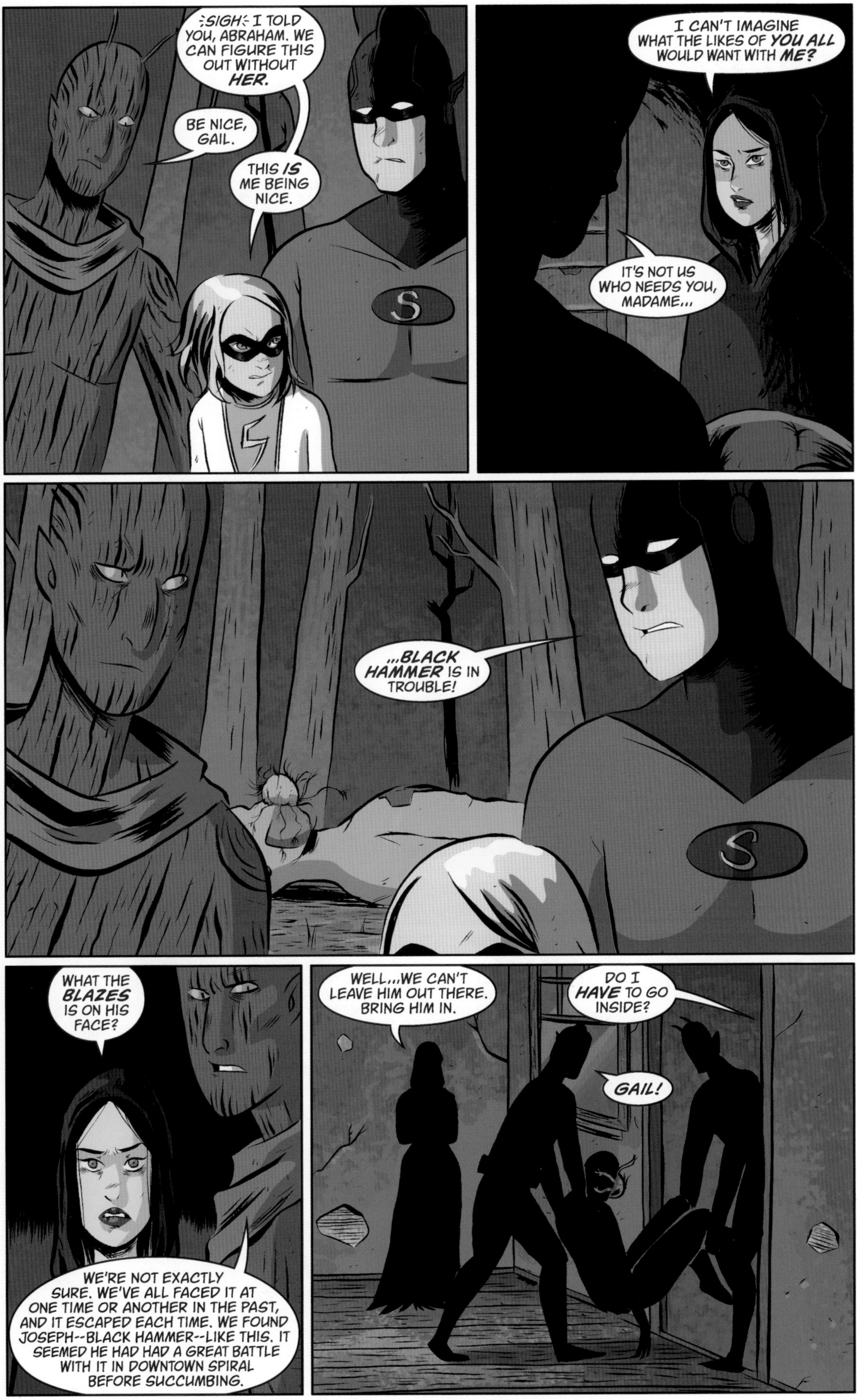

-SIGH- I TOLD YOU, ABRAHAM. WE CAN FIGURE THIS OUT WITHOUT HER.
BE NICE, GAIL.
THIS IS ME BEING NICE.
I CAN'T IMAGINE WHAT THE LIKES OF YOU ALL WOULD WANT WITH ME?
IT'S NOT US WHO NEEDS YOU, MADAME...
...BLACK HAMMER IS IN TROUBLE!
WHAT THE BLAZES IS ON HIS FACE?
WE'RE NOT EXACTLY SURE. WE'VE ALL FACED IT AT ONE TIME OR ANOTHER IN THE PAST, AND IT ESCAPED EACH TIME. WE FOUND JOSEPH--BLACK HAMMER--LIKE THIS. IT SEEMED HE HAD HAD A GREAT BATTLE WITH IT IN DOWNTOWN SPIRAL BEFORE SUCCUMBING.
WELL...WE CAN'T LEAVE HIM OUT THERE. BRING HIM IN.
DO I HAVE TO GO INSIDE?
GAIL!

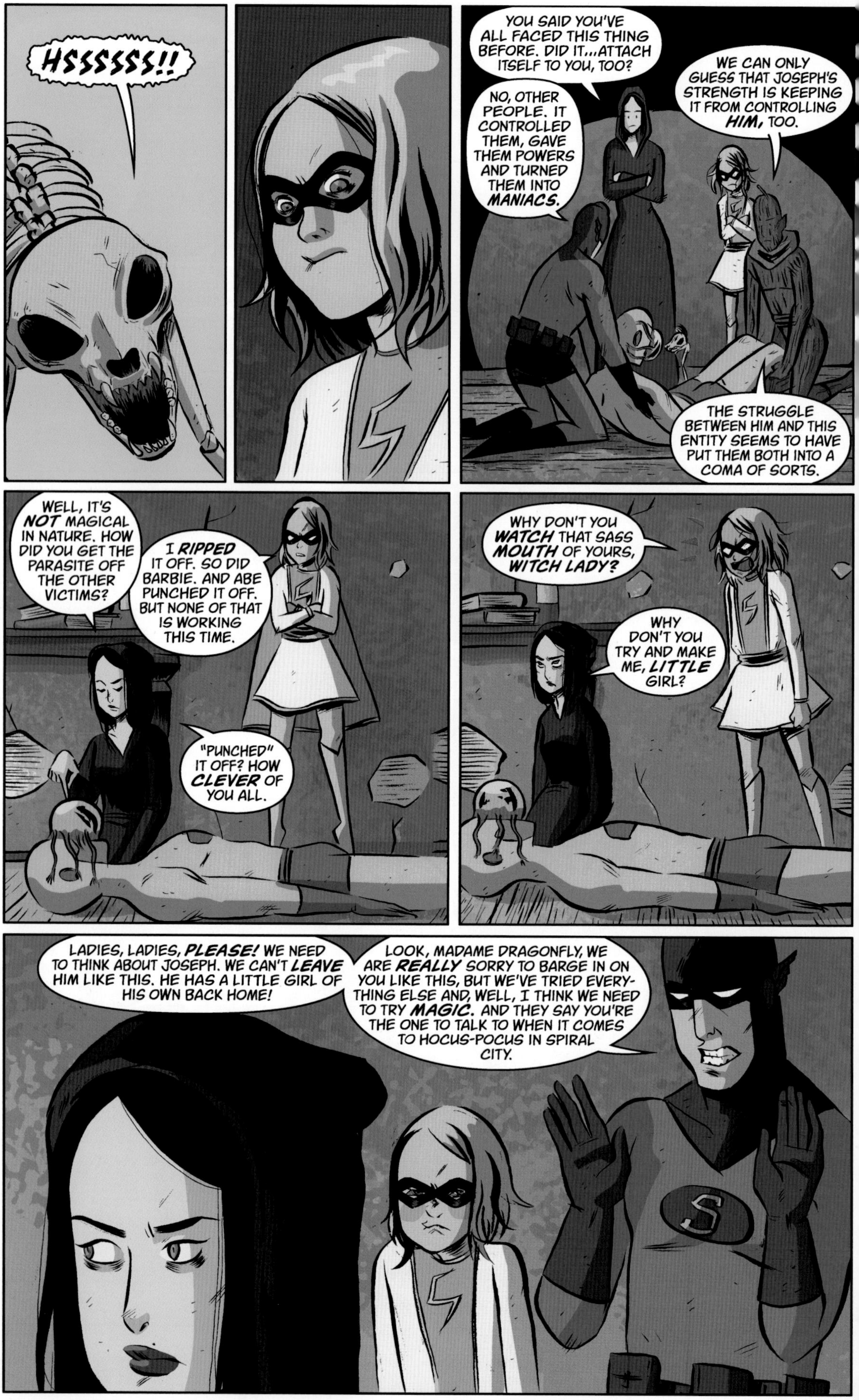
HSSSSSS!!
YOU SAID YOU'VE ALL FACED THIS THING BEFORE. DID IT...ATTACH ITSELF TO YOU, TOO?
NO, OTHER PEOPLE. IT CONTROLLED THEM, GAVE THEM POWERS AND TURNED THEM INTO MANIACS.
WE CAN ONLY GUESS THAT JOSEPH'S STRENGTH IS KEEPING IT FROM CONTROLLING HIM, TOO.
THE STRUGGLE BETWEEN HIM AND THIS ENTITY SEEMS TO HAVE PUT THEM BOTH INTO A COMA OF SORTS.
WELL, IT'S NOT MAGICAL IN NATURE. HOW DID YOU GET THE PARASITE OFF THE OTHER VICTIMS?
I RIPPED IT OFF. SO DID BARBIE. AND ABE PUNCHED IT OFF. BUT NONE OF THAT IS WORKING THIS TIME.
"PUNCHED" IT OFF? HOW CLEVER OF YOU ALL.
WHY DON'T YOU WATCH THAT SASS MOUTH OF YOURS, WITCH LADY?
WHY DON'T YOU TRY AND MAKE ME, LITTLE GIRL?
LADIES, LADIES, PLEASE! WE NEED TO THINK ABOUT JOSEPH. WE CAN'T LEAVE HIM LIKE THIS. HE HAS A LITTLE GIRL OF HIS OWN BACK HOME!
LOOK, MADAME DRAGONFLY, WE ARE REALLY SORRY TO BARGE IN ON YOU LIKE THIS, BUT WE'VE TRIED EVERY-THING ELSE AND, WELL, I THINK WE NEED TO TRY MAGIC. AND THEY SAY YOU'RE THE ONE TO TALK TO WHEN IT COMES TO HOCUS-POCUS IN SPIRAL CITY.

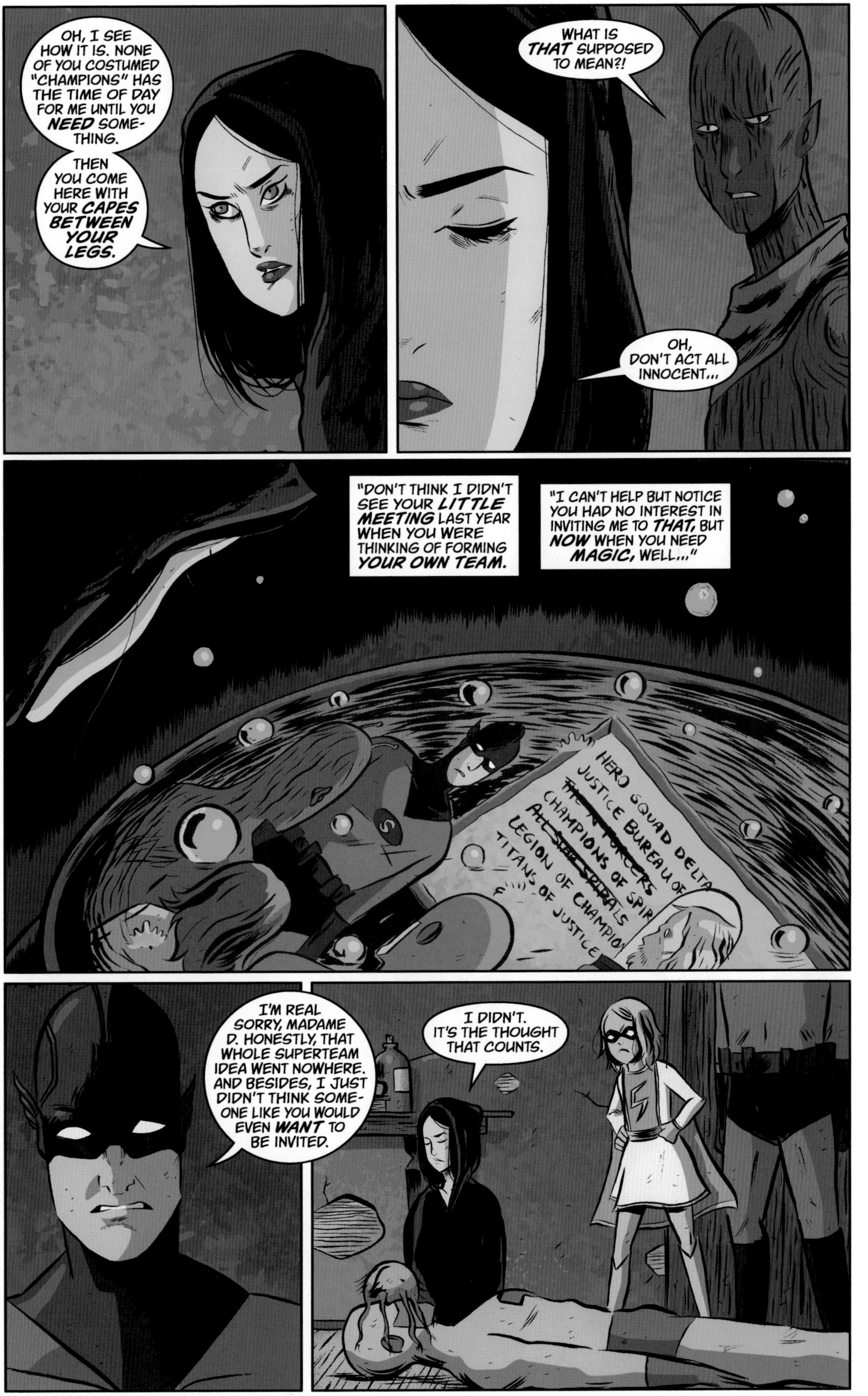
OH, I SEE HOW IT IS. NONE OF YOU COSTUMED "CHAMPIONS" HAS THE TIME OF DAY FOR ME UNTIL YOU NEED SOME-THING.
THEN YOU COME HERE WITH YOUR CAPES BETWEEN YOUR LEGS.
WHAT IS THAT SUPPOSED TO MEAN?!
OH, DON'T ACT ALL INNOCENT...
"DON'T THINK I DIDN'T SEE YOUR LITTLE MEETING LAST YEAR WHEN YOU WERE THINKING OF FORMING YOUR OWN TEAM.
"I CAN'T HELP BUT NOTICE YOU HAD NO INTEREST IN INVITING ME TO THAT, BUT NOW WHEN YOU NEED MAGIC, WELL..."
HERO SQUAD DELTA
JUSTICE BUREAU OF
CHAMPIONS OF SPIR
LEGION OF CHAMPIO
TITANS OF JUSTICE
I'M REAL SORRY, MADAME D. HONESTLY, THAT WHOLE SUPERTEAM IDEA WENT NOWHERE. AND BESIDES, I JUST DIDN'T THINK SOME-ONE LIKE YOU WOULD EVEN WANT TO BE INVITED.
I DIDN'T. IT'S THE THOUGHT THAT COUNTS.

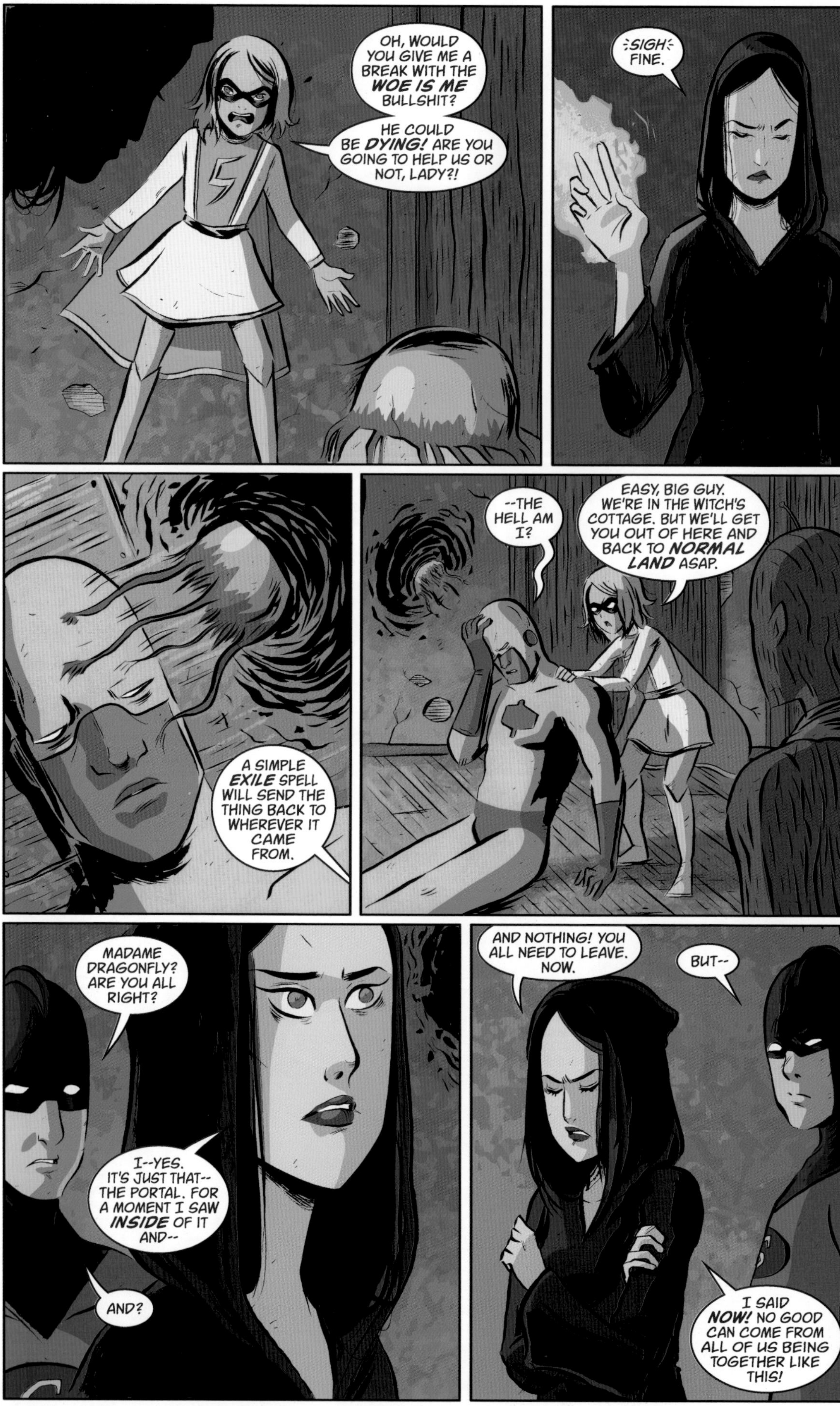
OH, WOULD YOU GIVE ME A BREAK WITH THE WOE IS ME BULLSHIT?
HE COULD BE DYING! ARE YOU GOING TO HELP US OR NOT, LADY?!
SIGH FINE.
A SIMPLE EXILE SPELL WILL SEND THE THING BACK TO WHEREVER IT CAME FROM.
--THE HELL AM I?
EASY, BIG GUY. WE'RE IN THE WITCH'S COTTAGE. BUT WE'LL GET YOU OUT OF HERE AND BACK TO NORMAL LAND ASAP.
MADAME DRAGONFLY? ARE YOU ALL RIGHT?
I--YES. IT'S JUST THAT-- THE PORTAL. FOR A MOMENT I SAW INSIDE OF IT AND--
AND?
AND NOTHING! YOU ALL NEED TO LEAVE. NOW.
BUT--
I SAID NOW! NO GOOD CAN COME FROM ALL OF US BEING TOGETHER LIKE THIS!

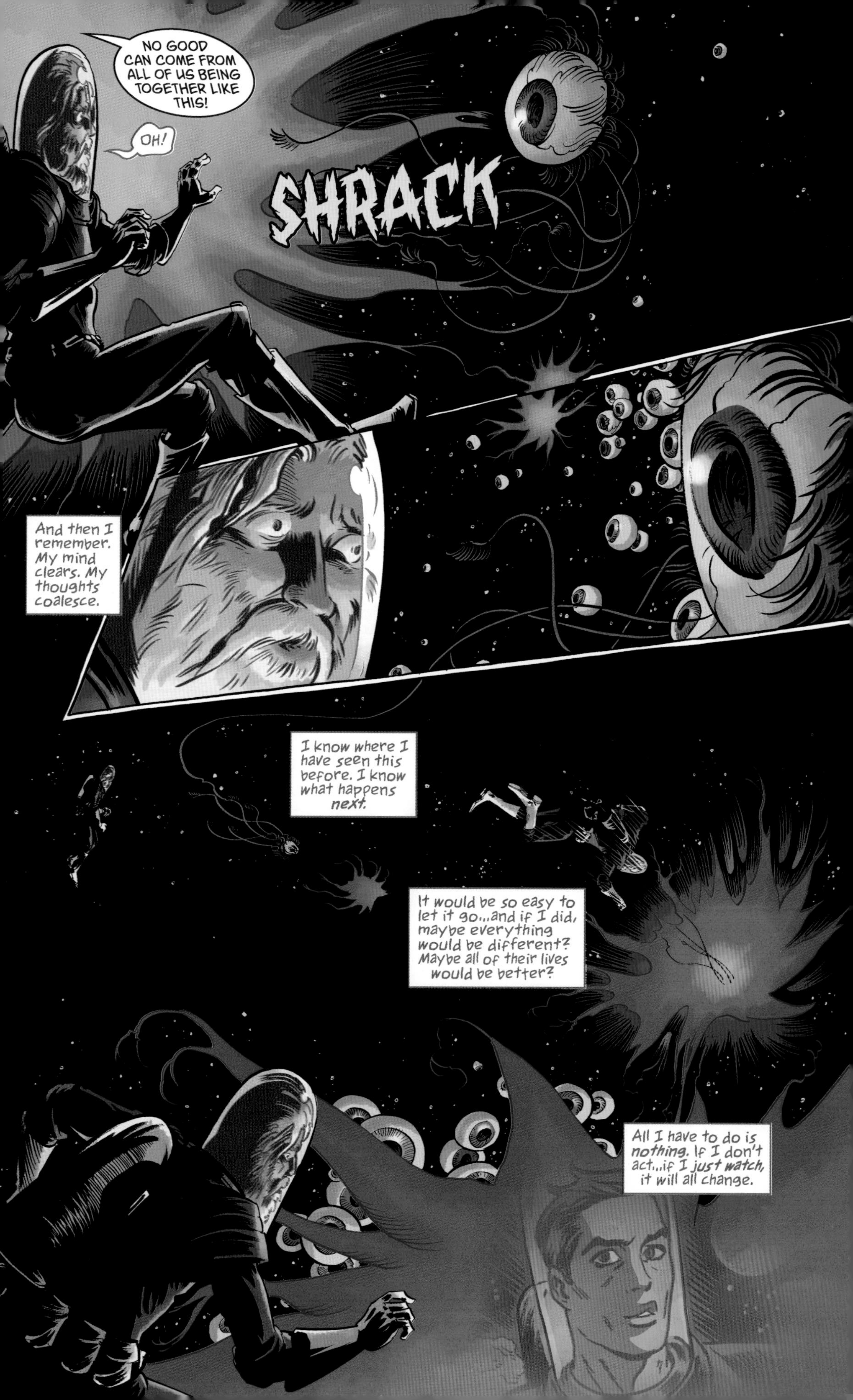
NO GOOD CAN COME FROM ALL OF US BEING TOGETHER LIKE THIS!
OH!
SHRACK
And then I remember. My mind clears. My thoughts coalesce.
I know where I have seen this before. I know what happens *next*.
It would be so easy to let it go...and if I did, maybe everything would be different? Maybe all of their lives would be better?
All I have to do is *nothing*. If I don't act...if I *just watch*, it will all change.

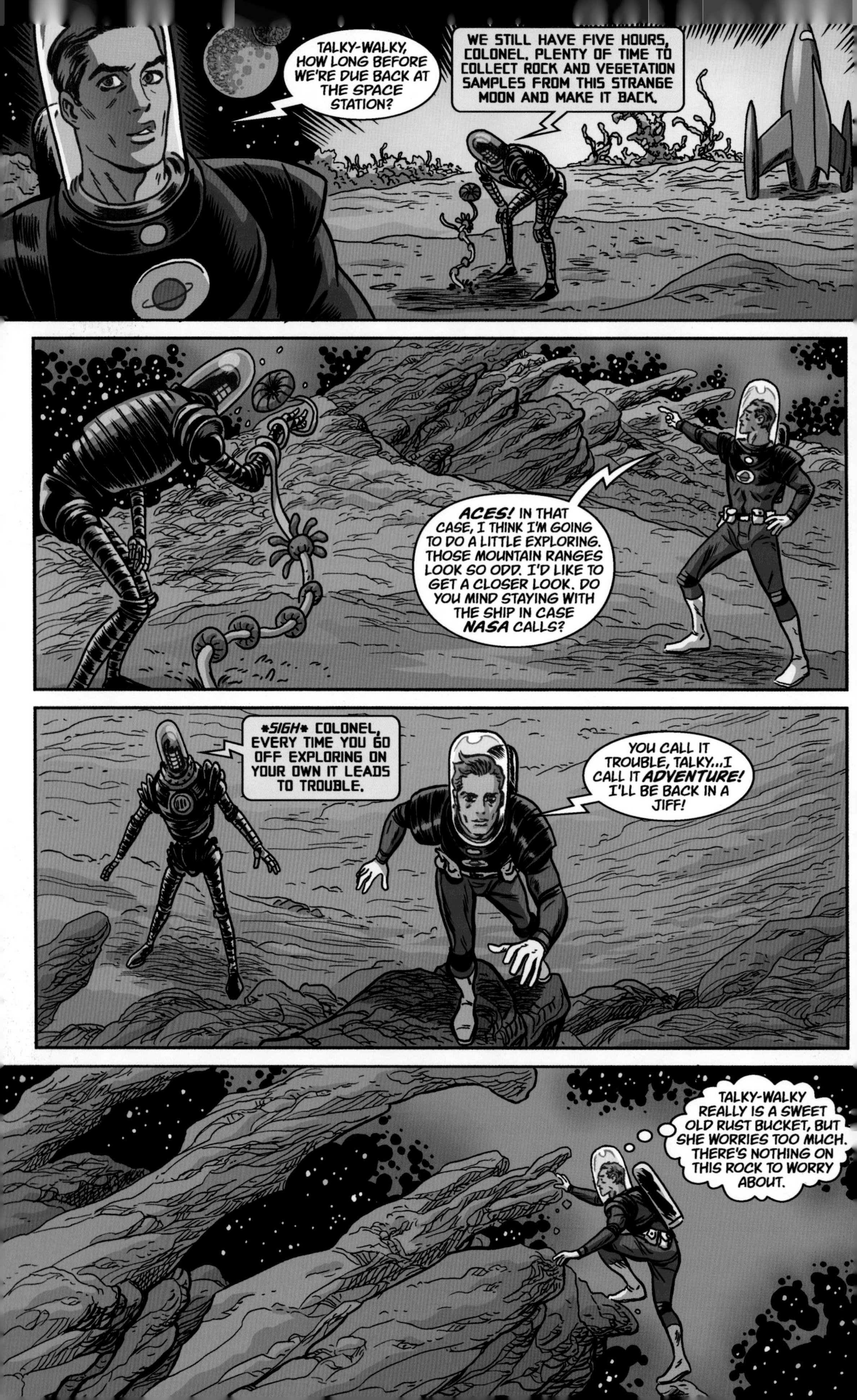
TALKY-WALKY, HOW LONG BEFORE WE'RE DUE BACK AT THE SPACE STATION?
WE STILL HAVE FIVE HOURS, COLONEL. PLENTY OF TIME TO COLLECT ROCK AND VEGETATION SAMPLES FROM THIS STRANGE MOON AND MAKE IT BACK.
ACES! IN THAT CASE, I THINK I'M GOING TO DO A LITTLE EXPLORING. THOSE MOUNTAIN RANGES LOOK SO ODD. I'D LIKE TO GET A CLOSER LOOK. DO YOU MIND STAYING WITH THE SHIP IN CASE NASA CALLS?
SIGH COLONEL, EVERY TIME YOU GO OFF EXPLORING ON YOUR OWN IT LEADS TO TROUBLE.
YOU CALL IT TROUBLE, TALKY...I CALL IT ADVENTURE! I'LL BE BACK IN A JIFF!
TALKY-WALKY REALLY IS A SWEET OLD RUST BUCKET, BUT SHE WORRIES TOO MUCH. THERE'S NOTHING ON THIS ROCK TO WORRY ABOUT.

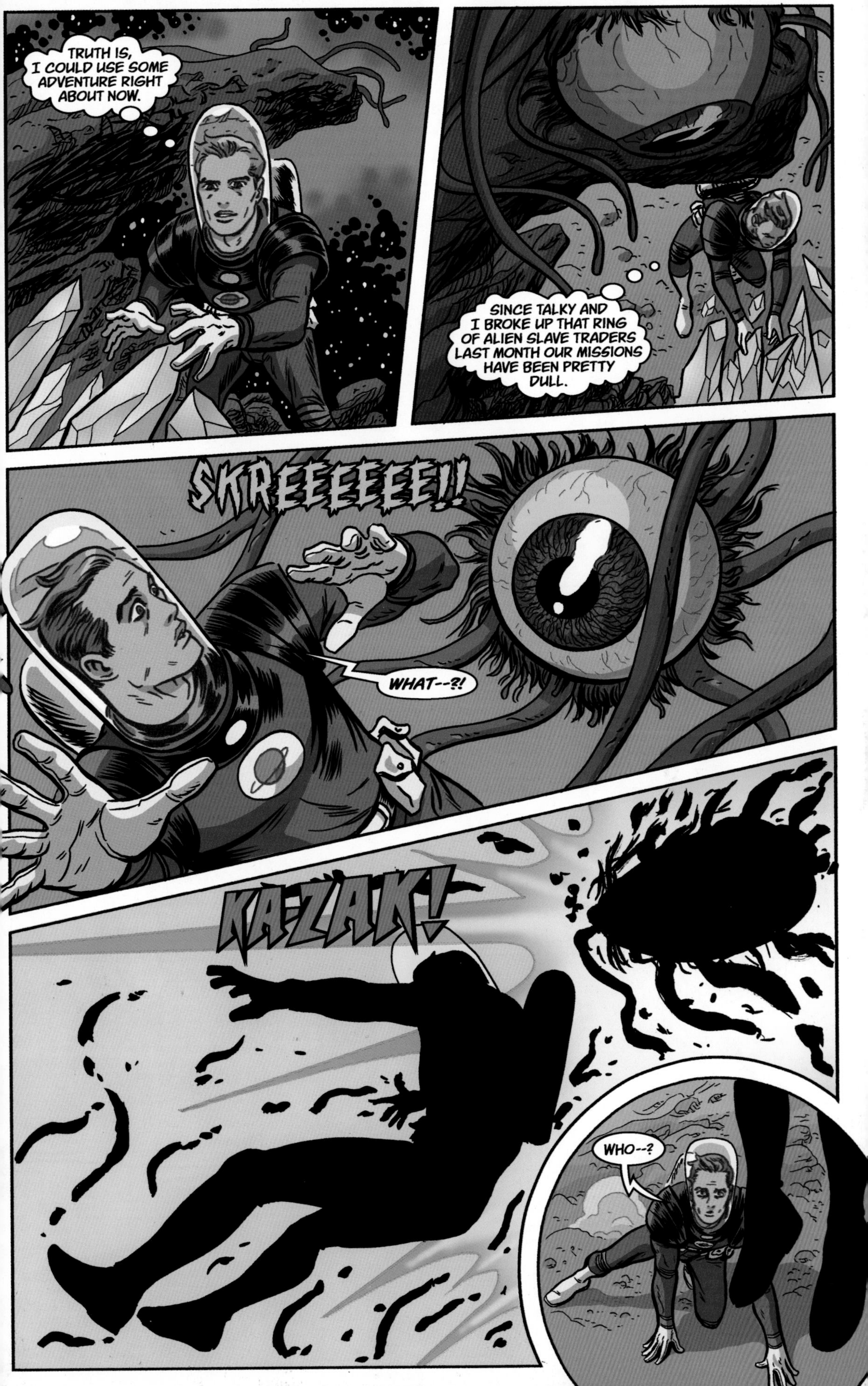
TRUTH IS, I COULD USE SOME ADVENTURE RIGHT ABOUT NOW.
SINCE TALKY AND I BROKE UP THAT RING OF ALIEN SLAVE TRADERS LAST MONTH OUR MISSIONS HAVE BEEN PRETTY DULL.
SKREEEEEEE!!
WHAT--?!
KA-ZAK!
WHO--?

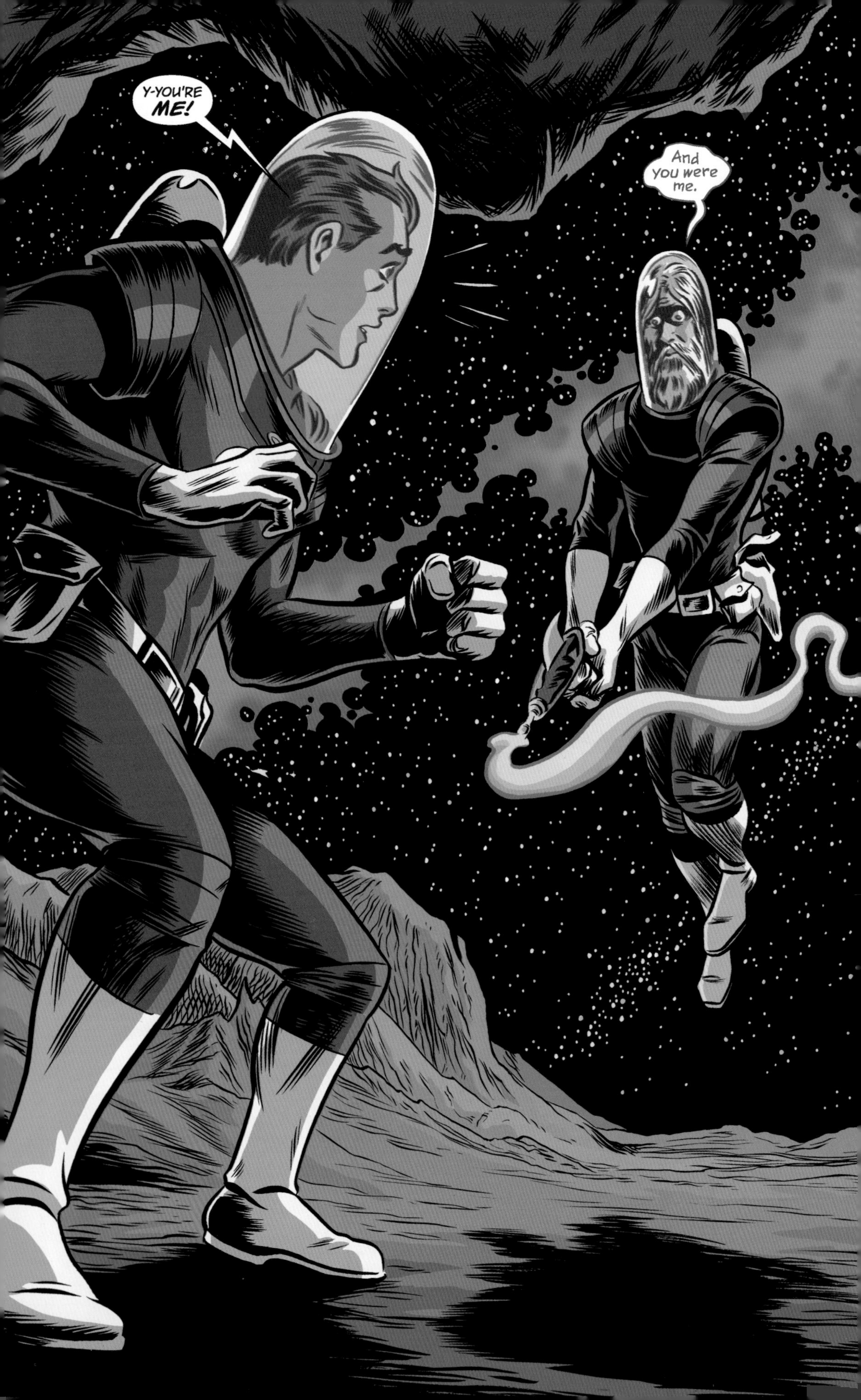
Y-YOU'RE ME!
And you were me.

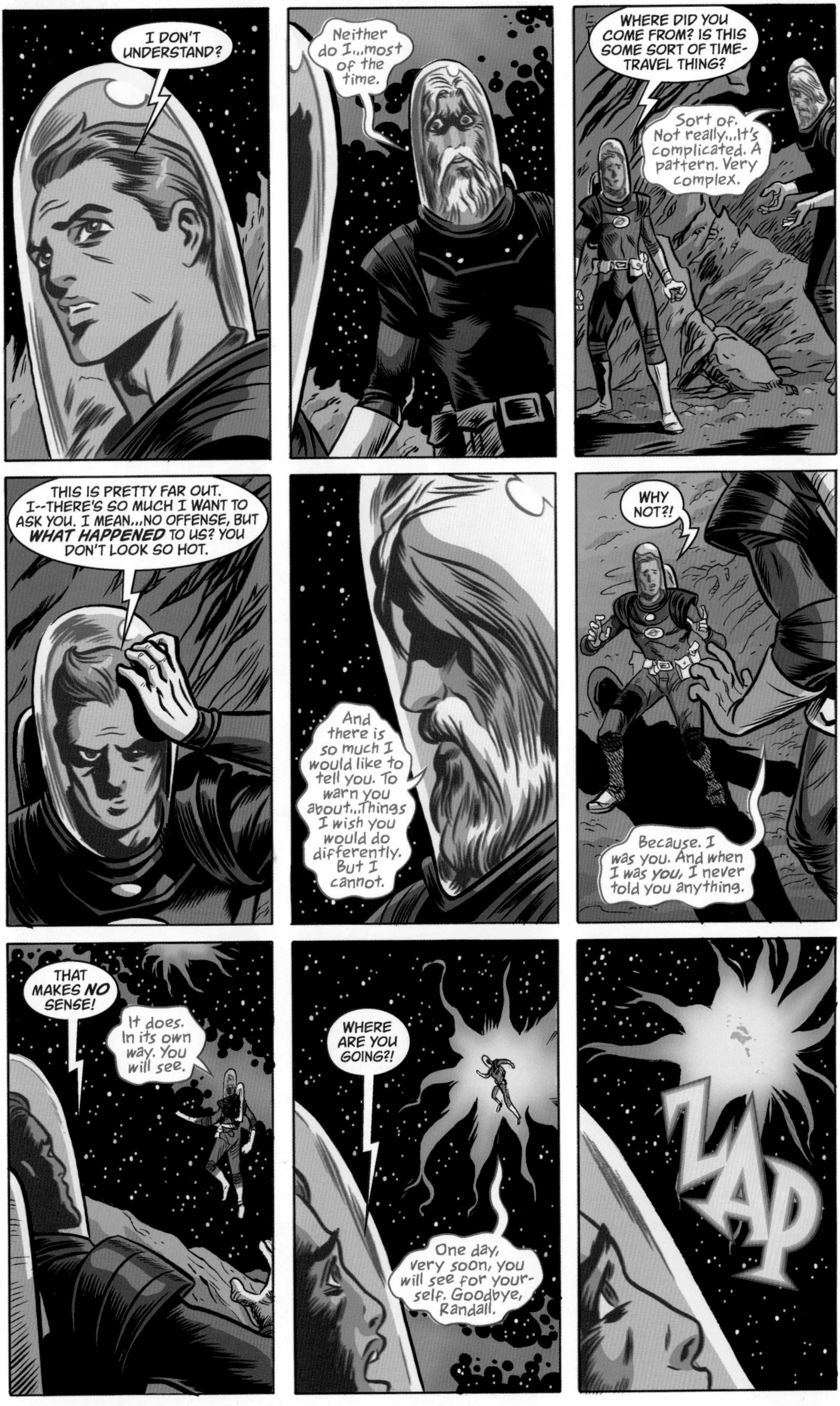
I DON'T UNDERSTAND?
Neither do I...most of the time.
WHERE DID YOU COME FROM? IS THIS SOME SORT OF TIME-TRAVEL THING?
Sort of. Not really...It's complicated. A pattern. Very complex.
THIS IS PRETTY FAR OUT. I--THERE'S SO MUCH I WANT TO ASK YOU. I MEAN...NO OFFENSE, BUT WHAT HAPPENED TO US? YOU DON'T LOOK SO HOT.
And there is so much I would like to tell you. To warn you about...Things I wish you would do differently. But I cannot.
WHY NOT?!
Because. I was you. And when I was you, I never told you anything.
THAT MAKES NO SENSE!
It does. In its own way. You will see.
WHERE ARE YOU GOING?!
One day, very soon, you will see for yourself. Goodbye, Randall.
ZAP

It is all a pattern. Things happen that must happen. We cannot *change* this pattern. As much as we might like to, we cannot alter our paths.

All we can do is regret.

COLONEL? ARE YOU ALL RIGHT?

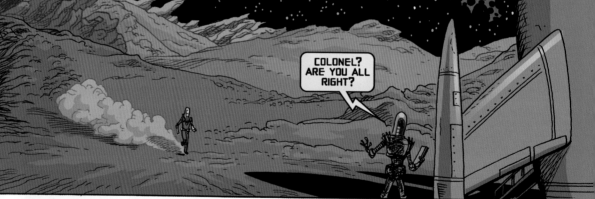

COLONEL? ARE YOU ALL RIGHT?

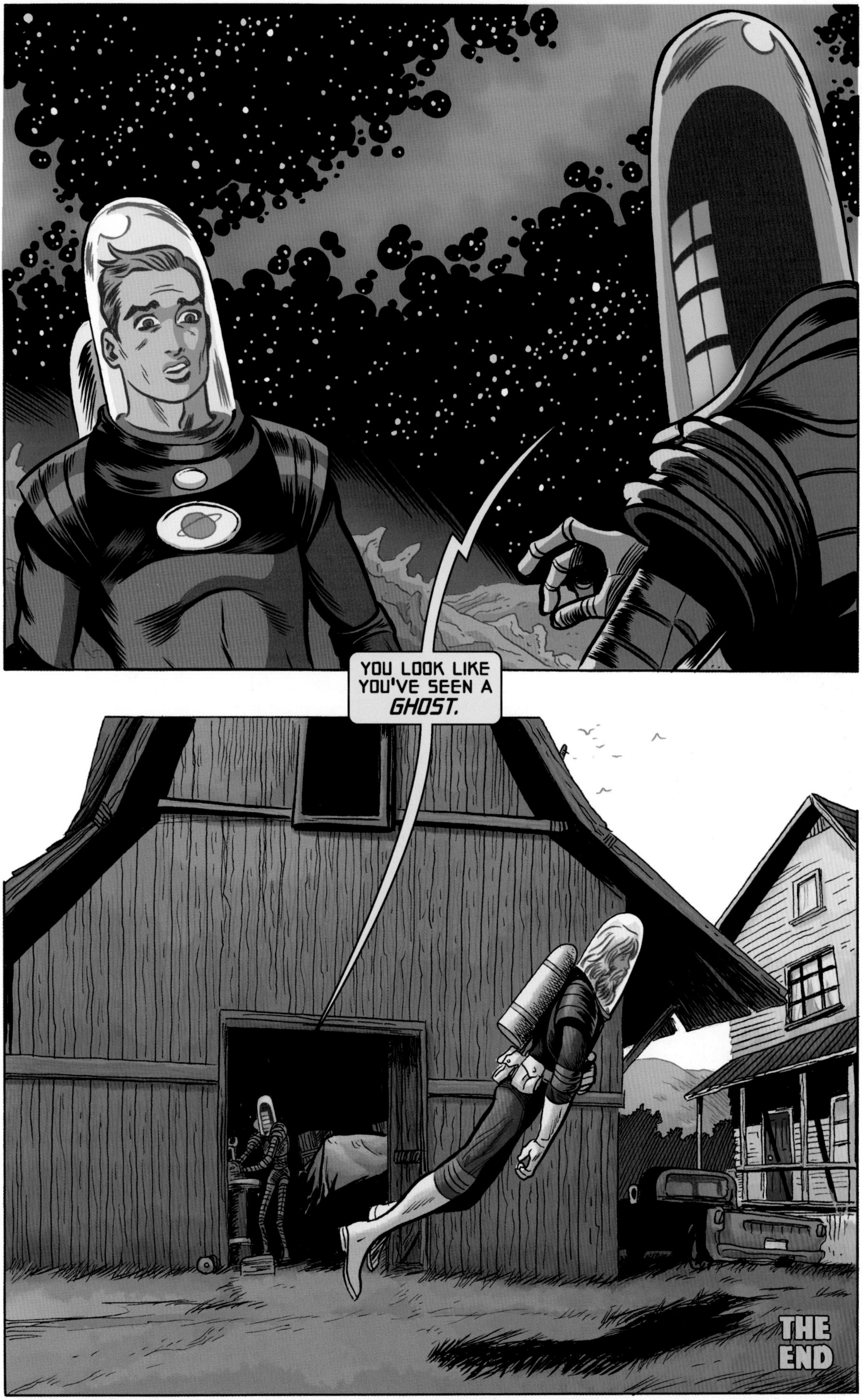
YOU LOOK LIKE YOU'VE SEEN A GHOST.
THE END

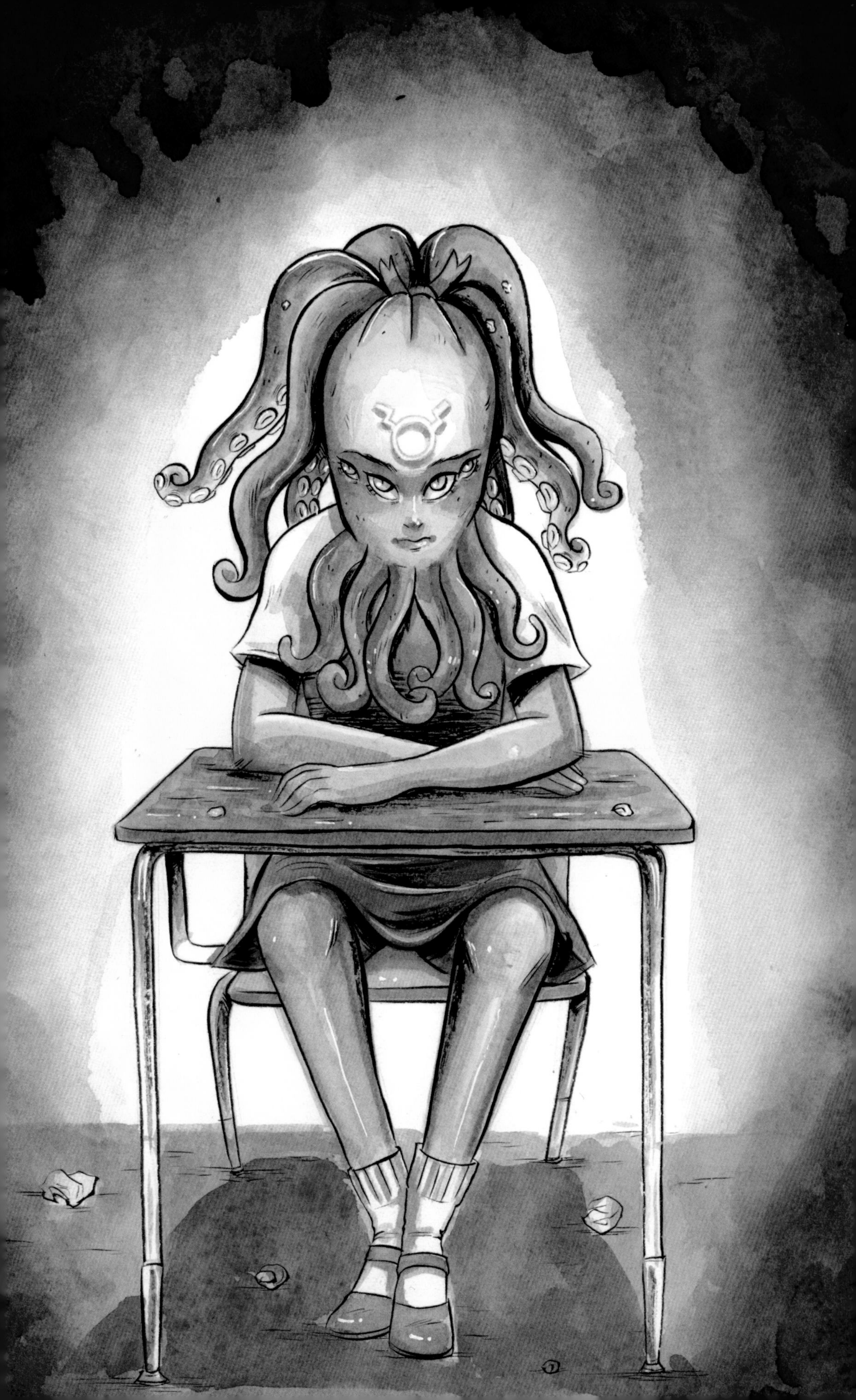

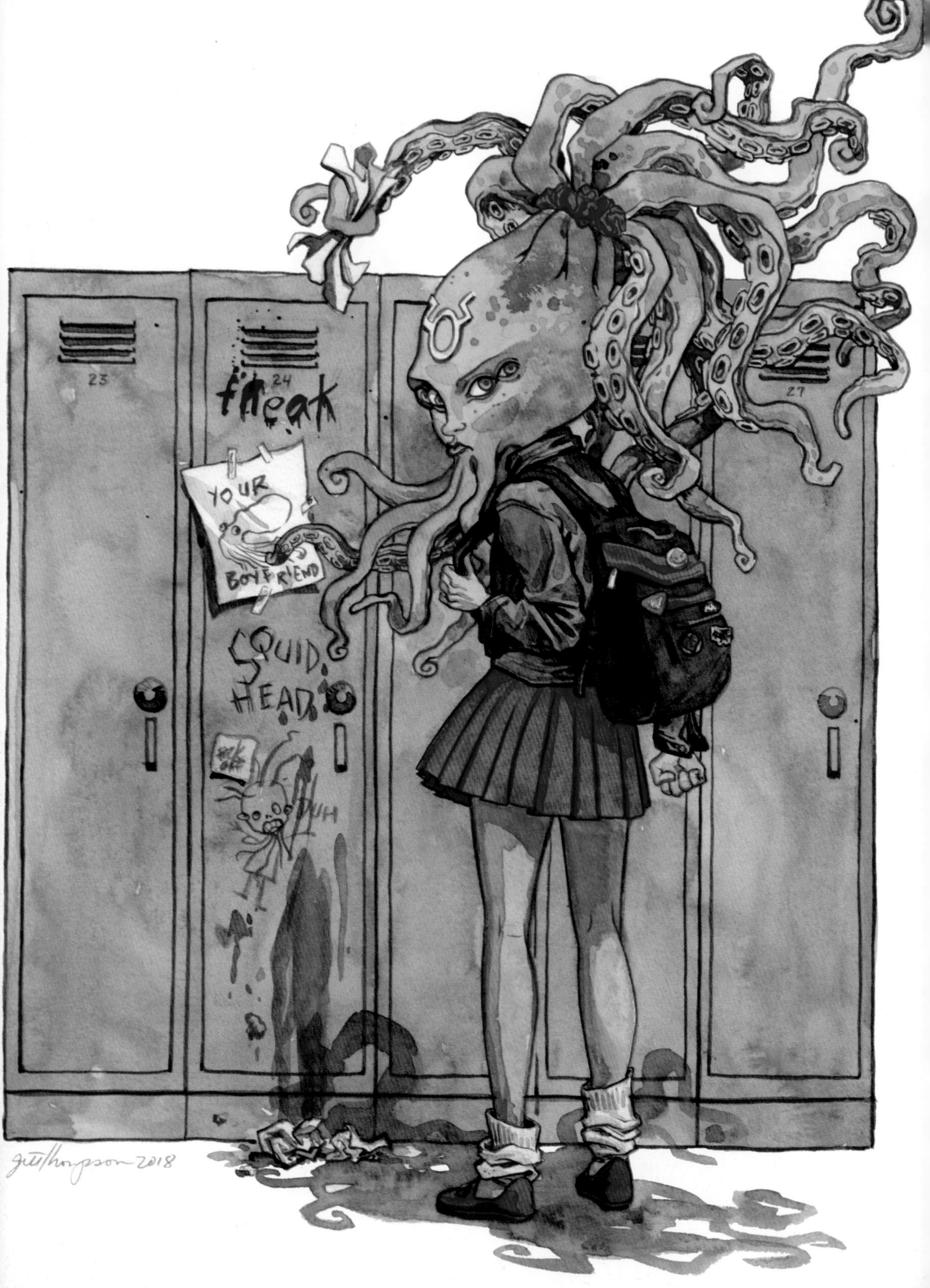
23
24
freak
YOUR
BOYFRIEND
SQUID HEAD
DUH
27

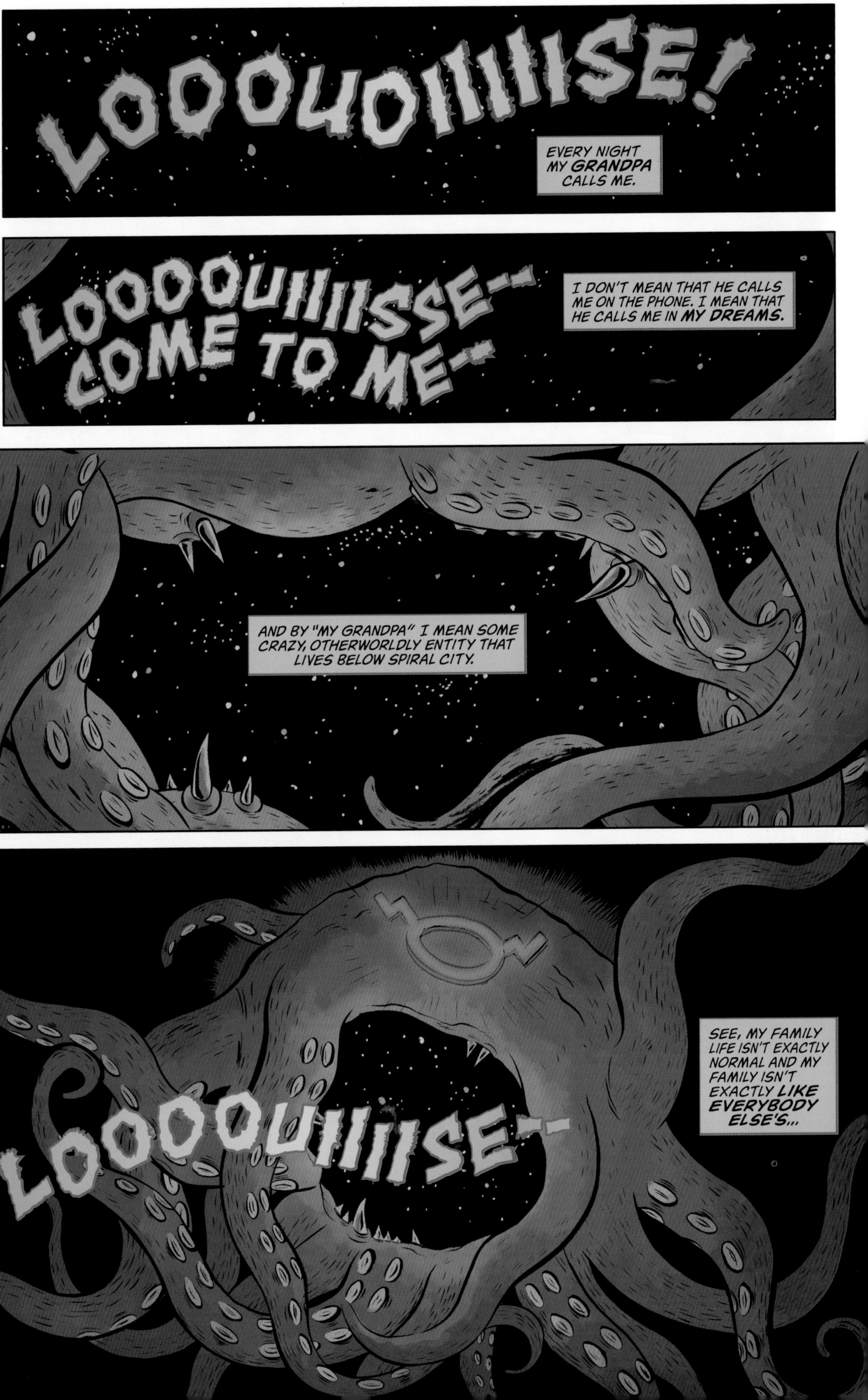
LOOOUOIIIIISE!
EVERY NIGHT MY GRANDPA CALLS ME.
LOOOOUIIIISSE-- COME TO ME--
I DON'T MEAN THAT HE CALLS ME ON THE PHONE. I MEAN THAT HE CALLS ME IN MY DREAMS.
AND BY "MY GRANDPA" I MEAN SOME CRAZY, OTHERWORLDLY ENTITY THAT LIVES BELOW SPIRAL CITY.
SEE, MY FAMILY LIFE ISN'T EXACTLY NORMAL AND MY FAMILY ISN'T EXACTLY LIKE EVERYBODY ELSE'S...
LOOOOUIIIISE--

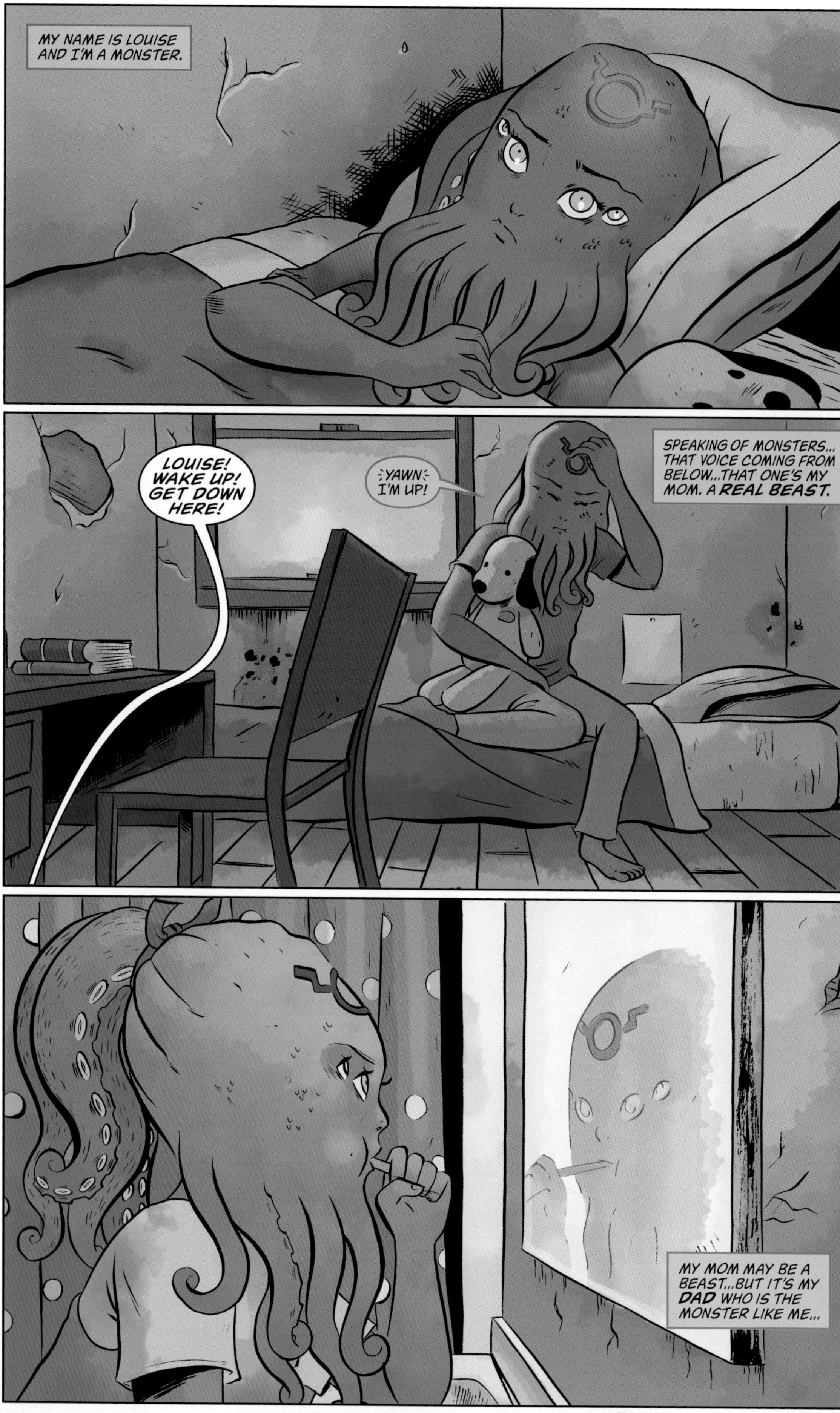
MY NAME IS LOUISE AND I'M A MONSTER.
LOUISE! WAKE UP! GET DOWN HERE!
YAWN I'M UP!
SPEAKING OF MONSTERS... THAT VOICE COMING FROM BELOW...THAT ONE'S MY MOM. A REAL BEAST.
MY MOM MAY BE A BEAST...BUT IT'S MY DAD WHO IS THE MONSTER LIKE ME...

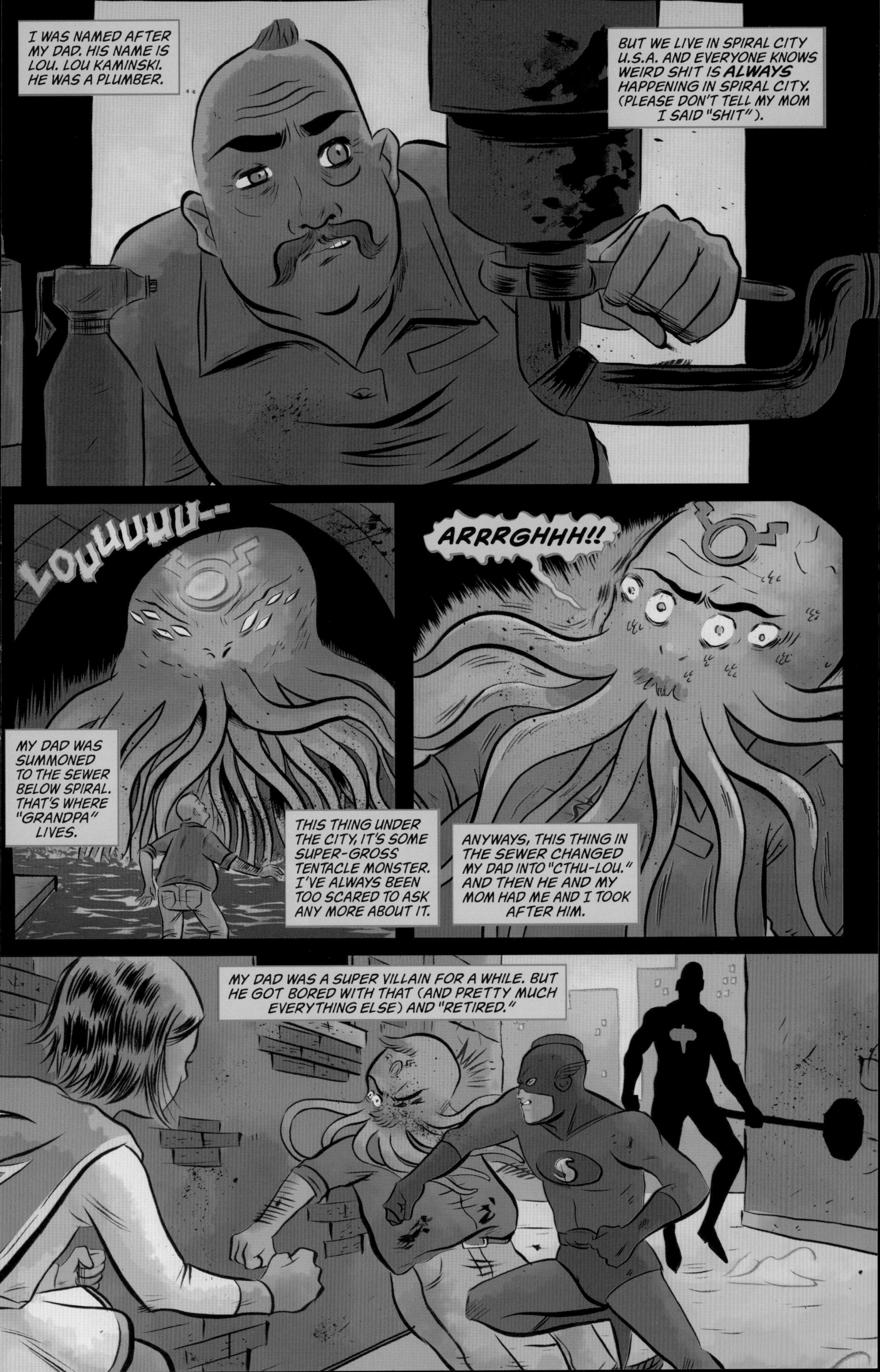

I WAS NAMED AFTER MY DAD. HIS NAME IS LOU. LOU KAMINSKI. HE WAS A PLUMBER.
BUT WE LIVE IN SPIRAL CITY U.S.A. AND EVERYONE KNOWS WEIRD SHIT IS **ALWAYS** HAPPENING IN SPIRAL CITY. (PLEASE DON'T TELL MY MOM I SAID "SHIT").
LOUUUUU--
MY DAD WAS SUMMONED TO THE SEWER BELOW SPIRAL. THAT'S WHERE "GRANDPA" LIVES.
THIS THING UNDER THE CITY, IT'S SOME SUPER-GROSS TENTACLE MONSTER. I'VE ALWAYS BEEN TOO SCARED TO ASK ANY MORE ABOUT IT.
ARRRGHHH!!
ANYWAYS, THIS THING IN THE SEWER CHANGED MY DAD INTO "CTHU-LOU." AND THEN HE AND MY MOM HAD ME AND I TOOK AFTER HIM.
MY DAD WAS A SUPER VILLAIN FOR A WHILE. BUT HE GOT BORED WITH THAT (AND PRETTY MUCH EVERYTHING ELSE) AND "RETIRED."

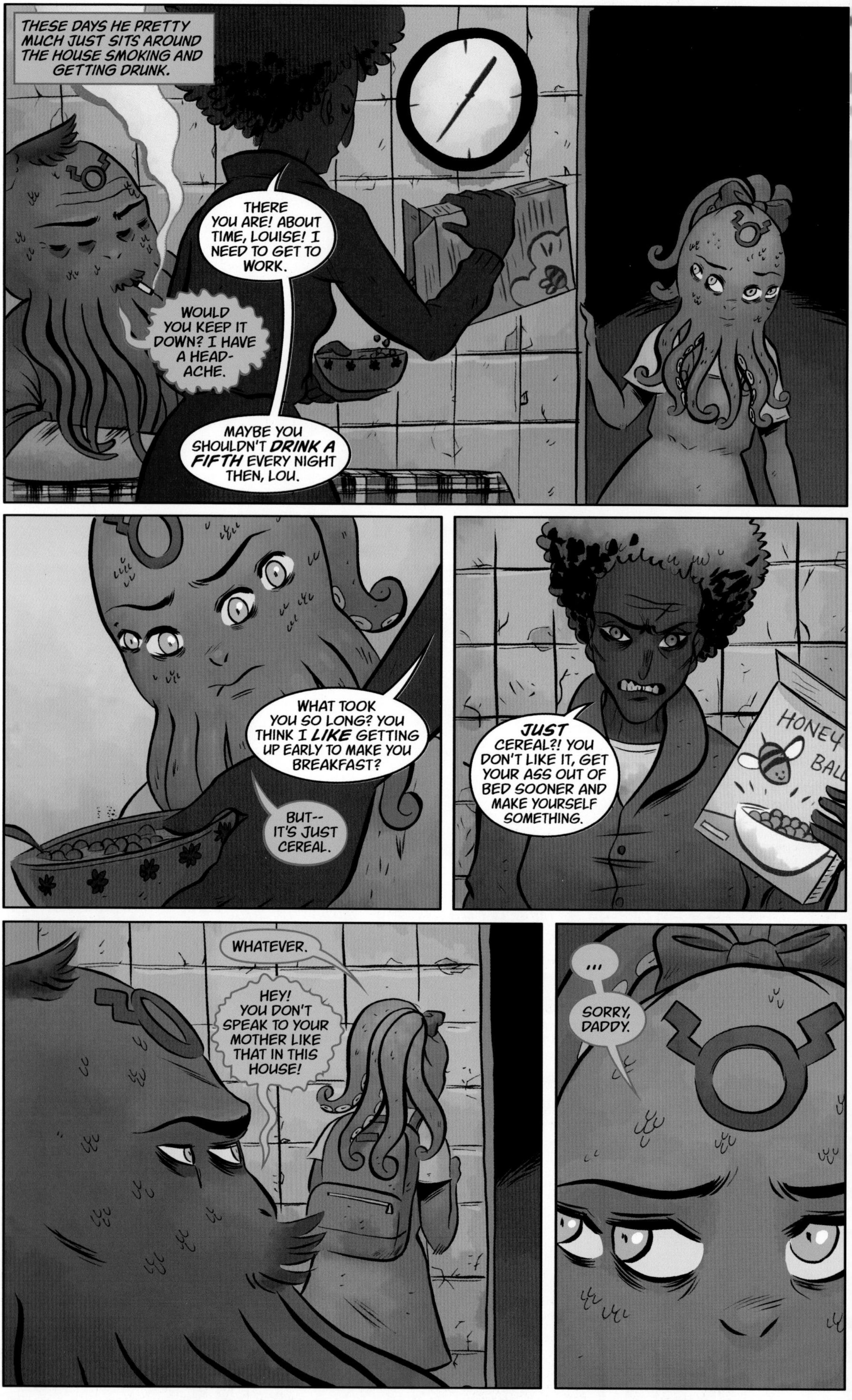
THESE DAYS HE PRETTY MUCH JUST SITS AROUND THE HOUSE SMOKING AND GETTING DRUNK.
THERE YOU ARE! ABOUT TIME, LOUISE! I NEED TO GET TO WORK.
WOULD YOU KEEP IT DOWN? I HAVE A HEAD-ACHE.
MAYBE YOU SHOULDN'T DRINK A FIFTH EVERY NIGHT THEN, LOU.
WHAT TOOK YOU SO LONG? YOU THINK I LIKE GETTING UP EARLY TO MAKE YOU BREAKFAST?
BUT-- IT'S JUST CEREAL.
JUST CEREAL?! YOU DON'T LIKE IT, GET YOUR ASS OUT OF BED SOONER AND MAKE YOURSELF SOMETHING.
WHATEVER.
HEY! YOU DON'T SPEAK TO YOUR MOTHER LIKE THAT IN THIS HOUSE!
...
SORRY, DADDY.

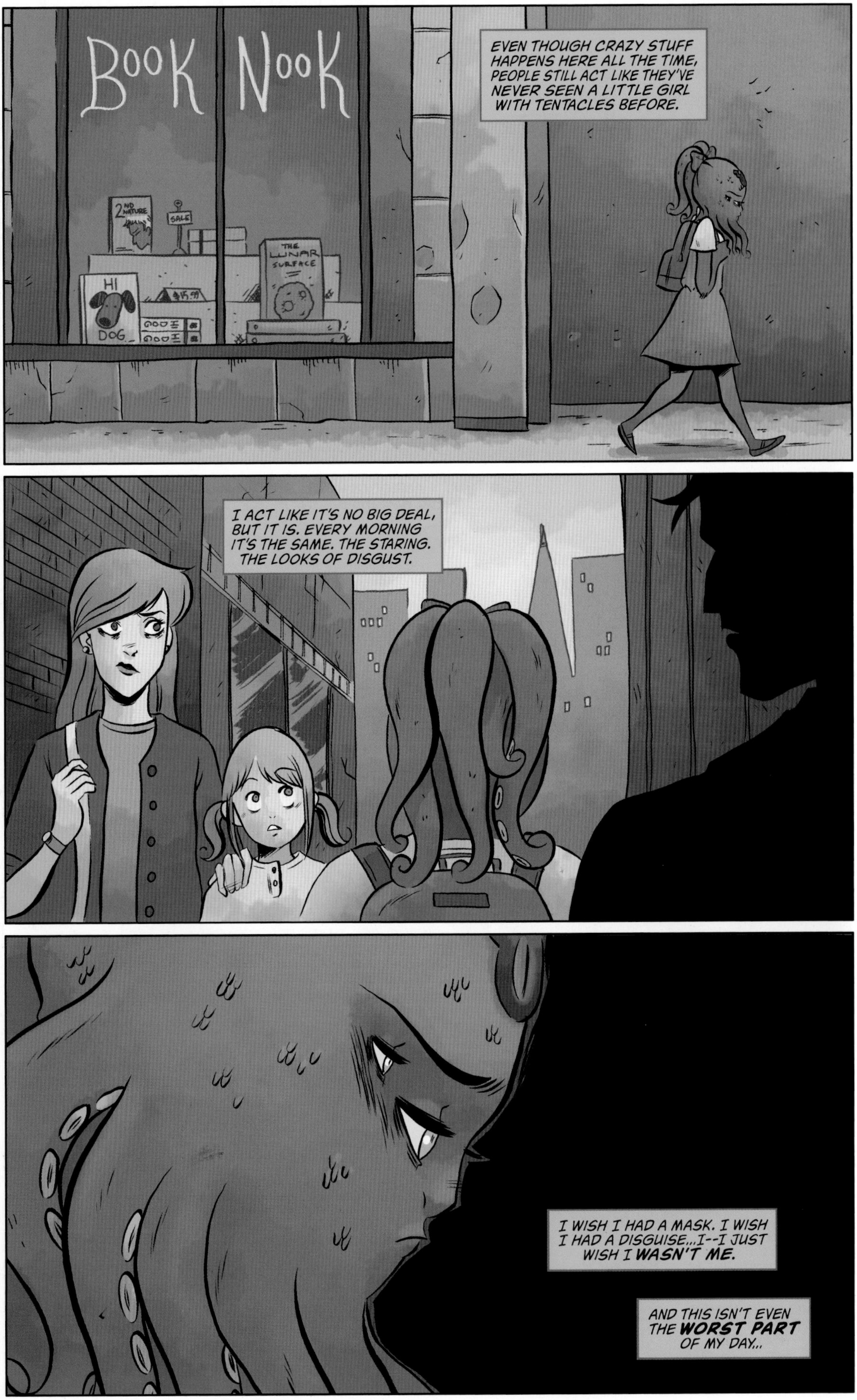
BOOK NOOK
EVEN THOUGH CRAZY STUFF HAPPENS HERE ALL THE TIME, PEOPLE STILL ACT LIKE THEY'VE NEVER SEEN A LITTLE GIRL WITH TENTACLES BEFORE.
I ACT LIKE IT'S NO BIG DEAL, BUT IT IS. EVERY MORNING IT'S THE SAME. THE STARING. THE LOOKS OF DISGUST.
I WISH I HAD A MASK. I WISH I HAD A DISGUISE...I--I JUST WISH I WASN'T ME.
AND THIS ISN'T EVEN THE WORST PART OF MY DAY...

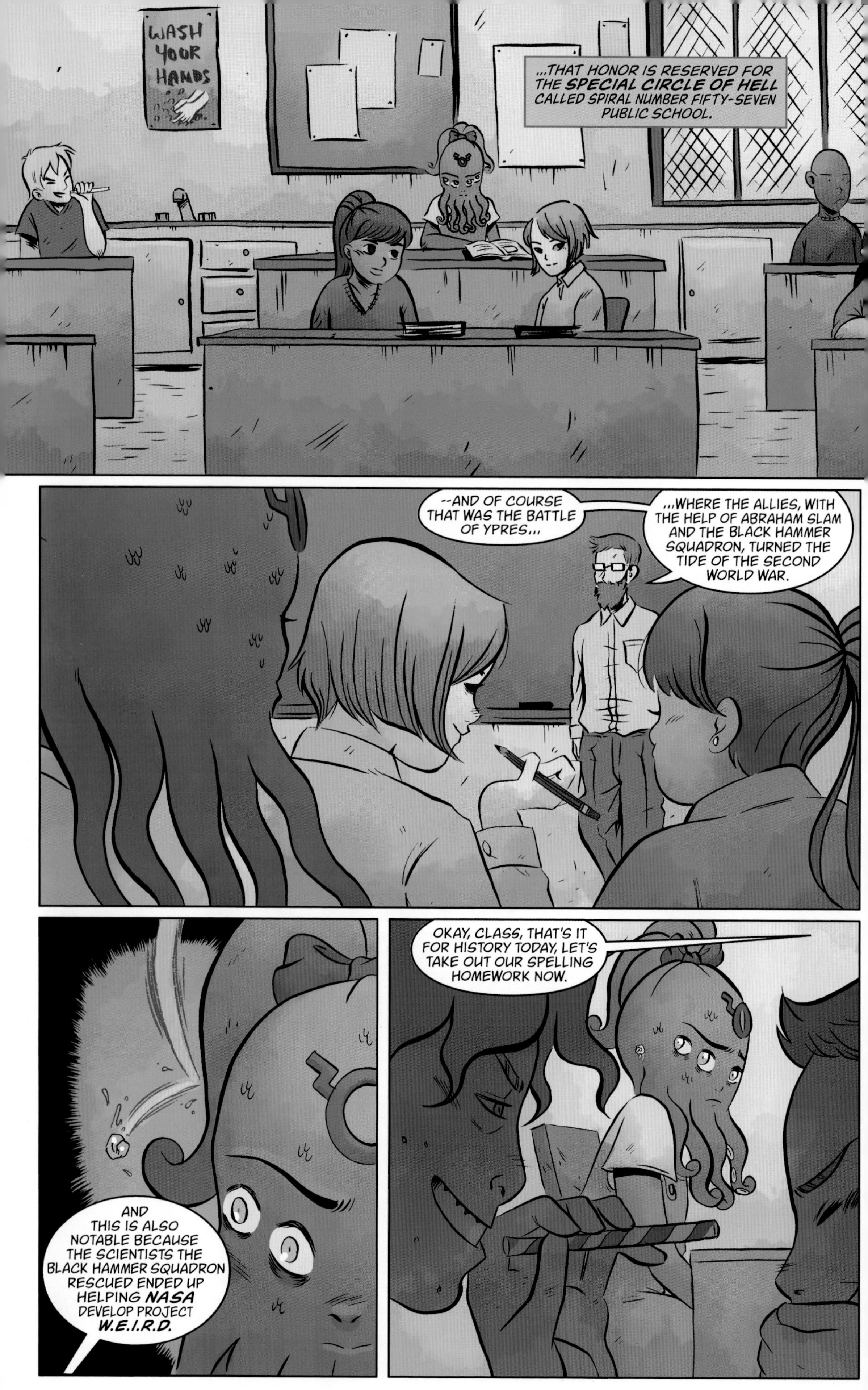
WASH YOUR HANDS
...THAT HONOR IS RESERVED FOR THE SPECIAL CIRCLE OF HELL CALLED SPIRAL NUMBER FIFTY-SEVEN PUBLIC SCHOOL.
--AND OF COURSE THAT WAS THE BATTLE OF YPRES...
...WHERE THE ALLIES, WITH THE HELP OF ABRAHAM SLAM AND THE BLACK HAMMER SQUADRON, TURNED THE TIDE OF THE SECOND WORLD WAR.
AND THIS IS ALSO NOTABLE BECAUSE THE SCIENTISTS THE BLACK HAMMER SQUADRON RESCUED ENDED UP HELPING NASA DEVELOP PROJECT W.E.I.R.D.
OKAY, CLASS, THAT'S IT FOR HISTORY TODAY, LET'S TAKE OUT OUR SPELLING HOMEWORK NOW.

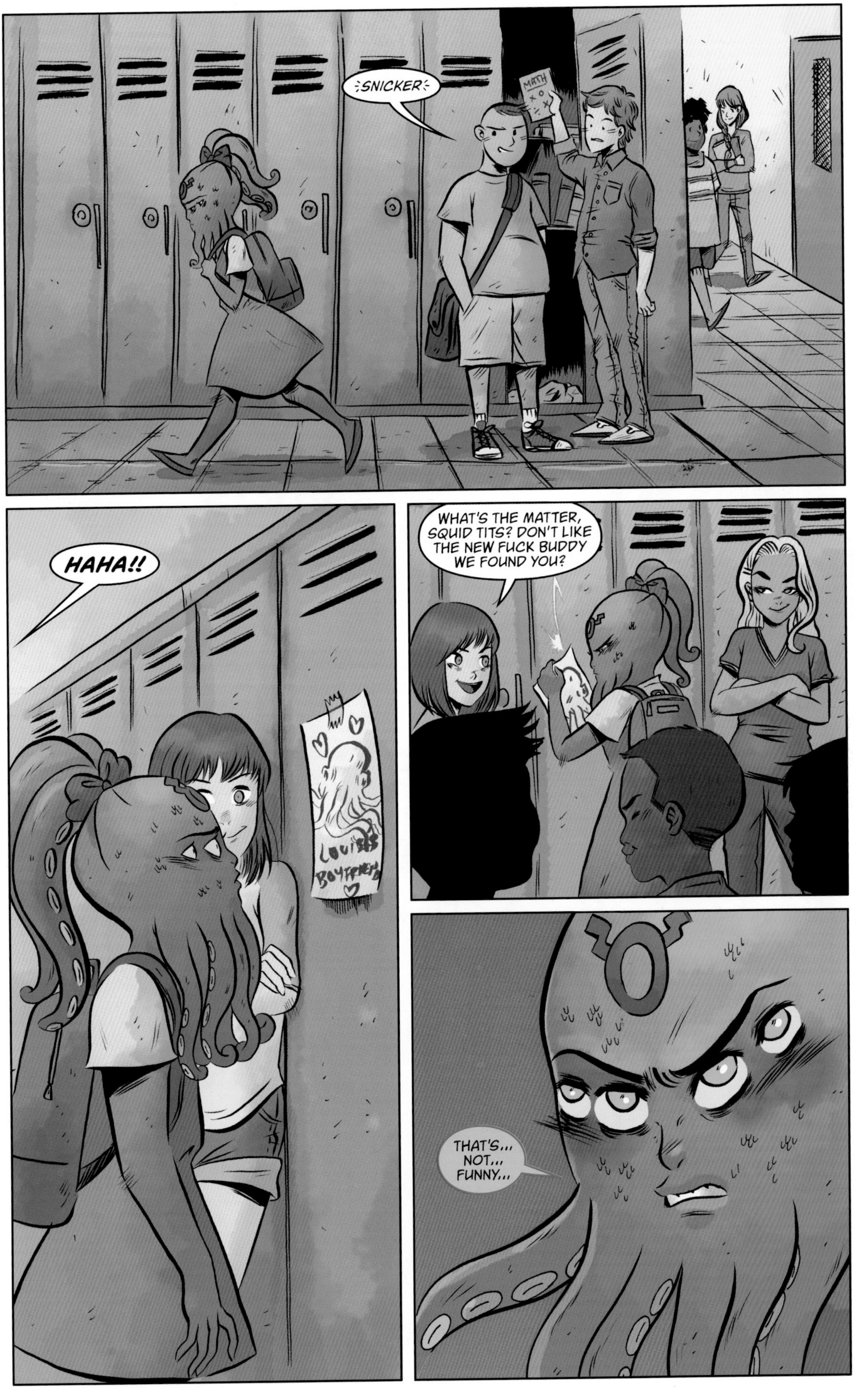
SNICKER
MATH
HAHA!!
WHAT'S THE MATTER, SQUID TITS? DON'T LIKE THE NEW FUCK BUDDY WE FOUND YOU?
THAT'S... NOT... FUNNY...

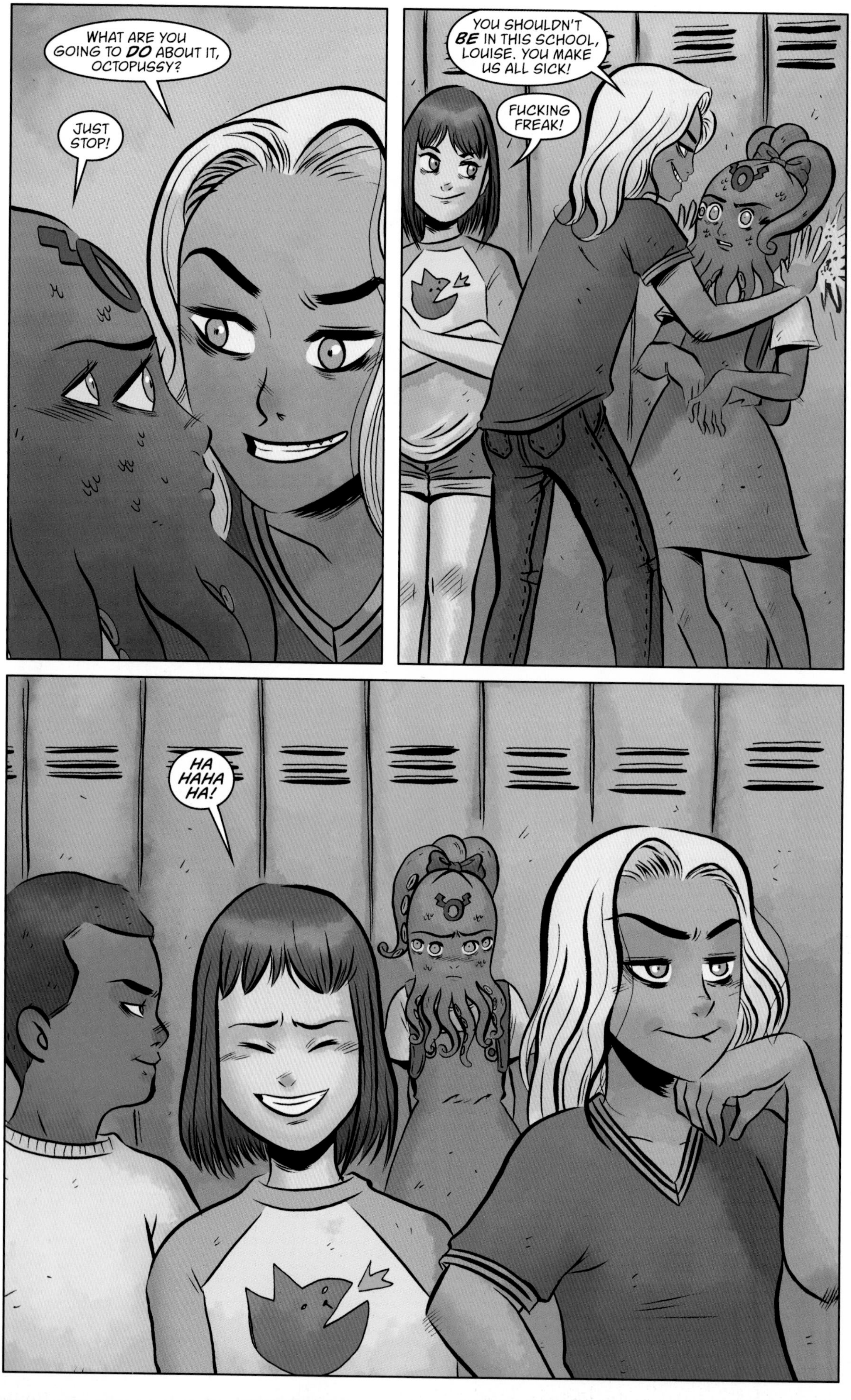
WHAT ARE YOU GOING TO DO ABOUT IT, OCTOPUSSY?
JUST STOP!
YOU SHOULDN'T BE IN THIS SCHOOL, LOUISE. YOU MAKE US ALL SICK!
FUCKING FREAK!
HA HAHAHA HA!

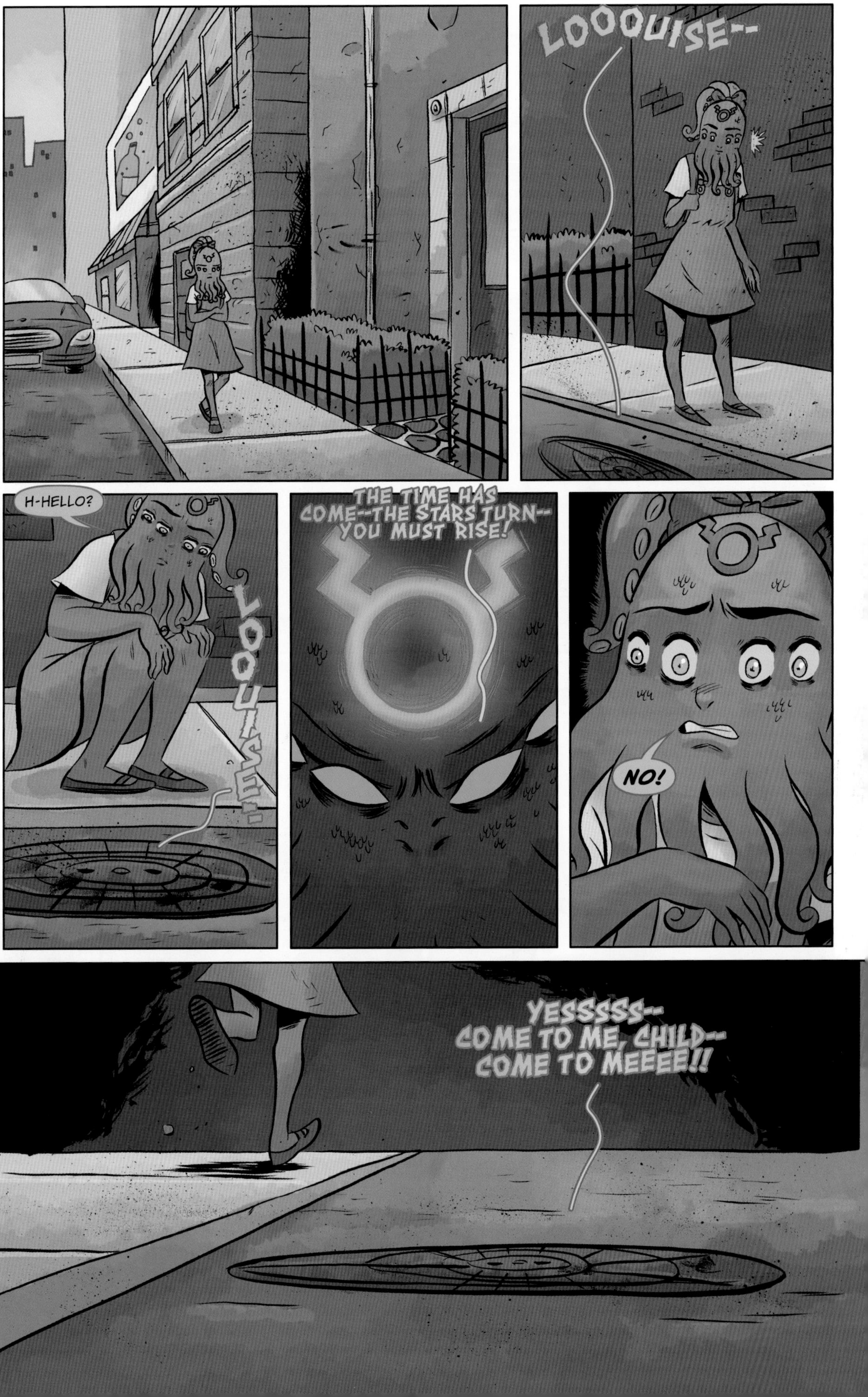
LOOOUISE--
H-HELLO?
LOOOUISE--!
THE TIME HAS
COME--THE STARS TURN--
YOU MUST RISE!
NO!
YESSSSS--
COME TO ME, CHILD--
COME TO MEEEE!!

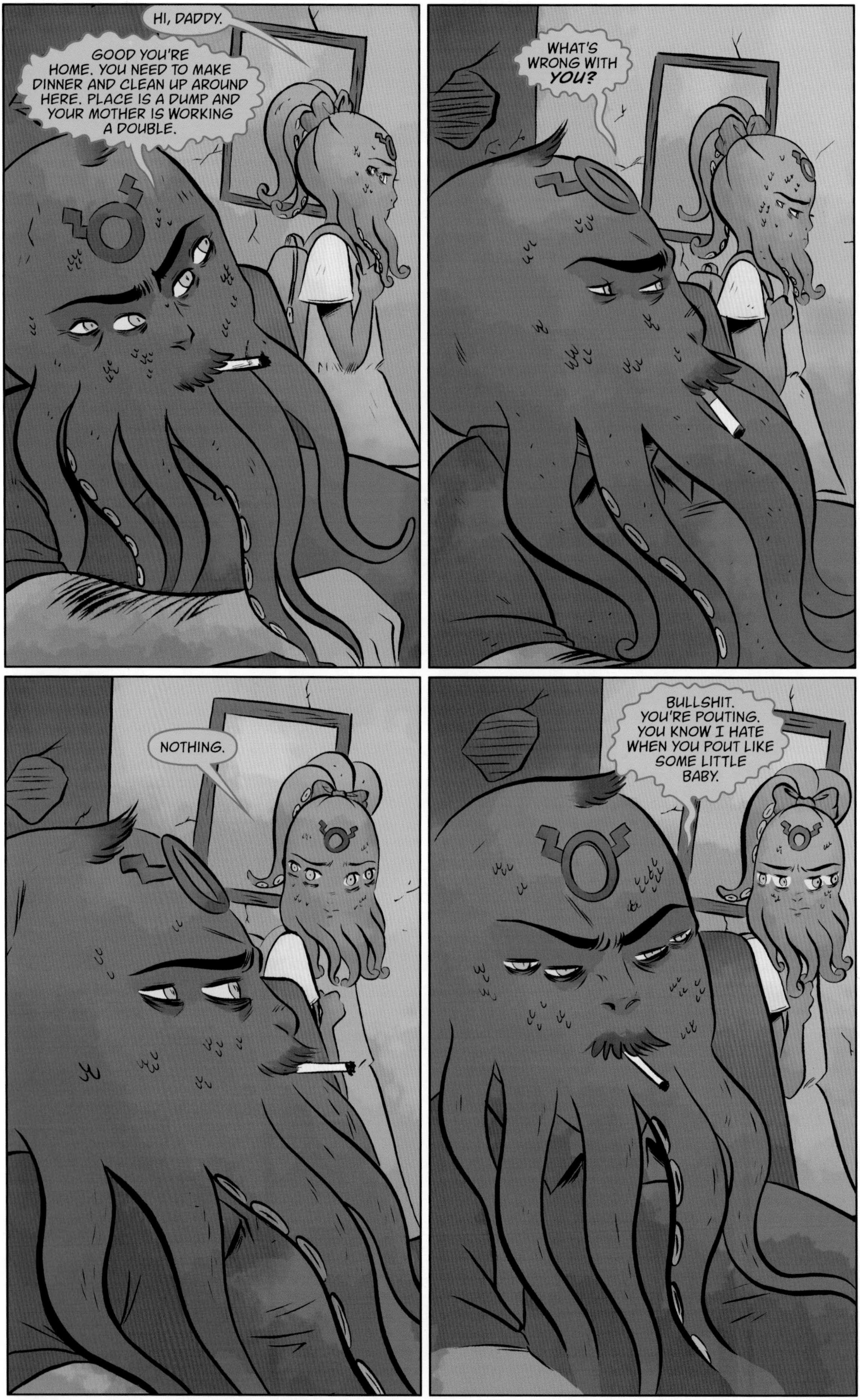
HI, DADDY.
GOOD YOU'RE HOME. YOU NEED TO MAKE DINNER AND CLEAN UP AROUND HERE. PLACE IS A DUMP AND YOUR MOTHER IS WORKING A DOUBLE.
WHAT'S WRONG WITH *YOU?*
NOTHING.
BULLSHIT. YOU'RE POUTING. YOU KNOW I HATE WHEN YOU POUT LIKE SOME LITTLE BABY.

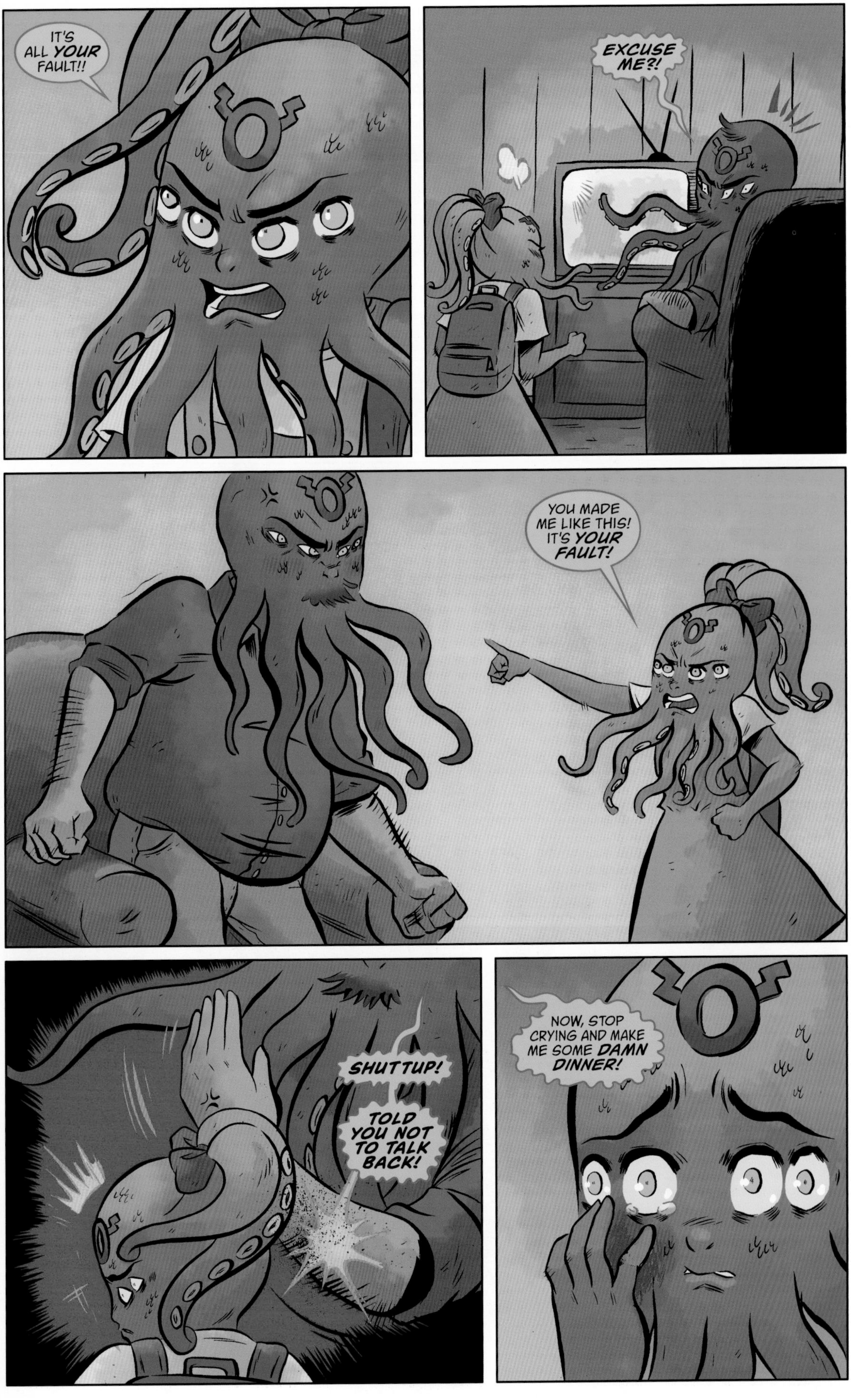
IT'S ALL YOUR FAULT!!
EXCUSE ME?!
YOU MADE ME LIKE THIS! IT'S YOUR FAULT!
SHUTTUP!
TOLD YOU NOT TO TALK BACK!
NOW, STOP CRYING AND MAKE ME SOME DAMN DINNER!

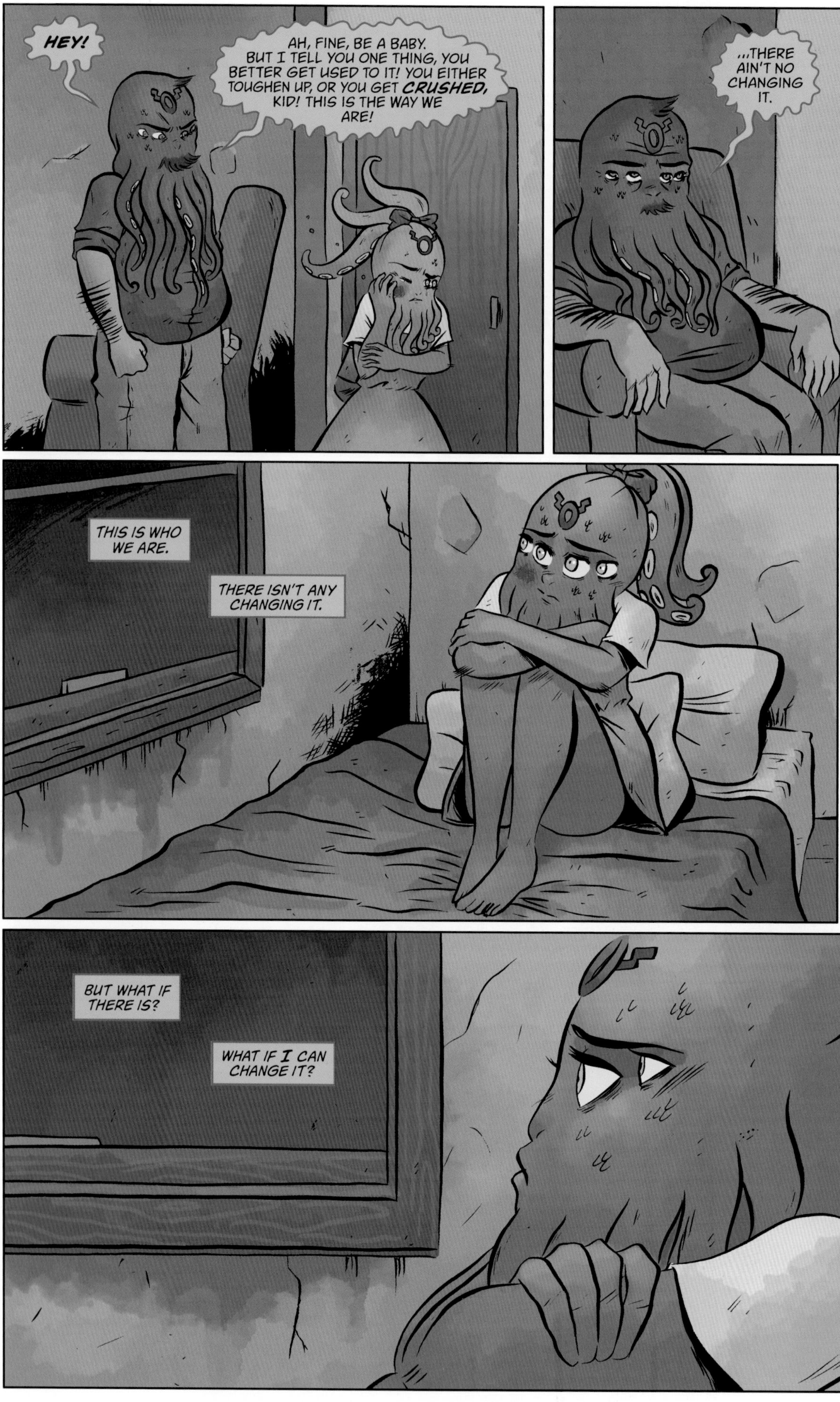
HEY!
AH, FINE, BE A BABY. BUT I TELL YOU ONE THING, YOU BETTER GET USED TO IT! YOU EITHER TOUGHEN UP, OR YOU GET CRUSHED, KID! THIS IS THE WAY WE ARE!
...THERE AIN'T NO CHANGING IT.
THIS IS WHO WE ARE.
THERE ISN'T ANY CHANGING IT.
BUT WHAT IF THERE IS?
WHAT IF I CAN CHANGE IT?

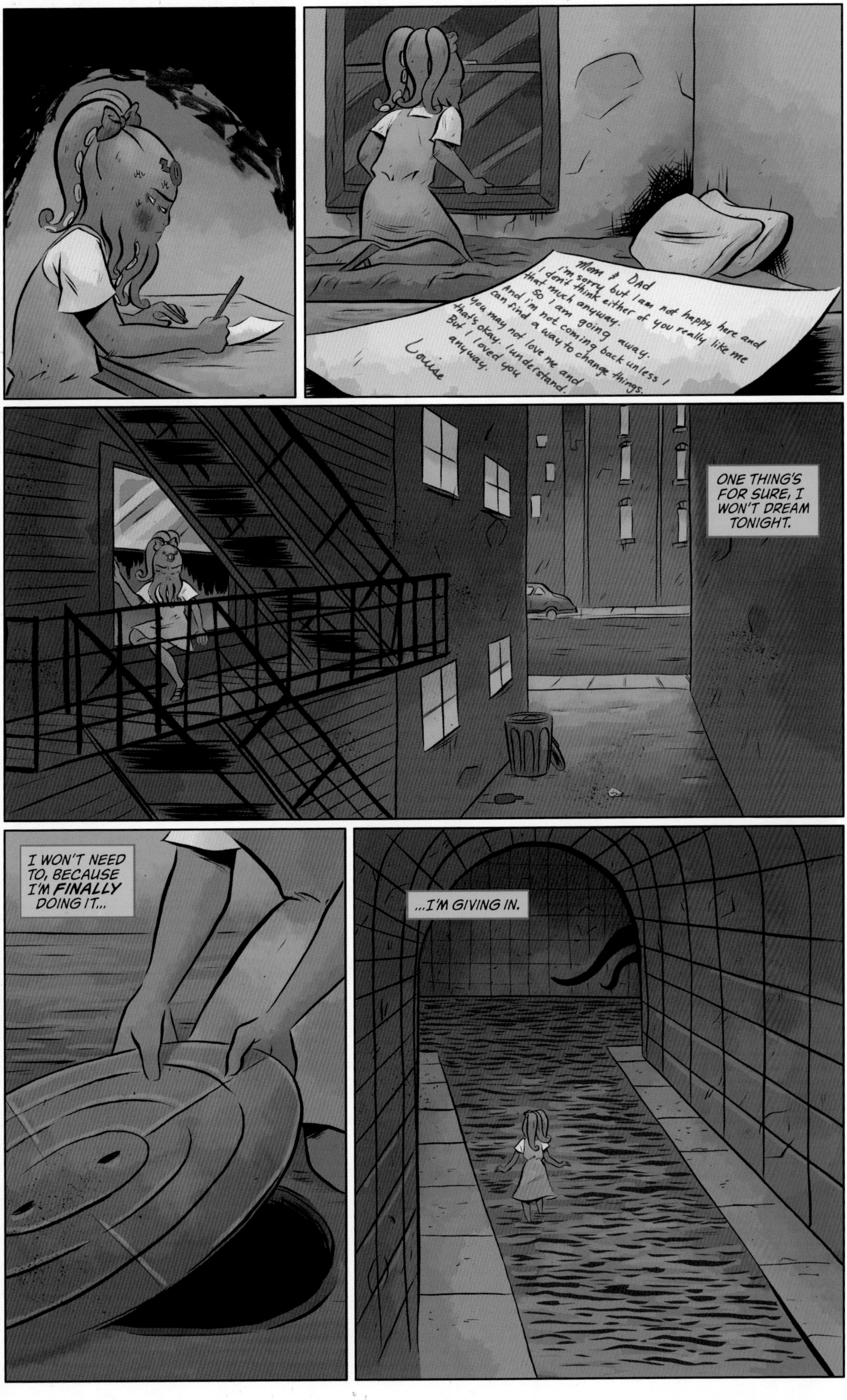
Mom & DAD
I'm sorry but I am not happy here and
I don't think either of you really like me
that much anyway.
So I am going away.
And I'm not coming back unless I
can find a way to change things.
You may not love me and
that's okay. I understand.
But I loved you
anyway.
Louise
ONE THING'S FOR SURE, I WON'T DREAM TONIGHT.
I WON'T NEED TO, BECAUSE I'M **FINALLY** DOING IT...
...I'M GIVING IN.

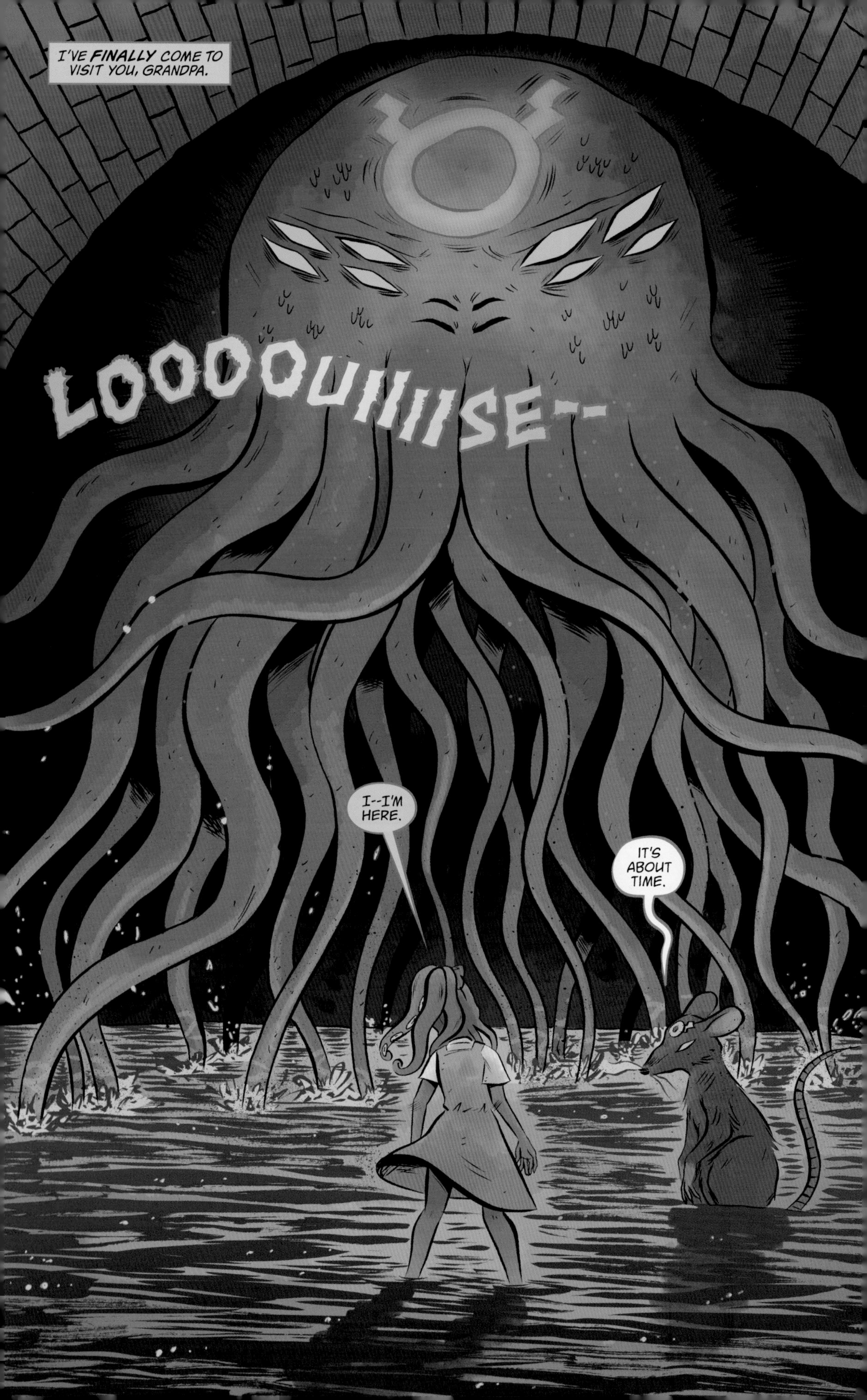
I'VE FINALLY COME TO VISIT YOU, GRANDPA.
LOOOOUIIIISE--
I--I'M HERE.
IT'S ABOUT TIME.

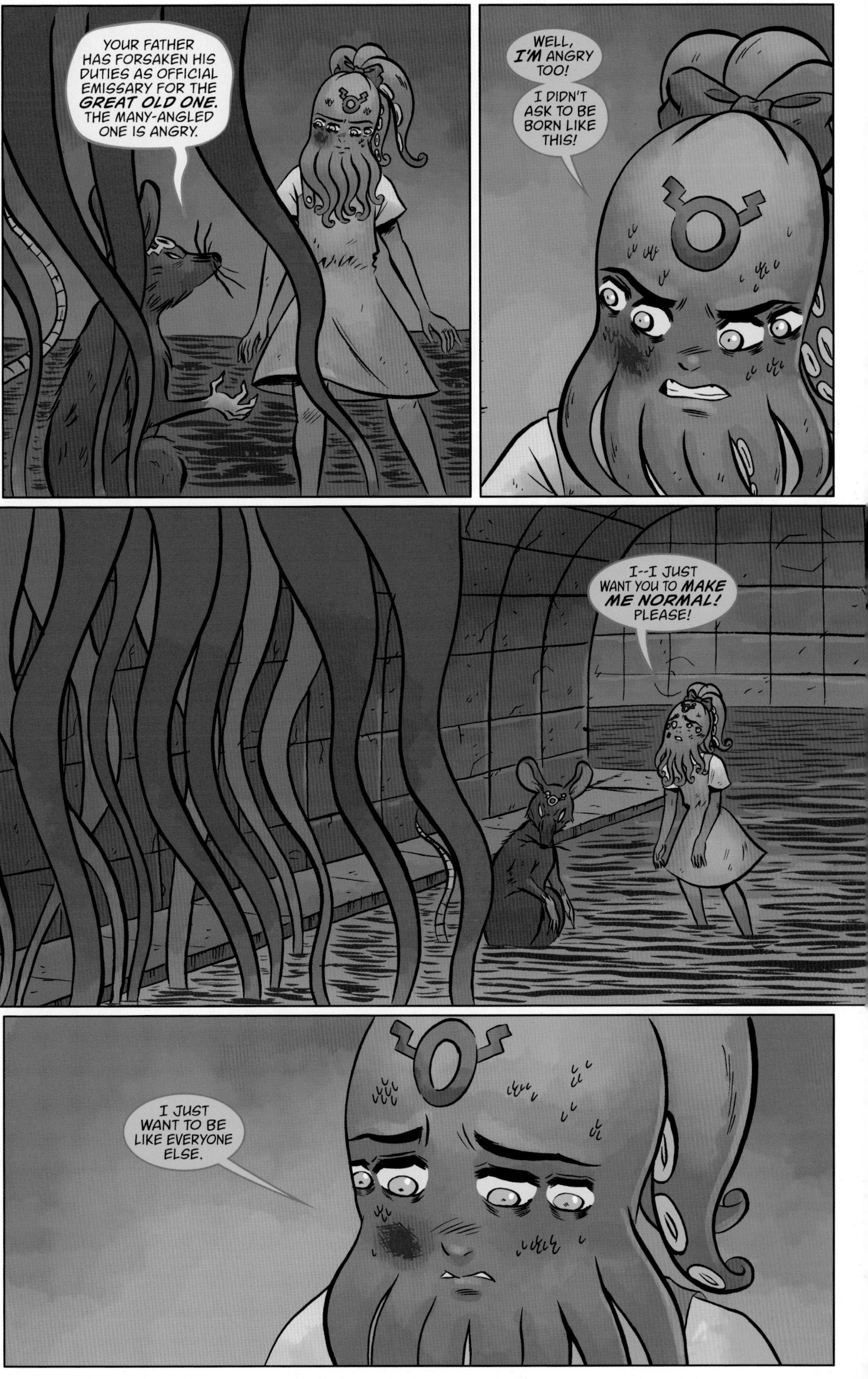
YOUR FATHER HAS FORSAKEN HIS DUTIES AS OFFICIAL EMISSARY FOR THE **GREAT OLD ONE**. THE MANY-ANGLED ONE IS ANGRY.
WELL, ***I'M*** ANGRY TOO!
I DIDN'T ASK TO BE BORN LIKE THIS!
I--I JUST WANT YOU TO ***MAKE ME NORMAL!*** PLEASE!
I JUST WANT TO BE LIKE EVERYONE ELSE.

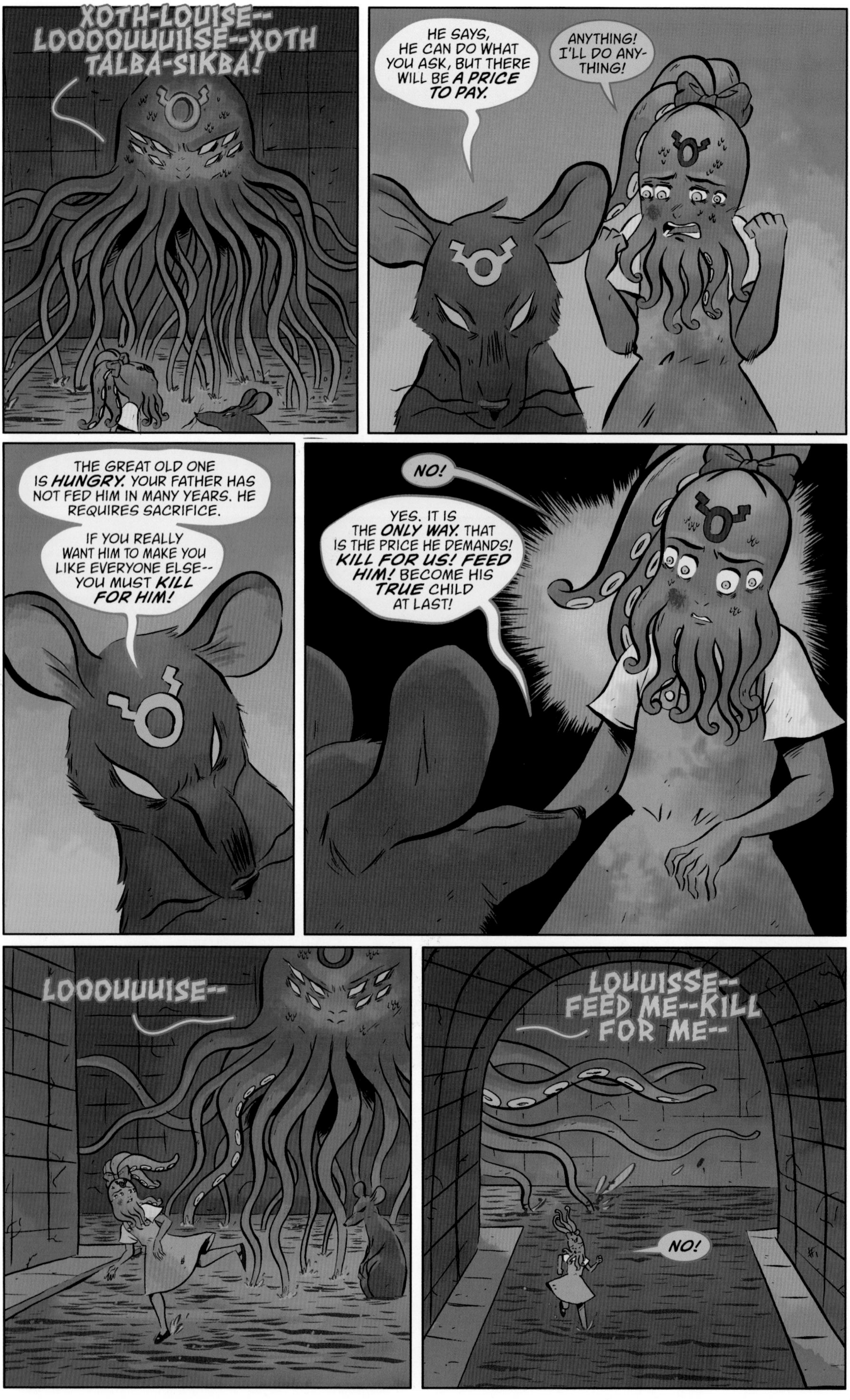
XOTH-LOUISE--
LOOOOUUUIISE--XOTH
TALBA-SIKBA!
HE SAYS, HE CAN DO WHAT YOU ASK, BUT THERE WILL BE A PRICE TO PAY.
ANYTHING! I'LL DO ANYTHING!
THE GREAT OLD ONE IS HUNGRY. YOUR FATHER HAS NOT FED HIM IN MANY YEARS. HE REQUIRES SACRIFICE.
IF YOU REALLY WANT HIM TO MAKE YOU LIKE EVERYONE ELSE-- YOU MUST KILL FOR HIM!
NO!
YES. IT IS THE ONLY WAY. THAT IS THE PRICE HE DEMANDS! KILL FOR US! FEED HIM! BECOME HIS TRUE CHILD AT LAST!
LOOOUUUISE--
LOUUISSE--
FEED ME--KILL
FOR ME--
NO!

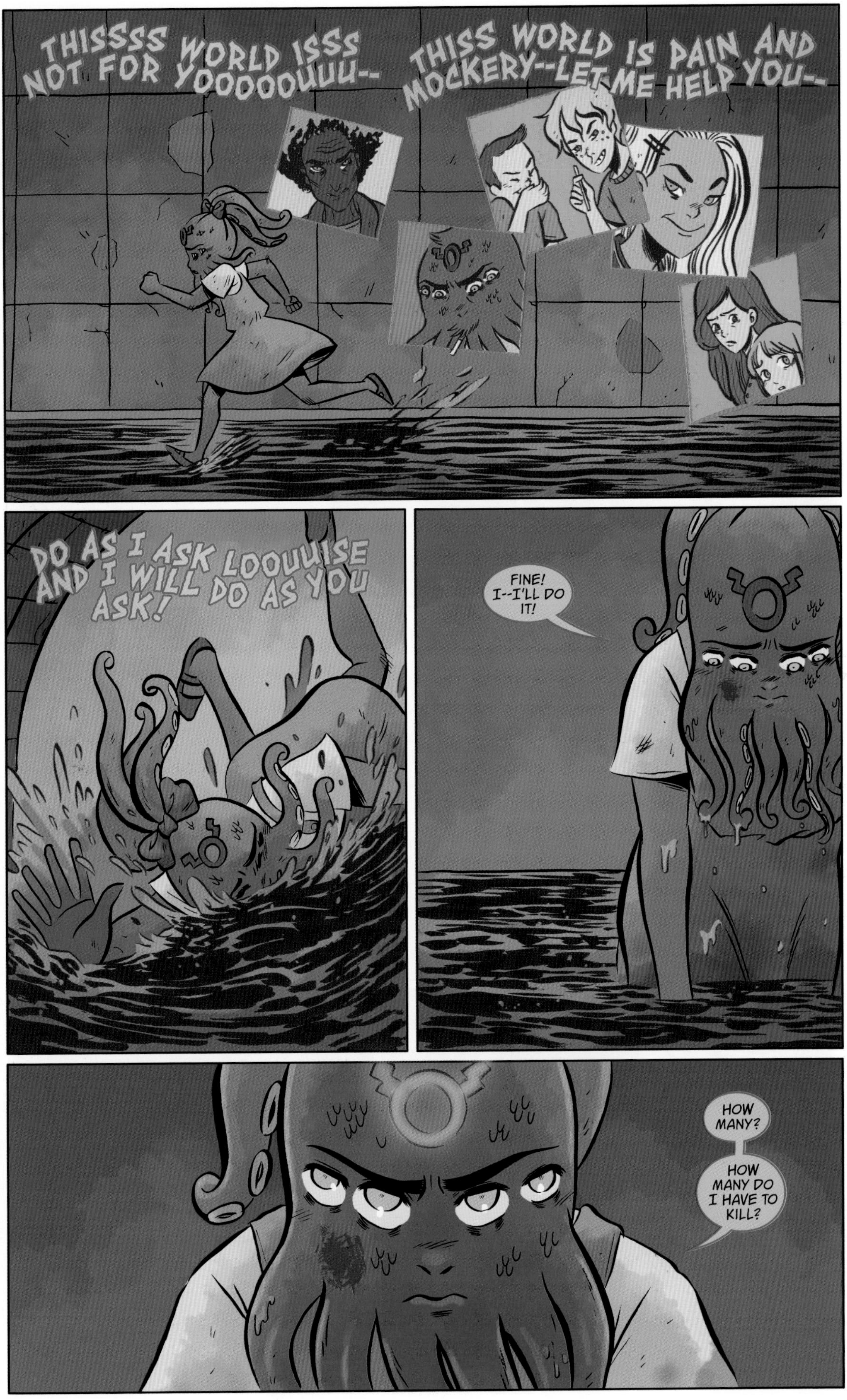
THISSSS WORLD ISSS NOT FOR YOOOOOUUU--
THISS WORLD IS PAIN AND MOCKERY--LET ME HELP YOU--
DO AS I ASK LOOUUISE AND I WILL DO AS YOU ASK!
FINE! I--I'LL DO IT!
HOW MANY?
HOW MANY DO I HAVE TO KILL?

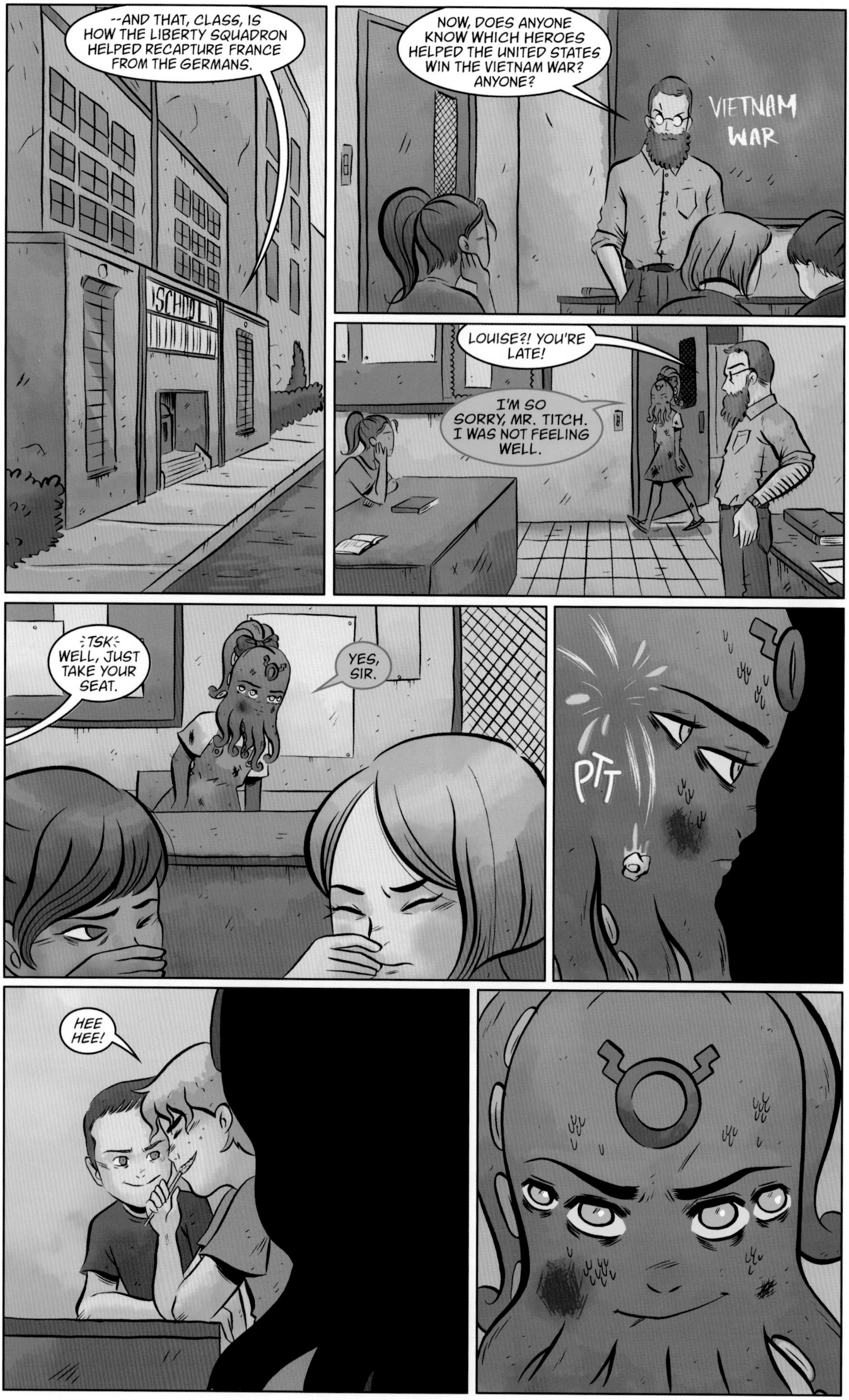

--AND THAT, CLASS, IS HOW THE LIBERTY SQUADRON HELPED RECAPTURE FRANCE FROM THE GERMANS.
SCHOOL
NOW, DOES ANYONE KNOW WHICH HEROES HELPED THE UNITED STATES WIN THE VIETNAM WAR? ANYONE?
VIETNAM WAR
LOUISE?! YOU'RE LATE!
I'M SO SORRY, MR. TITCH. I WAS NOT FEELING WELL.
TSK
WELL, JUST TAKE YOUR SEAT.
YES, SIR.
PTT
HEE HEE!

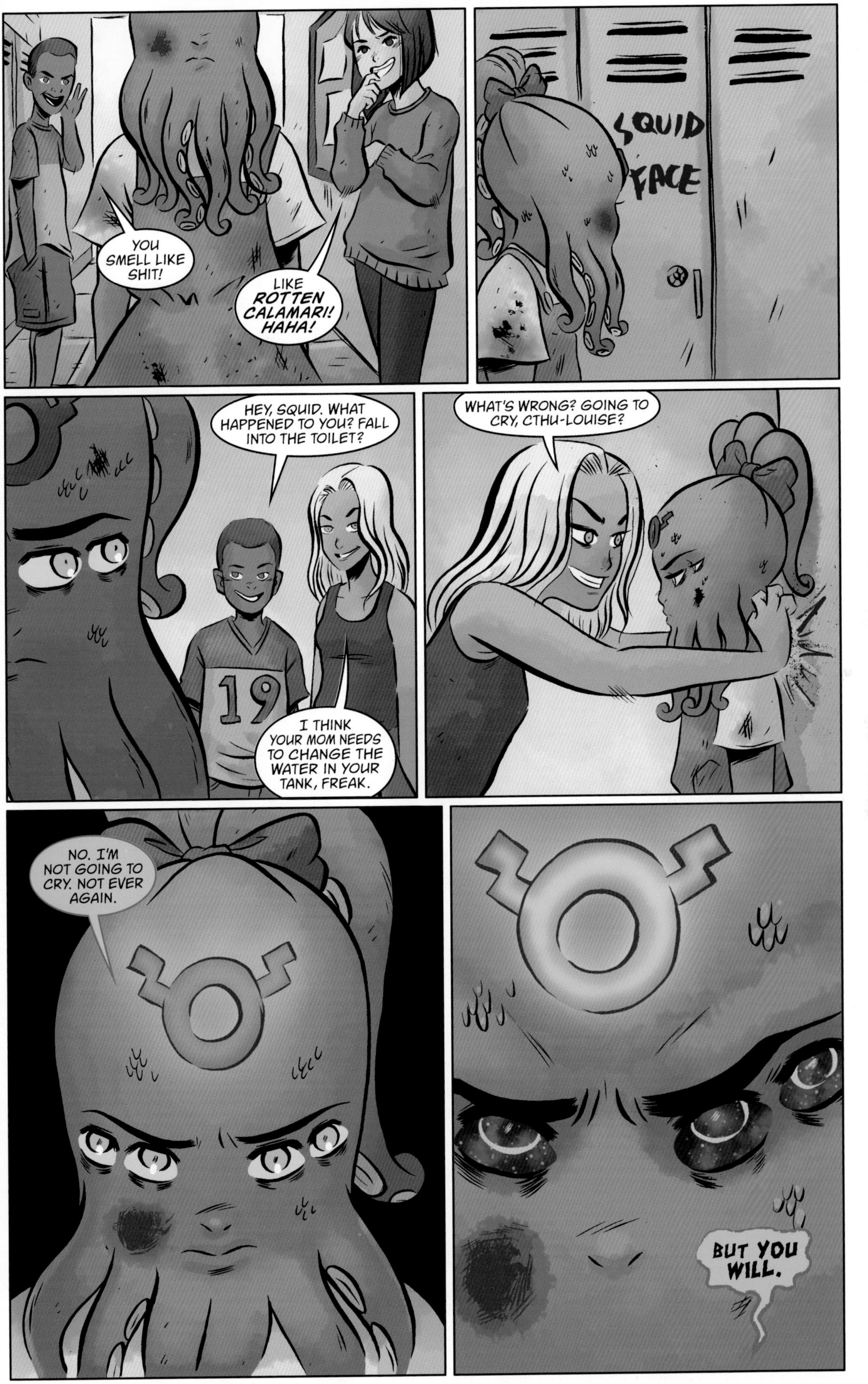
YOU SMELL LIKE SHIT!
LIKE ROTTEN CALAMARI! HAHA!
SQUID FACE
HEY, SQUID. WHAT HAPPENED TO YOU? FALL INTO THE TOILET?
I THINK YOUR MOM NEEDS TO CHANGE THE WATER IN YOUR TANK, FREAK.
19
WHAT'S WRONG? GOING TO CRY, CTHU-LOUISE?
NO. I'M NOT GOING TO CRY. NOT EVER AGAIN.
BUT YOU WILL.

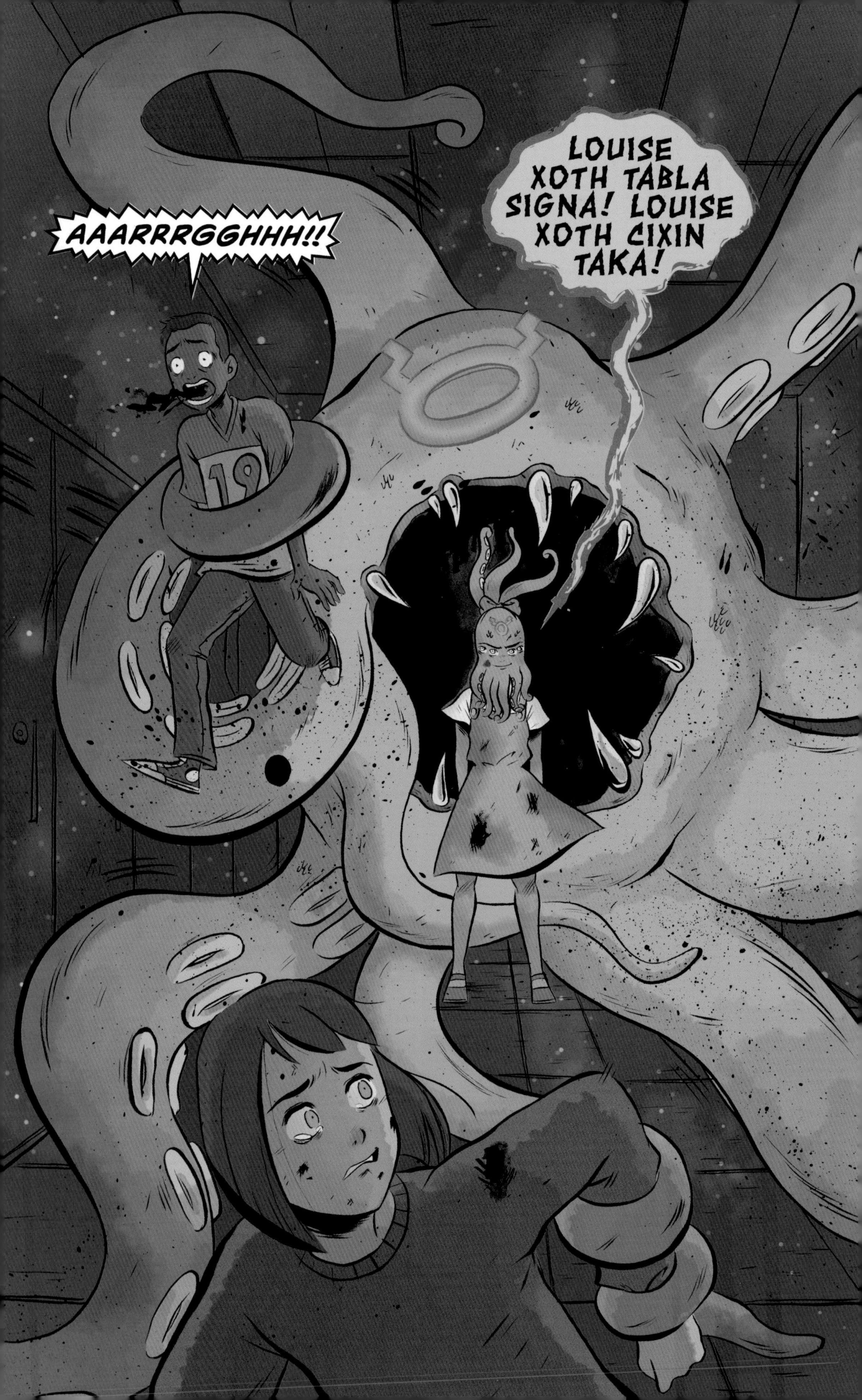
AAARRRGGHHH!!
LOUISE XOTH TABLA SIGNA! LOUISE XOTH CIXIN TAKA!

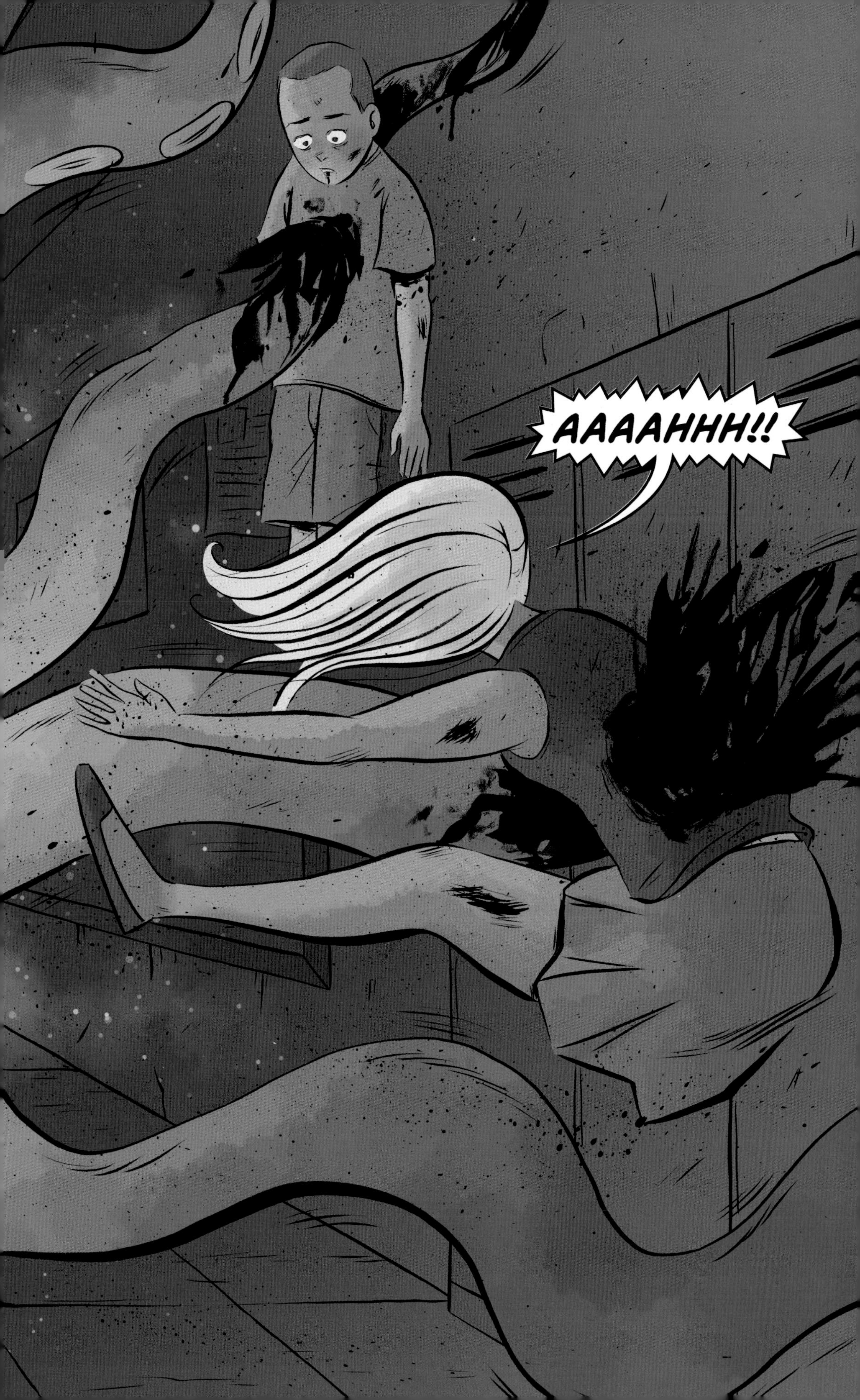
AAAAHHH!!

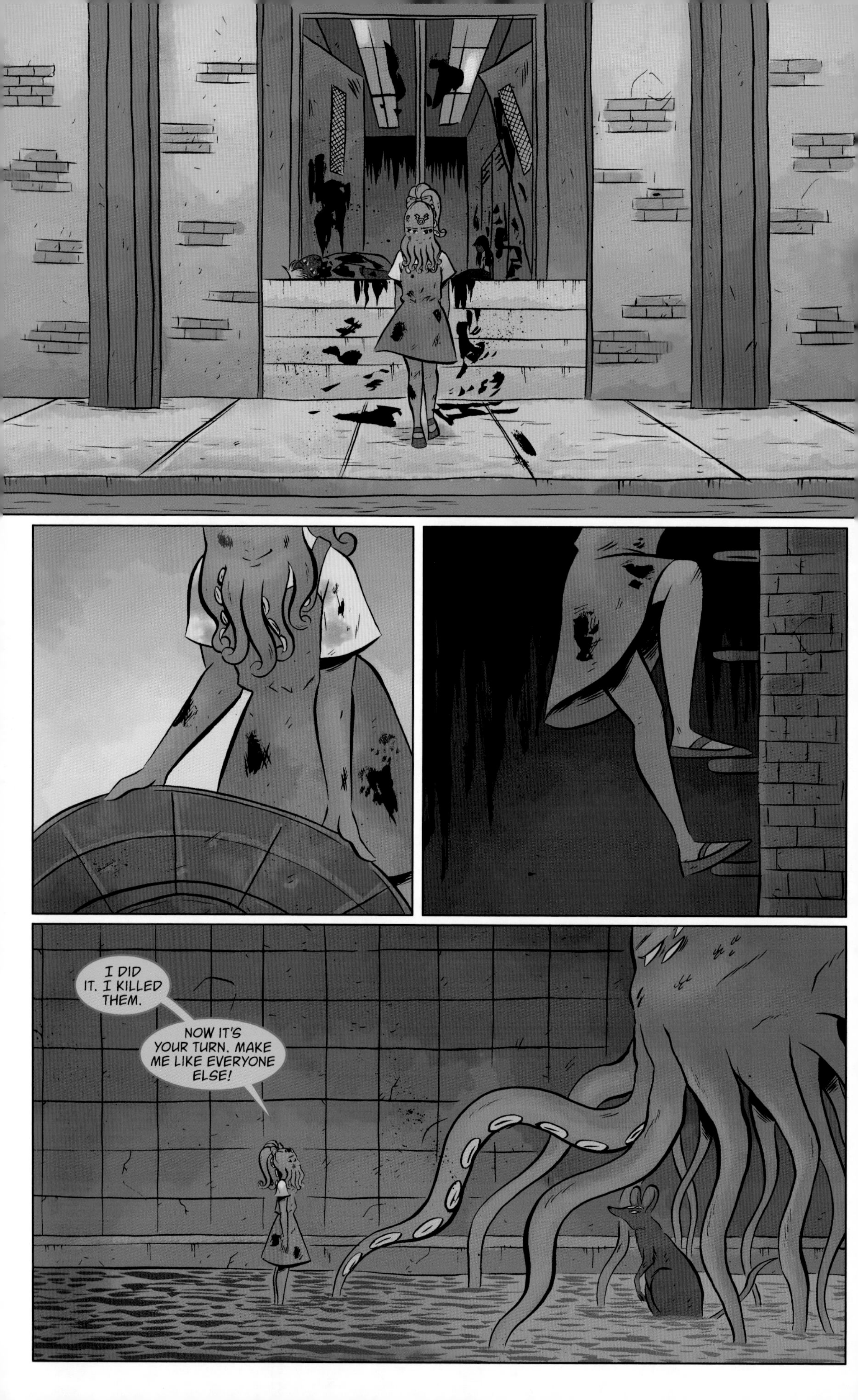
I DID IT. I KILLED THEM.
NOW IT'S YOUR TURN. MAKE ME LIKE EVERYONE ELSE!

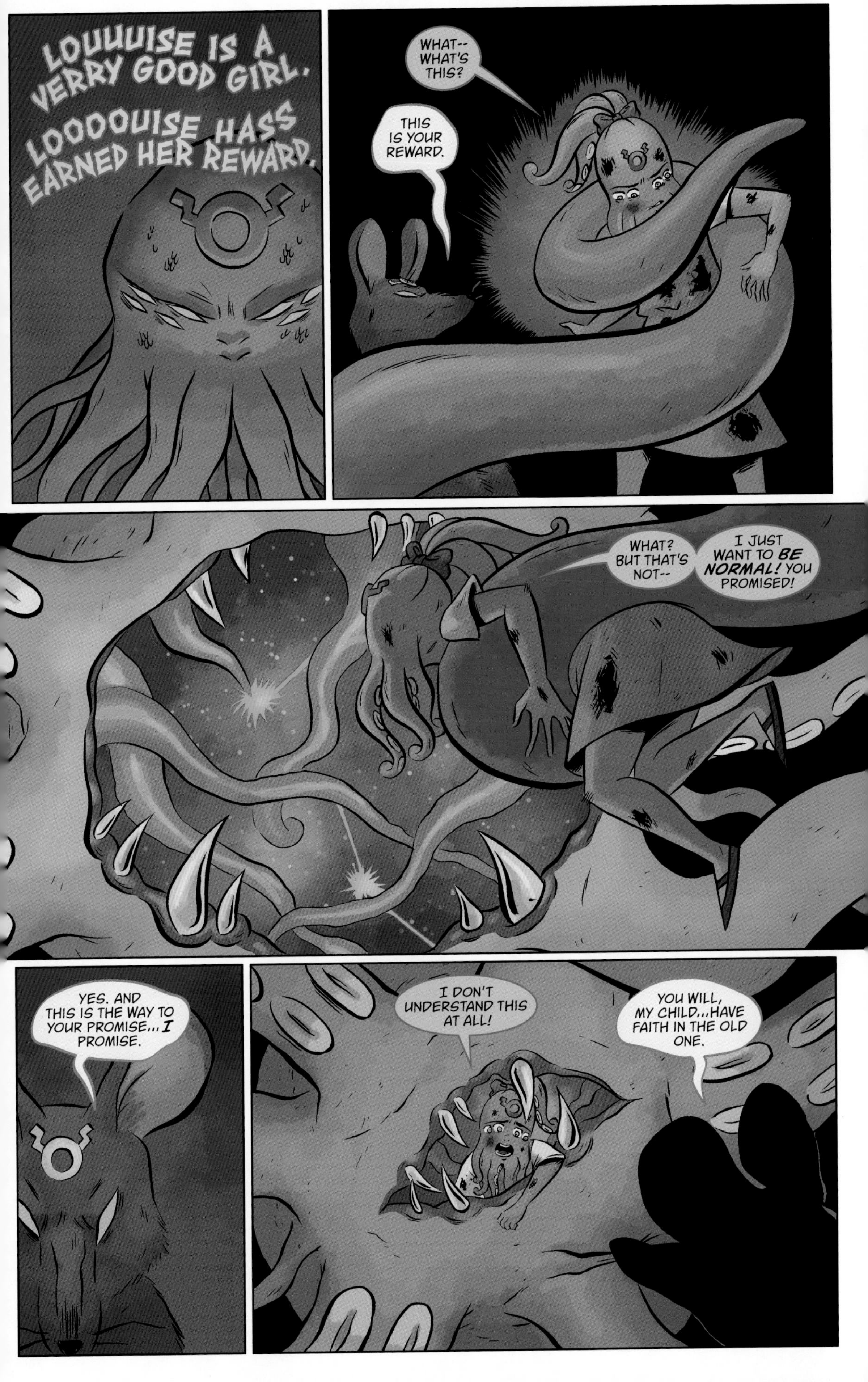
LOUUUISE IS A VERRY GOOD GIRL.
LOOOOUISE HASS EARNED HER REWARD.
WHAT-- WHAT'S THIS?
THIS IS YOUR REWARD.
WHAT? BUT THAT'S NOT--
I JUST WANT TO ***BE NORMAL!*** YOU PROMISED!
YES. AND THIS IS THE WAY TO YOUR PROMISE... *I* PROMISE.
I DON'T UNDERSTAND THIS AT ALL!
YOU WILL, MY CHILD...HAVE FAITH IN THE OLD ONE.

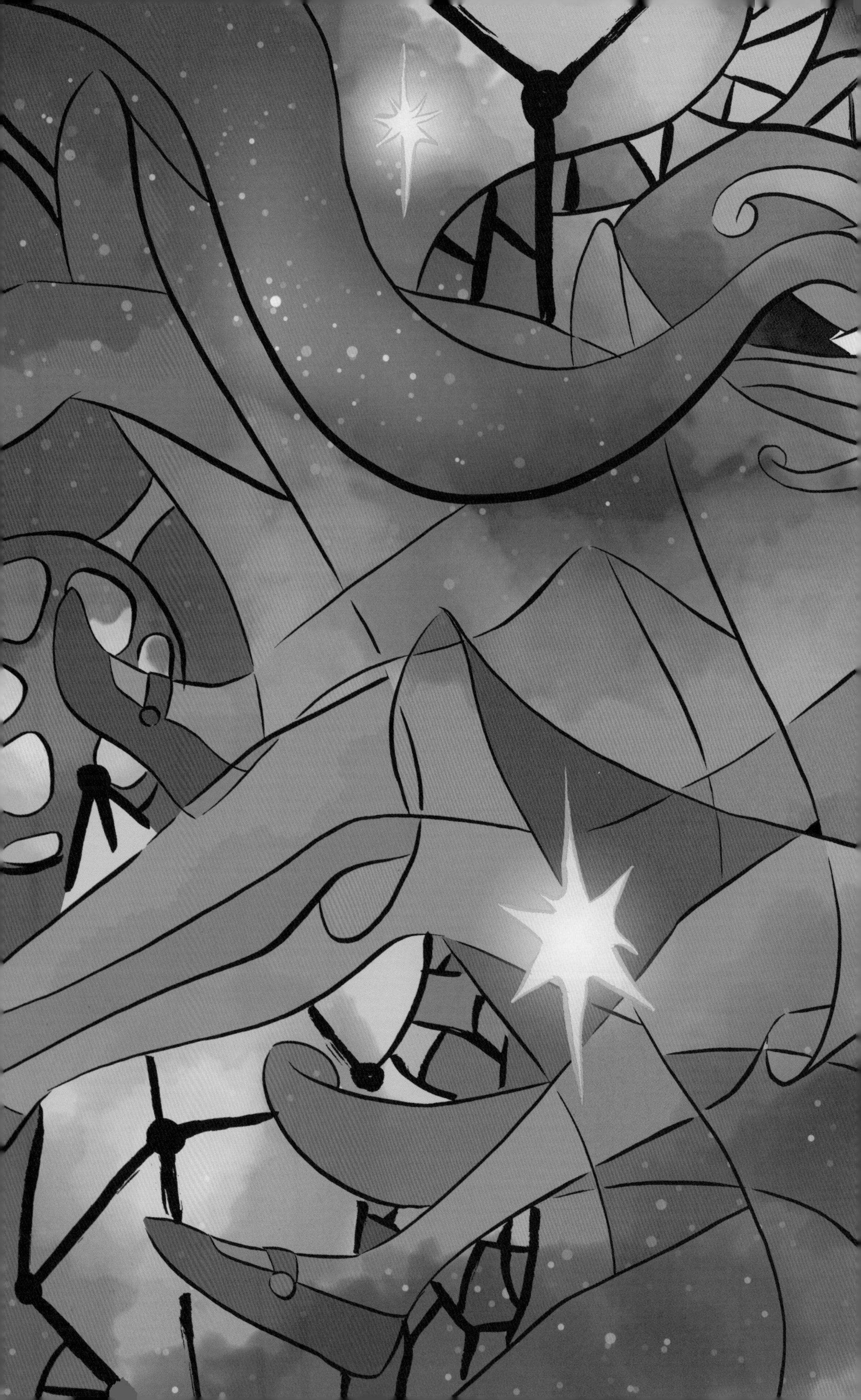

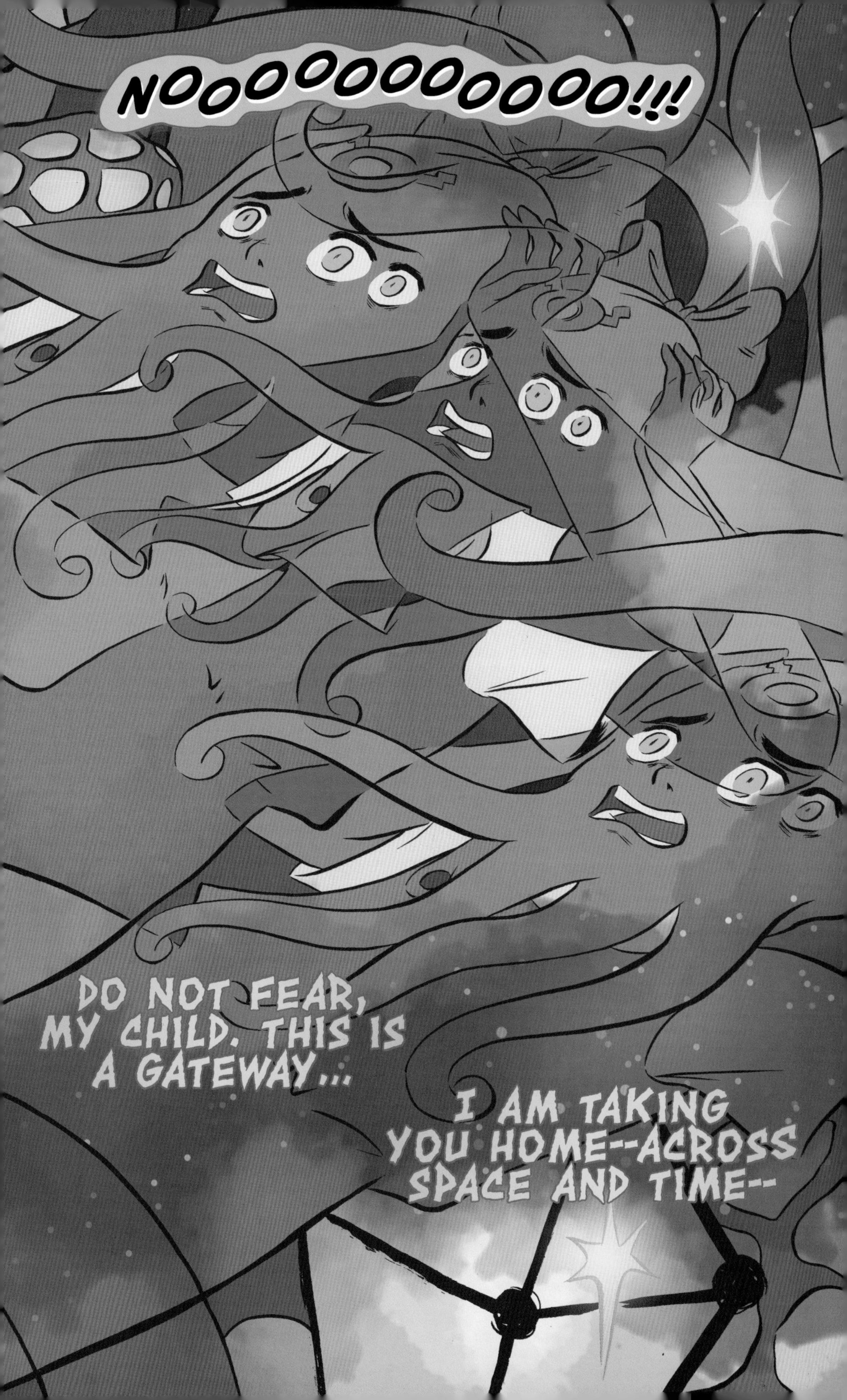
NOOOOOOOOOOOOO!!!
DO NOT FEAR, MY CHILD. THIS IS A GATEWAY...
I AM TAKING YOU HOME--ACROSS SPACE AND TIME--

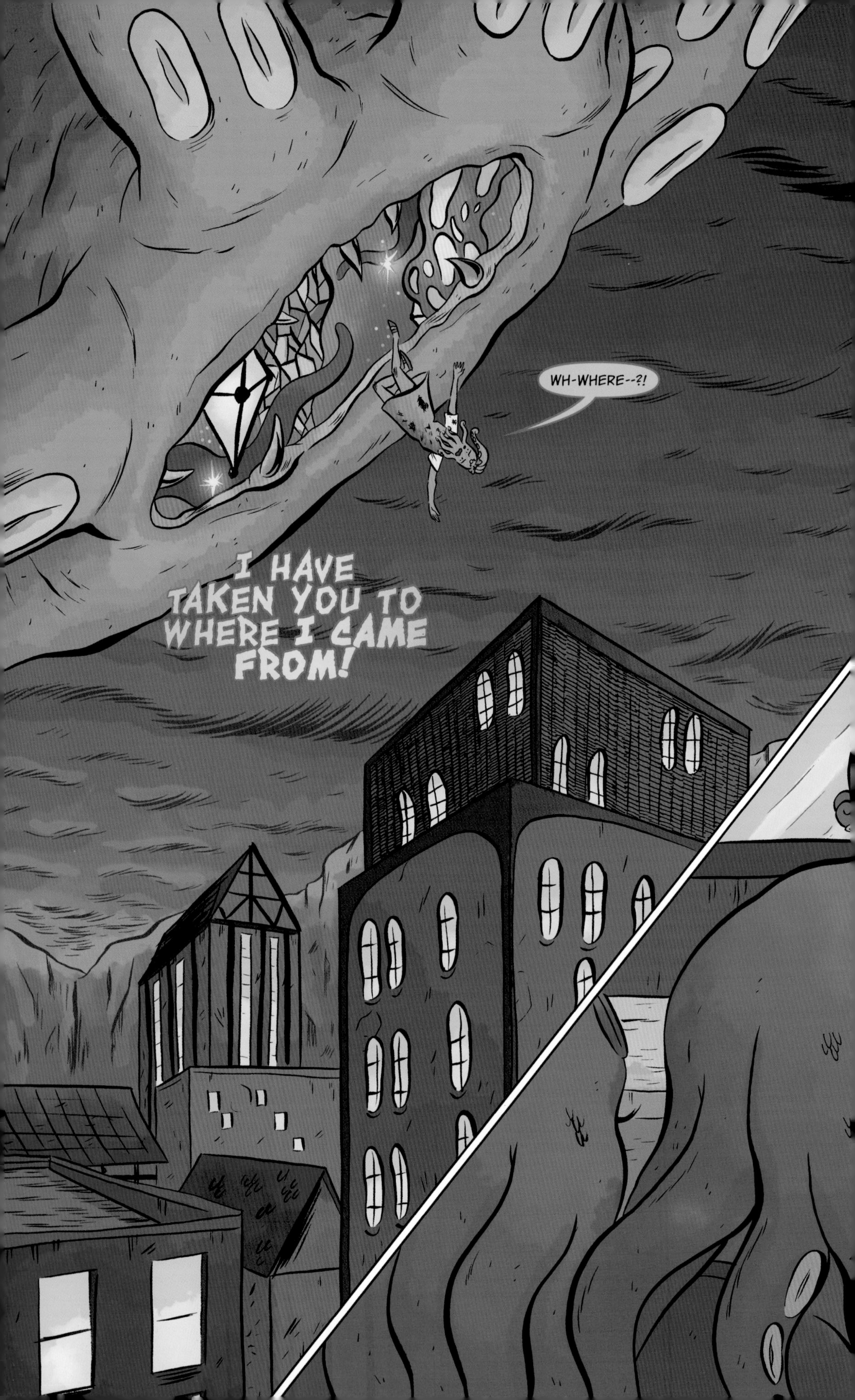
WH-WHERE--?!
I HAVE TAKEN YOU TO WHERE I CAME FROM!

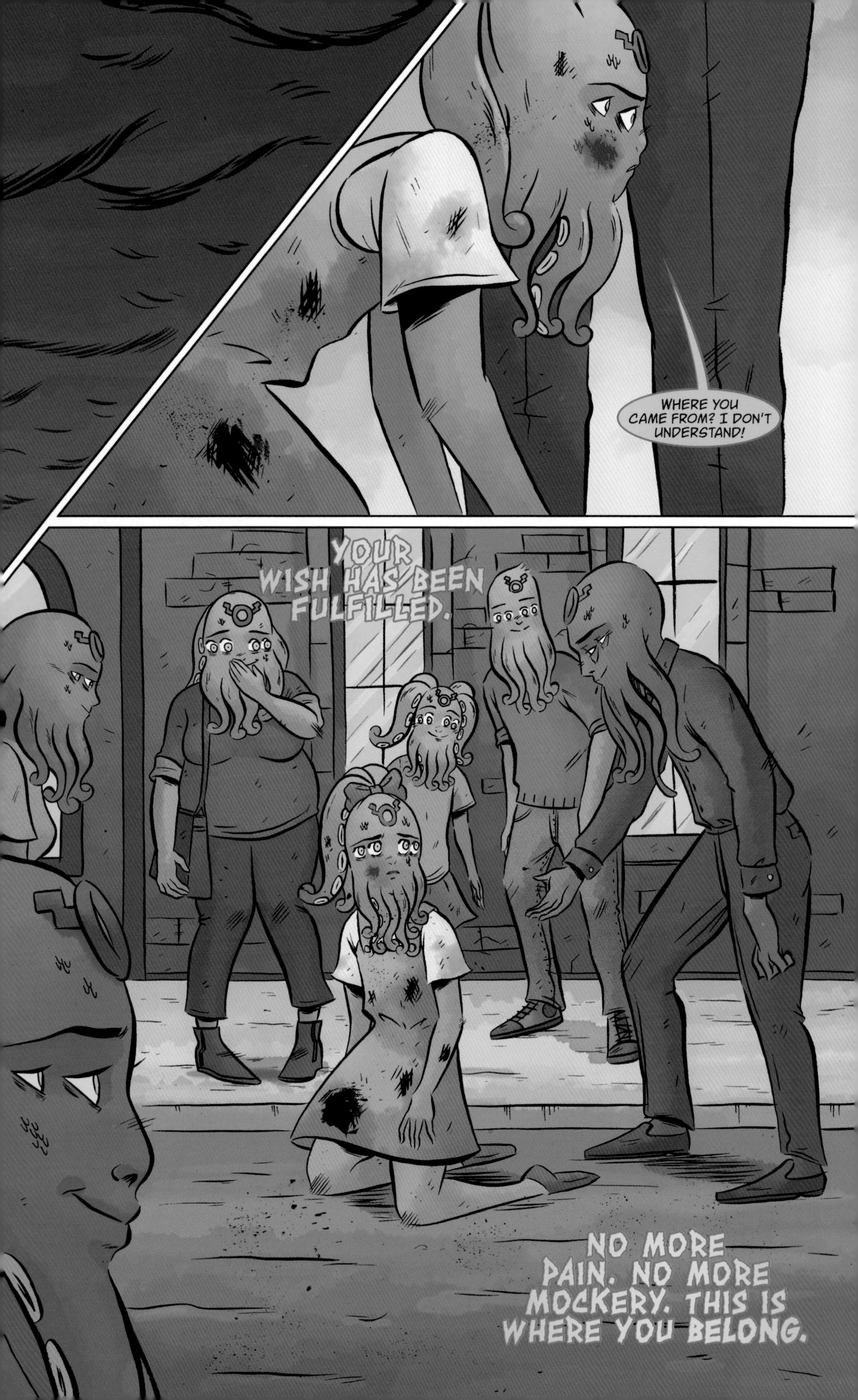
WHERE YOU CAME FROM? I DON'T UNDERSTAND!
YOUR WISH HAS BEEN FULFILLED.
NO MORE PAIN. NO MORE MOCKERY. THIS IS WHERE YOU BELONG.

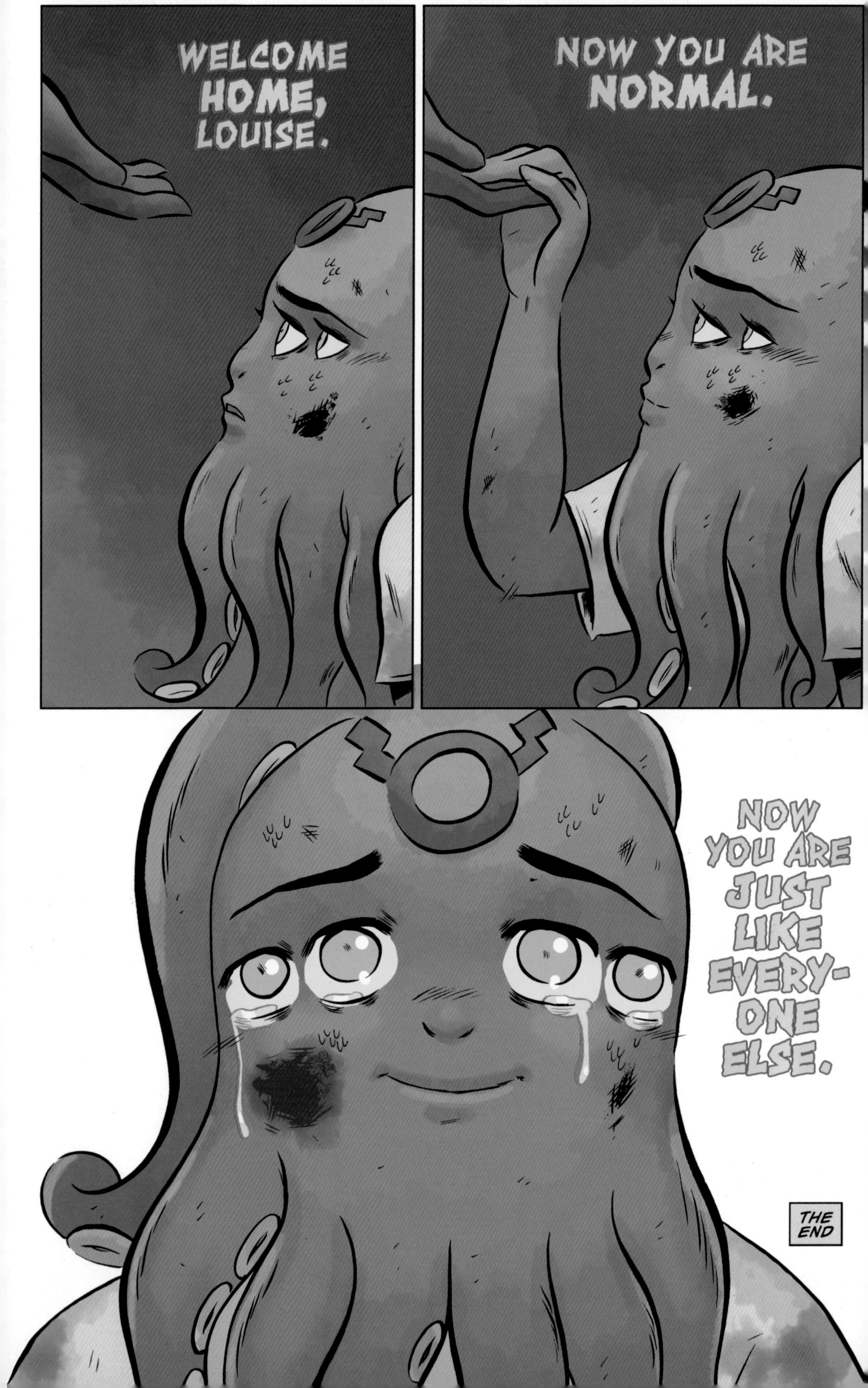
WELCOME HOME, LOUISE.
NOW YOU ARE NORMAL.
NOW YOU ARE JUST LIKE EVERY-ONE ELSE.
THE END

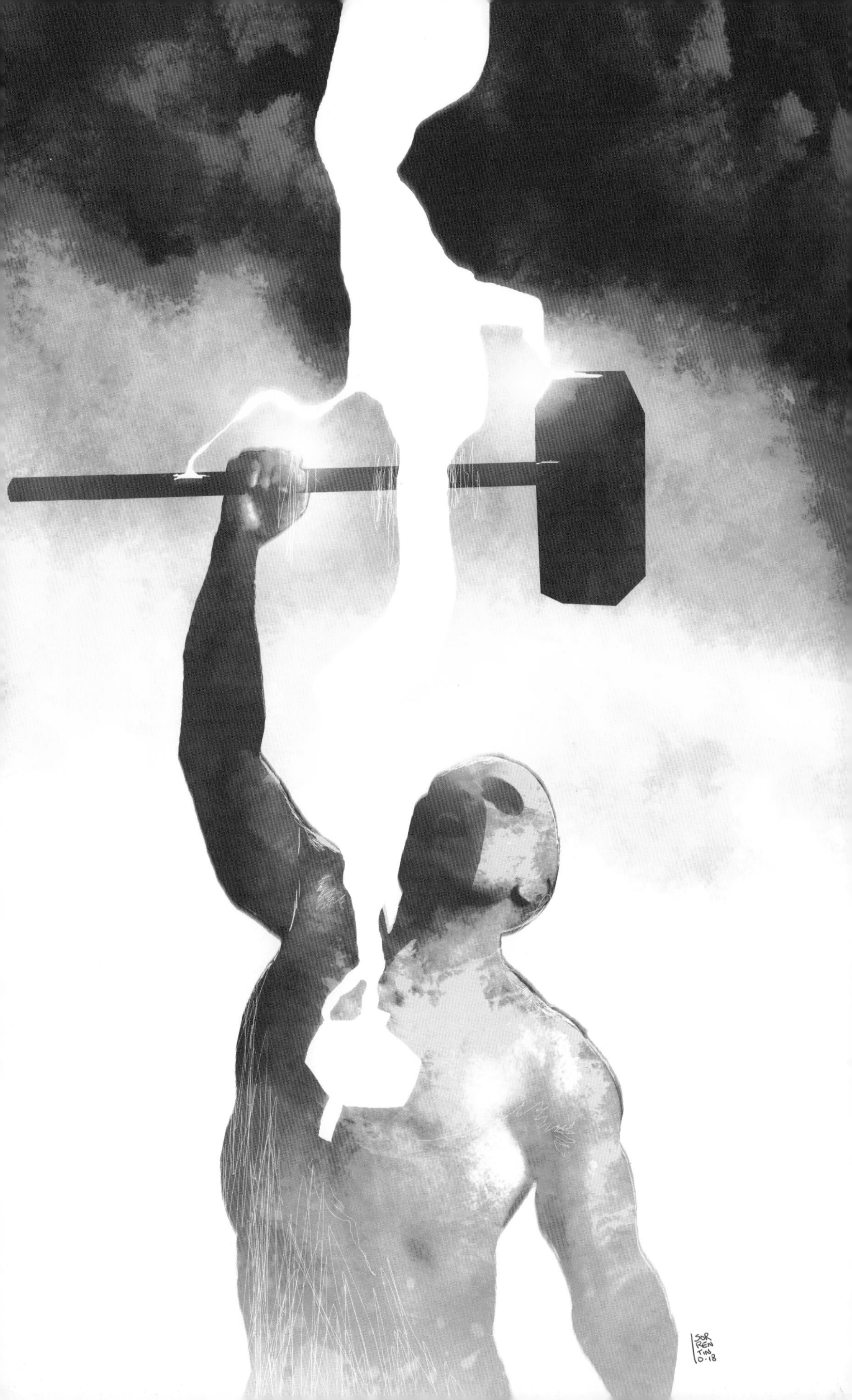
SOR
REN
TIN
O·18

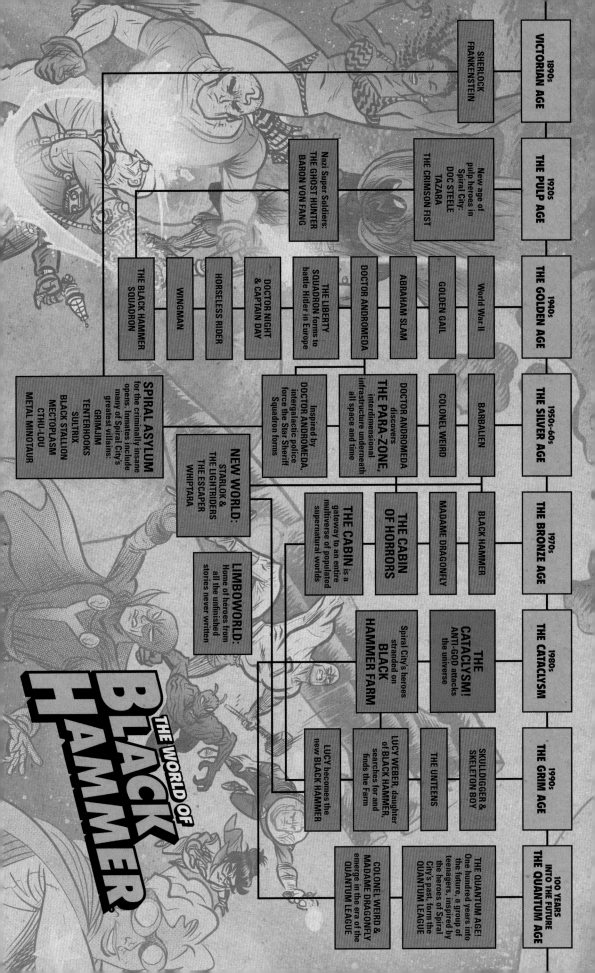

THE WORLD OF BLACK HAMMER

1890s VICTORIAN AGE
- SHERLOCK FRANKENSTEIN

1920s THE PULP AGE
- New age of pulp heroes in Spiral City: DOC STEELE, TAZARA, THE CRIMSON FIST
- Nazi Super Soldiers: THE GHOST HUNTER, BARON VON FANG

1940s THE GOLDEN AGE
- World War II
- GOLDEN GAIL
- ABRAHAM SLAM
- DOCTOR ANDROMEDA
- THE LIBERTY SQUADRON forms to battle Hitler in Europe
- DOCTOR NIGHT & CAPTAIN DAY
- HORSELESS RIDER
- WINGMAN
- THE BLACK HAMMER SQUADRON

1950s–60s THE SILVER AGE
- BARBALIEN
- COLONEL WEIRD
- DOCTOR ANDROMEDA discovers THE PARA-ZONE, interdimensional infrastructure underneath all space and time
- Inspired by DOCTOR ANDROMEDA, intergalactic police force the Star Sheriff Squadron forms
- SPIRAL ASYLUM for the criminally insane opens. Inmates include many of Spiral City's greatest villains: GRIMJIM, TENTERHOOKS, SULTRIX, BLACK STALLION, MECTOPLASM, CTHU-LOU, METAL MINOTAUR
- NEW WORLD: STARLOK & THE LIGHTRIDERS, THE ESCAPER, WHIPTARA

1970s THE BRONZE AGE
- BLACK HAMMER
- MADAME DRAGONFLY
- THE CABIN OF HORRORS
- THE CABIN is a gateway to an entire multiverse of populated supernatural worlds
- LIMBOWORLD: Home of heroes from all the unfinished stories never written

1980s THE CATACLYSM
- THE CATACLYSM! ANTI-GOD attacks the universe
- Spiral City's heroes stranded on BLACK HAMMER FARM

1990s THE GRIM AGE
- SKULLDIGGER & SKELETON BOY
- THE UNTEENS
- LUCY WEBER, daughter of BLACK HAMMER, searches for and finds the Farm
- LUCY becomes the new BLACK HAMMER

100 YEARS INTO THE FUTURE THE QUANTUM AGE
- THE QUANTUM AGE! One hundred years into the future, a group of teenagers, inspired by the heroes of Spiral City's past, form the QUANTUM LEAGUE
- COLONEL WEIRD & MADAME DRAGONFLY emerge in the era of the QUANTUM LEAGUE

ABRAHAM SLAM

PERSONAL DATA

Alter Ego: *Abraham Slamkowski*
Occupation: *Professional Boxer; Farmer*
Marital Status: *Single*
Known Relatives: *Unknown*
Group Affiliation: *The Liberty Squadron*
Base of Operations: *Spiral City*
First Appearance: Black Hammer #1
Height: 6'2"   **Weight:** 240 lbs.
Eyes: Brown   **Hair:** Gray (formerly brown)

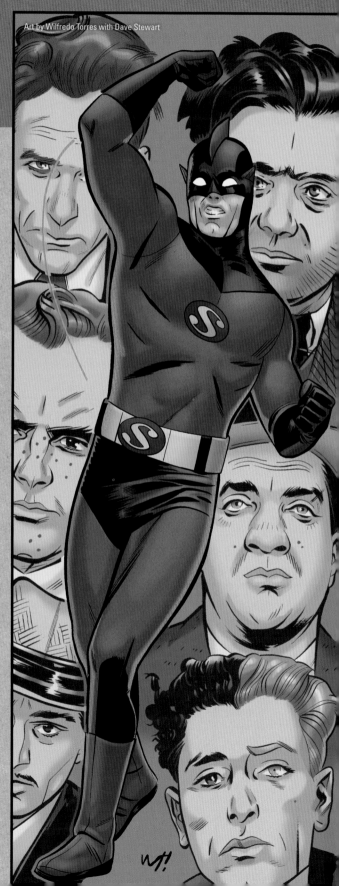

Art by Wilfredo Torres with Dave Stewart

HISTORY

Abraham Slamkowski was born to a poor family in the ghettos of Spiral City's Lower East Side. As a young man, he hoped to join the American troops in the fight against the Axis during World War II. However, he was designated unfit for service, due to being short sighted, frail, and having weak lungs. Bullied and looked down upon, Slamkowski had all but given up, until professional boxer Punch Sockingham took notice of his drive and strong spirit. Punch invited him into his gym, and the rest is history!

Under Punch's guidance, Slamkowski trained hard, built up a robust frame, and became an incredible fighter. He was well on his way to becoming the next great professional boxer and was christened "Abraham Slam" by Punch. Until, one day, a group of mobsters arrived at Sockingham Boxing Gym and shot Punch for his unpaid debts. Slamkowski reacted quickly and knocked the men unconscious, but it was too late . . . Punch died in his young protégé's arms.

Inspired by Punch's legacy and now under the guise of Abraham Slam, Slamkowski donned a flamboyant costume and began fighting crime on the streets of Spiral City. His first target: the mob responsible for Punch's murder. Slamkowski eventually joined the other Golden Age heroes as a part of the Liberty Squadron (see "The Liberty Squadron"). Together, they would head to Europe and battle the Nazi forces—playing a key role in the Axis's demise. Slamkowski finally achieved his lifelong dream of fighting for America.

As he continued through the Silver and Bronze Ages of heroes, Slamkowski aged and began questioning his relevancy. After nearly being defeated by the first iteration of Cthu-Lou (see "Cthu-Lou"), Black Hammer (see "Black Hammer I") had to step in and rescue him. Slamkowski may have been saved but his ego was deeply bruised. He decided he needed to upgrade his armor and weaponry in order to stay with the times. However, this eventually proved futile when he was once again defeated by a supervillain far outside his weight class. Abraham Slam finally decided to hang up his costume.

Nevertheless, during the first Cataclysm, Abraham Slam was called back into action alongside Earth's remaining heroes against the nefarious Anti-God (see "Anti-God"). When Black Hammer dealt his killing blow, Slamkowski and the other heroes mysteriously disappeared and are still missing . . .

POWERS & WEAPONS

Though he has no superpowers, Abraham Slam is a trained fighter and gymnast. He is remarkably strong and tough, as well as agile. Slamkowski is a gifted boxer and never backs down from a fight.

ANTI-GOD

PERSONAL DATA
Alter Ego: *None*
Occupation: *Conqueror*
Marital Status: *Single*
Known Relatives: *Starlok (twin brother)*
Group Affiliation: *None*
Base of Operations: *The Anti-Moon*
First Appearance: Black Hammer *#1*
Height: *∞* ***Weight:*** *∞*
Eyes: *Red* ***Hair:*** *∞*

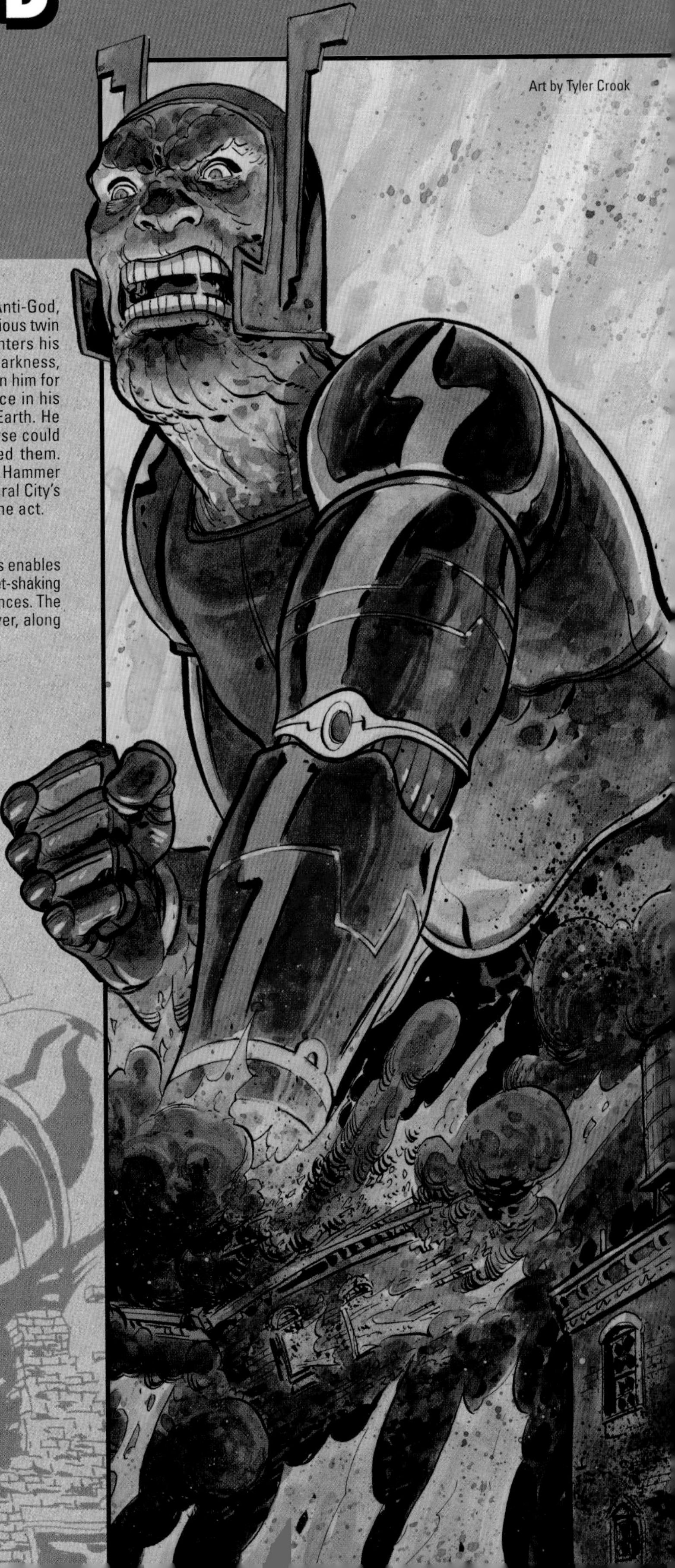

Art by Tyler Crook

HISTORY
Not much is known about the origins of Anti-God, only that he is Starlok's estranged and nefarious twin (see "Starlok & the Lightriders"). He counters his brother's heavenly light with apocalyptic darkness, and the balance of the universe depends on him for this. However Anti-God tipped that balance in his favor during the first Great Cataclysm on Earth. He took on the greatest heroes that the universe could throw at him, and he easily overpowered them. Anti-God was eventually defeated by Black Hammer (see "Black Hammer I") and the rest of Spiral City's heroes—disappearing alongside them in the act.

POWERS & WEAPONS
Anti-God can exploit vast cosmic power. This enables him to wield and reshape matter, unleash planet-shaking energy blasts, and teleport tremendous distances. The extent of his powers is unknowable, however, along with whether or not he can truly be killed.

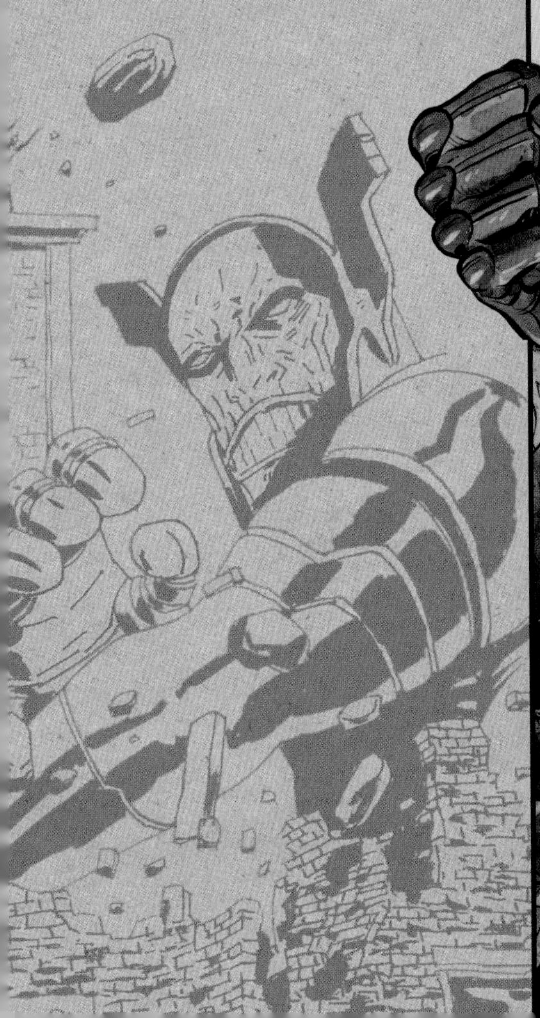

BARBALIEN

PERSONAL DATA

Alter Ego: Mark Markz
Occupation: Police Officer
Marital Status: Single
Known Relatives: Marv Marvz (father; deceased);
Myrt Myrtz (mother; deceased)
Group Affiliation: None
Base of Operations: Spiral City
First Appearance: Black Hammer #1
Height: 7'0" *Weight:* 300 lbs.
Eyes: Blue *Hair:* None

Art by Sina Grace

HISTORY

Mark Markz, a Martian diplomat from the red tribes of Mars, was looked down upon by his people for his pacifist views and for the rumors of his homosexuality. He, however, was a Martian of great wisdom and compassion. When a NASA spacecraft crash-landed on Mars, he championed words over war when debating the fate of the green planet, Earth. As a result, the Martians of Mars delegated Markz to be sent to Earth to infiltrate the humans and report back on his findings.

Landed on Earth, Markz quickly found himself in the middle of a police shootout at Spiral City's waterfront. After swiftly defeating the mobsters with his superior strength, Markz used his natural talent to shapeshift into a murdered cop and then dumped his corpse in the bay. He quickly picked up the English language and infiltrated Spiral City's police force. His Martian mission didn't last long, however, as Markz soon found himself falling in love with planet Earth and abandoned any espionage. He instead established a stellar career in the Spiral City police department. During his off hours, he fought crime on the streets as Barbalien, the Warlord of Mars.

Eventually, after years of close friendship with his police partner, Cole, Markz hoped that their partnership could become something more. He soon learned, however, that planet Earth was not so different from his home planet of Mars, after all. Cole rejected Markz in a furious rage and abandoned him on the street. Markz became the subject of cruel, homophobic harassment at his workplace. Eventually, he succumbed to the cruelty and turned in his badge. Blatant homophobia, ignorance, and hate had ended the career of one of Spiral City's finest policemen.

Markz wouldn't give up his superheroics, though. When Anti-God (see "Anti-God") appeared during the first Cataclysm, Markz joined in the fight alongside the remainder of Earth's heroes. He, too, disappeared in the aftermath of Anti-God's defeat and hasn't been seen since . . .

POWERS & WEAPONS

All Martians possess several innate abilities, including superior strength, speed, and agility. While they cannot fly, they are able to jump large distances. Martian skin is impervious to pain and damage. They can also change their shapes at will and impersonate others.

In addition to his superhuman abilities, Markz is also a highly skilled detective with above-average intelligence. He is an expert at all forms of hand-to-hand combat and is trained in the art of Martian warfare. He is a master swordsman and marksman and is often seen with his trusty sword and Martian blaster.

BLACK HAMMER I

PERSONAL DATA
Alter Ego: *Joseph Weber*
Occupation: *Police Officer; Social Worker*
Marital Status: *Married*
Known Relatives: *Lorraine Weber (wife); Lucy Weber (daughter)*
Group Affiliation: *The Lightriders*
Base of Operations: *Hall of Hammer*
First Appearance: Black Hammer *#1*
Height: *6'6" (6'0" as Joseph)*
Weight: *645 lbs. (240 lbs. as Joseph)*
Eyes: *Brown* ***Hair:*** *Black*

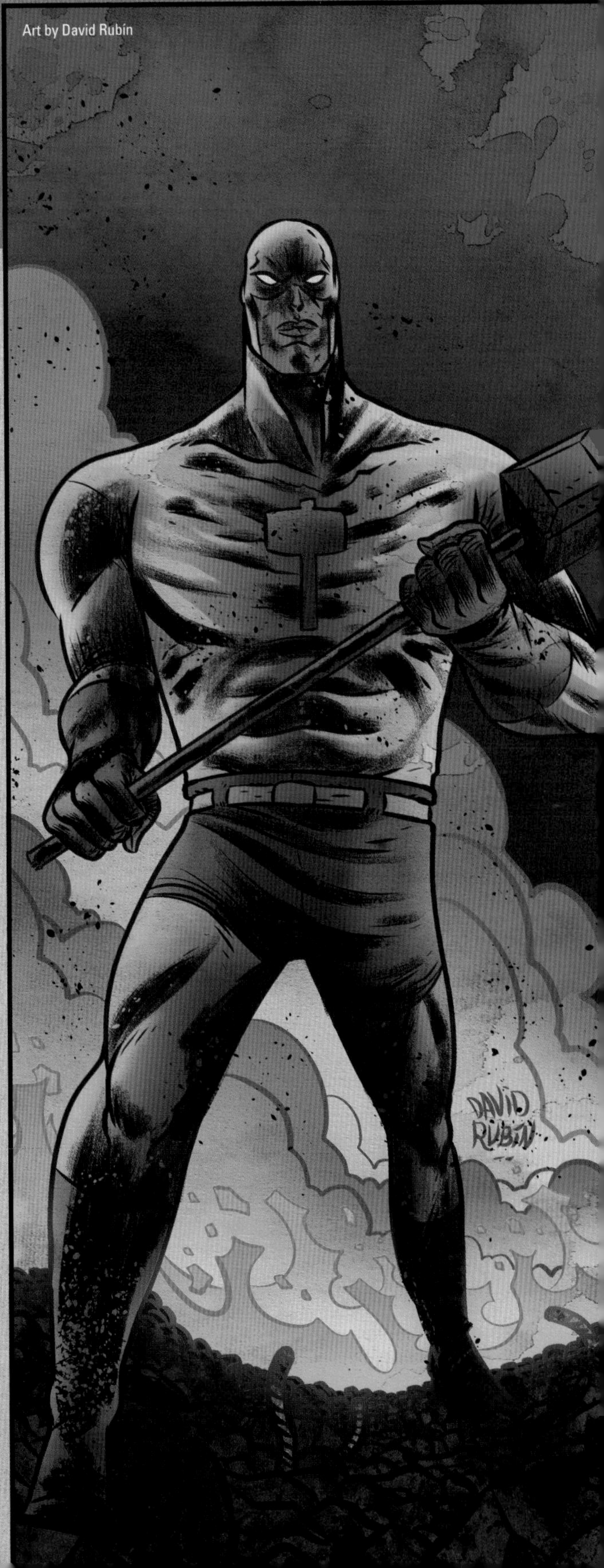
DAVID RUBIN
Art by David Rubín

HISTORY
Joe Weber was an involved community member within the poorer slums of Spiral City. One night, after volunteering at the local soup kitchen, Weber stumbled upon the murder of a costumed superhero. The dying man told Joe that someone worthy always needed to wield his black hammer. When the hammer seemed to call to him, Weber grabbed hold of it. He was immediately transformed into Black Hammer and teleported to a heavenly world just outside our own—New World.

On New World, Weber was quickly welcomed by Starlok (see "Starlok & the Lightriders") who introduced him to the Lightriders and his new role as Black Hammer. Weber refused to call New World his new home and ignored Starlok's pleas. He teleported himself back to Spiral City. Upon his return, he discovered that he had been missing for four months and his wife, Lorraine, was with child.

Lorraine soon gave birth to a little girl named Lucy (see Black Hammer II), and Weber dedicated his time to raising his family and protecting his city. Weber eventually embraced his role as Black Hammer by monitoring and protecting both Earth and New World from those with ill intent.

On Lucy's tenth birthday, Starlok summoned Weber to New World, where Anti-God (see "Anti-God") had easily laid waste to the Lightriders and would soon be upon Earth. Having missed out on far too much of his daughter's life due to superheroics, Weber rejected Starlok's plea once again and sat down for cake. Little did he know, that this rejection of his cosmic duties would lead to Anti-God's arrival on Earth and initiate the first Cataclysm. Weber left his daughter's side and assembled the remainder of Earth's heroes. Together they battled Anti-God, and Black Hammer dealt the killing blow to Anti-God's cranium. However, in the aftermath, Black Hammer and the other heroes disappeared and have been missing ever since . . .

POWERS & WEAPONS
Black Hammer acquires his superhuman abilities from the titular hammer that he wields. These abilities include flight, superhuman strength, invulnerability, teleportation, and control over lightning.

The black hammer itself is one of the finest weapons in the omniverse. It is nigh indestructible and seems to have a working mind of its own. The hammer is able to choose worthy wielders and pass on superhuman abilities.

BLACK HAMMER II

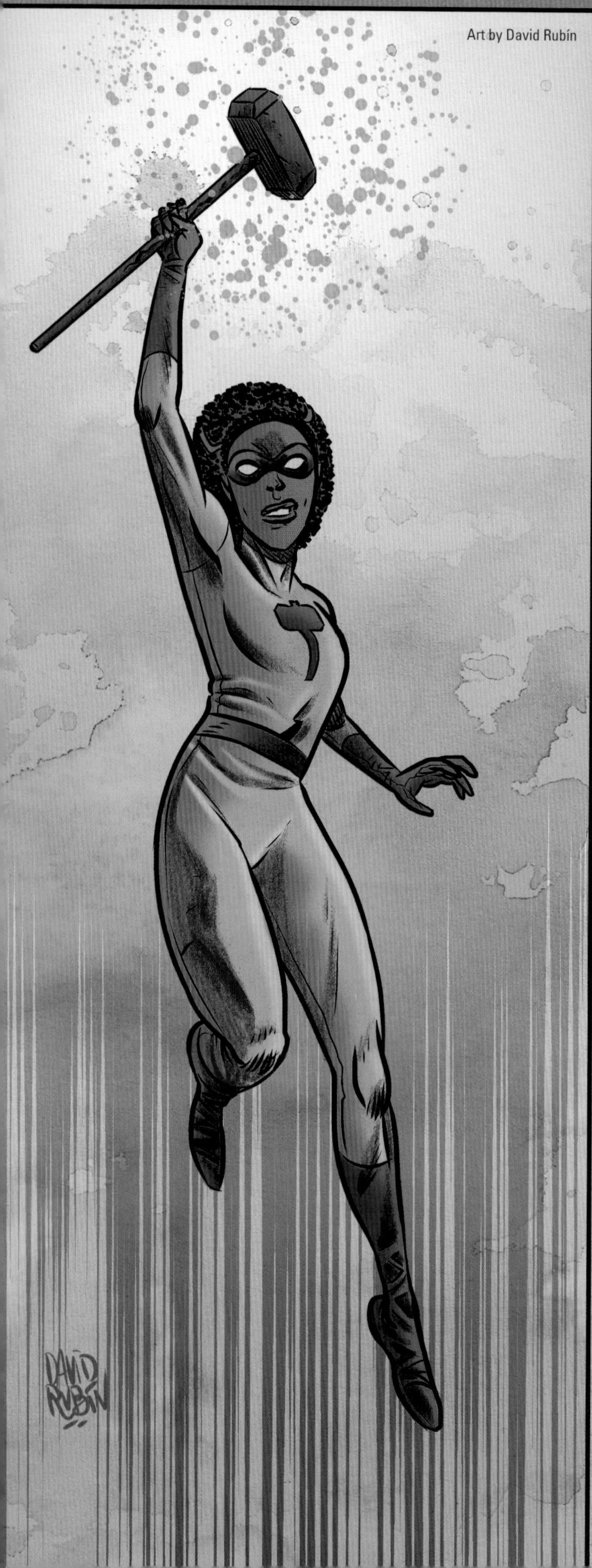
Art by David Rubín

PERSONAL DATA
Full Name: *Lucy Weber*
Occupation: *Journalist*
Marital Status: *Single*
Known Relatives: *Joseph Weber (father; deceased); Lorraine Weber (mother)*
Group Affiliation: *Global Planet Staff*
Base of Operations: *Spiral City*
First Appearance: Black Hammer *#1*
Height: *6'3" (5'9" as Lucy)*
Weight: *475lbs (154 lbs. as Lucy).*
Eyes: *Brown* ***Hair:*** *Black*

HISTORY

Born the daughter of Joseph Weber (see "Black Hammer I"), Lucy grew up under the influence of Earth's greatest hero. While her father was away saving the cosmos and Spiral City alike, Weber spent her time discovering a love for reading and writing. After the disappearance of her father during the first Cataclysm (see "Anti-God"), Weber dedicated the remainder of her adolescence searching for Black Hammer and the rest of Earth's missing heroes.

She attended journalism school at Spiral University and quickly became a gifted journalist. Her first story led her through a grocery list of Spiral City's greatest villains (see "Spiral City Asylum") and eventually into the hands of a reformed Sherlock Frankenstein (see "Sherlock Frankenstein"). Frankenstein had given up hope on finding the lost heroes, particularly his beloved Golden Gail (see "Golden Gail"), but Weber inspired the ghoulish doctor. As a result, Frankenstein began funding her search for the missing heroes.

Eventually, Lucy became a reporter at the Global Planet but never gave up searching for her father. She discovered a crashed probe that appeared to come from Colonel Weird's ship, and later tracked the cosmic doorway that it emerged from.

Soon after discovering that cosmic doorway, Weber herself disappeared . . .

POWERS & WEAPONS

Lucy eventually becomes Black Hammer, after picking up her father's fallen hammer, and acquires superhuman abilities. These abilities include flight, superhuman strength, invulnerability, teleportation, and control over lightning. Lucy also has a skilled investigative mind.

The black hammer itself is the one of the finest weapons in the omniverse. It is nigh indestructible and seems to have a working mind of its own. The hammer is able to choose worthy wielders and pass on superhuman abilities.

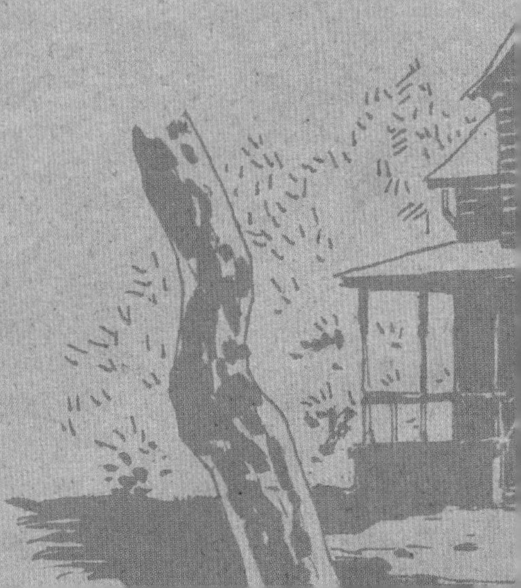

Art by Rich Tommaso

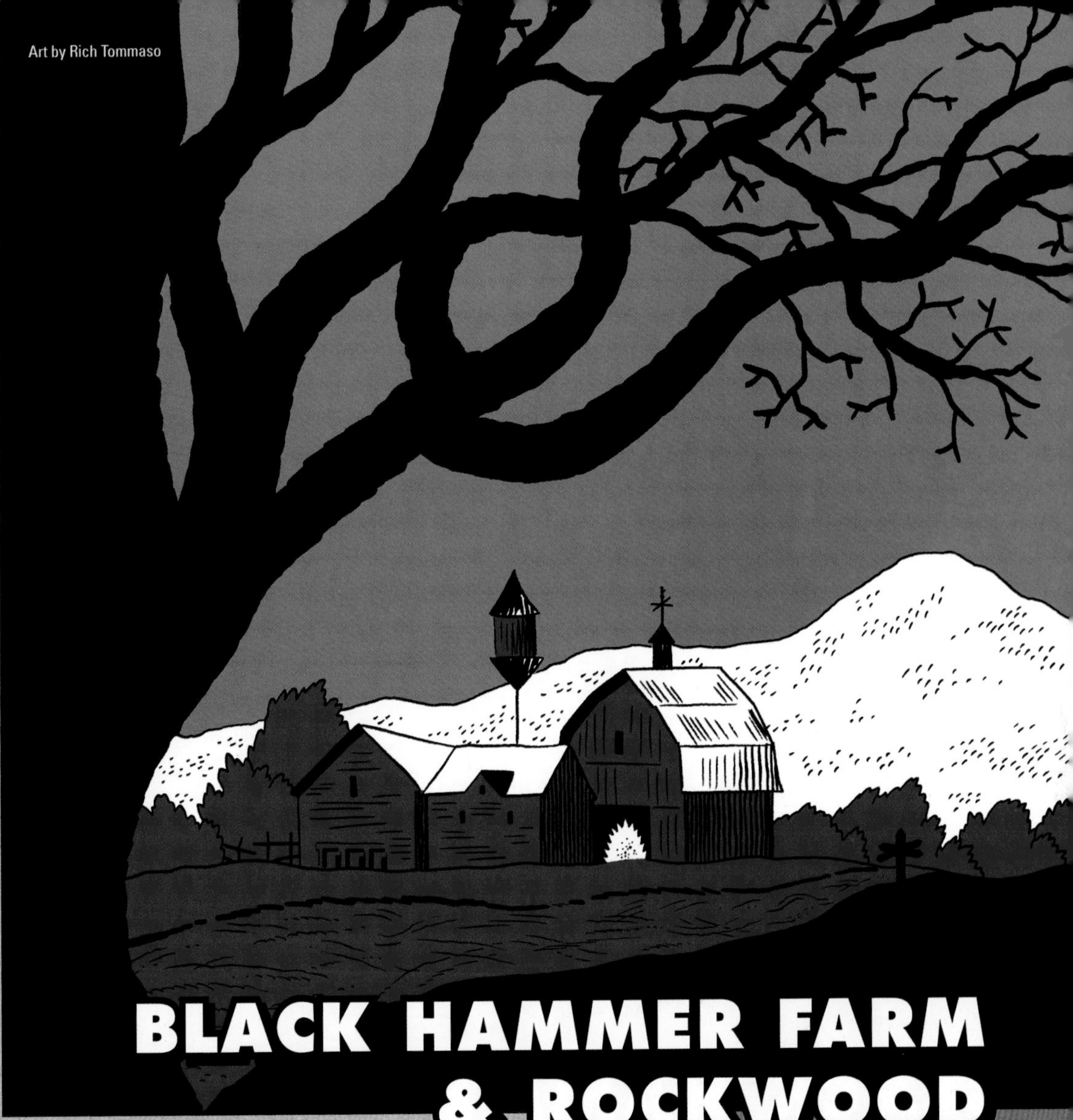

BLACK HAMMER FARM & ROCKWOOD

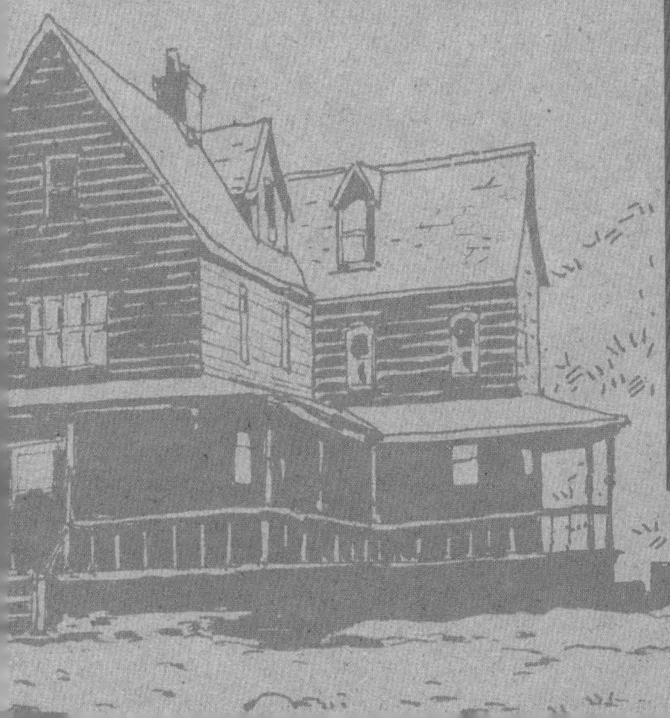

First Appearance: Black Hammer *#1*

HISTORY

While the small town of Rockwood may appear to be an unassuming, idyllic, and all-American municipality, it reveals itself to be a dreamy cage designed to imprison our wayward heroes. But don't worry, nothing ever goes wrong in Rockwood. No crime. No scandals. No wilting flowers. And **definitely** no liquified police officers. Rockwood is a perfect town with breathtaking prairie land and a flourishing techno scene. It is enclosed within a murderous dimensional bubble that holds everyone nice and snug within its lethal limits. Cross its boundaries and die! A great destination for the whole family after you've defeated a transdimensional conqueror and need to recover a healthy, harmonious balance. Life is dandy when you're a Rockwood vigilante.

On the outskirts of Rockwood lies an isolated farm . . . Black Hammer Farm, to be exact. It's the home of our wayward heroes—whether they like it or not!

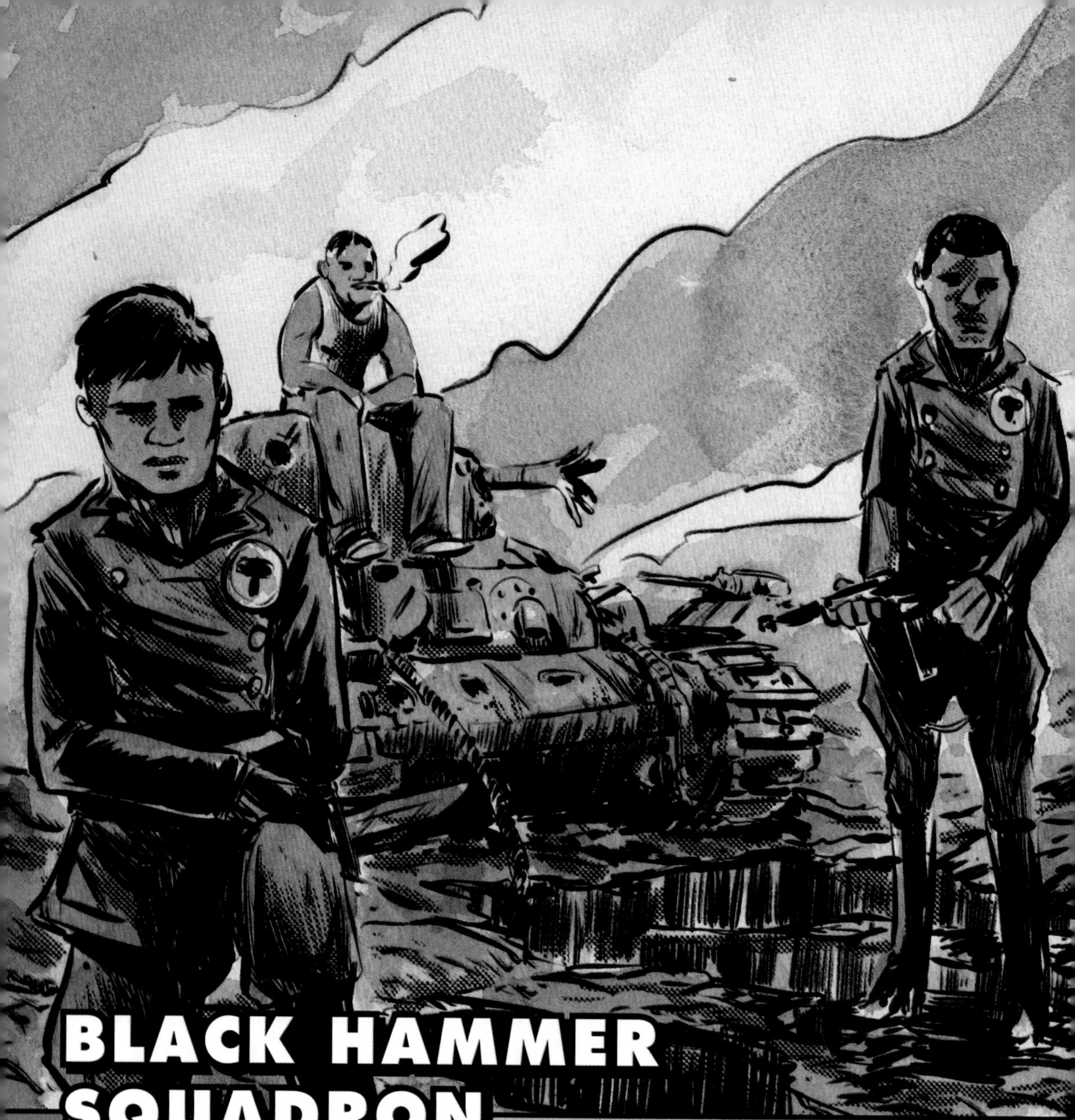

BLACK HAMMER SQUADRON

First Appearance: Black Hammer '45 #1

HISTORY

The Black Hammer Squadron was the greatest attack squadron of World War II, a unit forged and handpicked to tackle the war's most dangerous missions. Under the leadership of Sidney "Hammer" Hawthorne, the Squadron was able to handle and contain some of the worst atrocities that the Axis unleashed. They were the terror of the Nazi machine—defeating their dreaded Nachtwulf Patrol, the mystical Drachenkriegers, and even the Ghost Hunter himself (see "Ghost Hunter"). The Black Hammer Squadron stepped up when evil loomed and everybody else buried their noses in the sand!

The Squadron was made up exclusively of soldiers of color and often, due to this, the American media wasn't quite as appreciative as the rest of the world. In the aftermath of the war, it was Abraham Slam and the Liberty Squadron that received most of the American public's praise. Either way, the Squadron knew and understood the difference that they made in the war effort. They **always** gave back five times what they got, and then some.

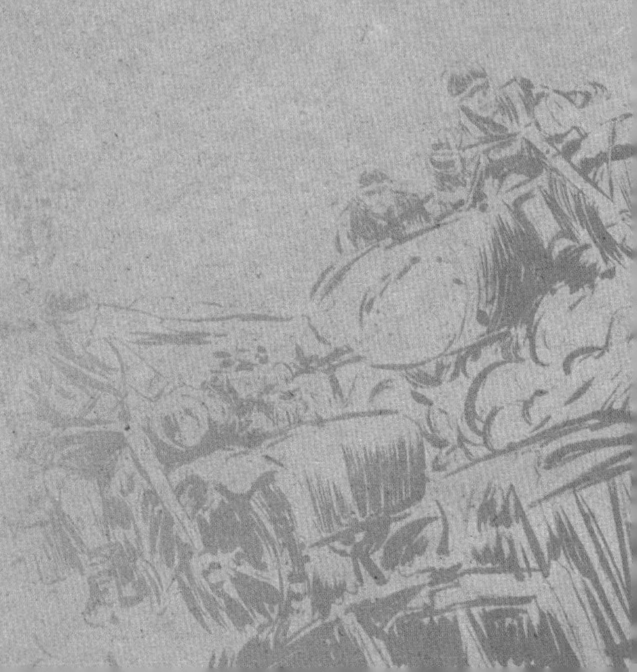

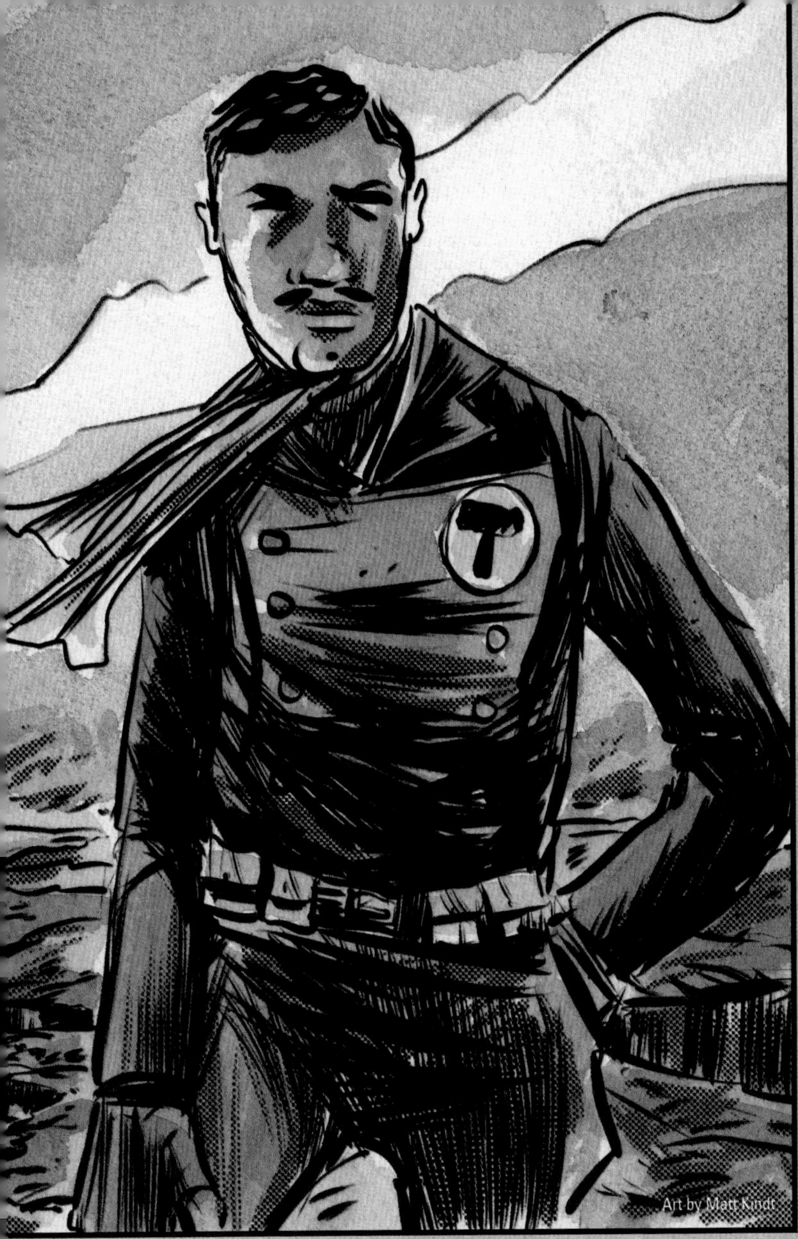
Art by Matt Kindt

MEMBERS

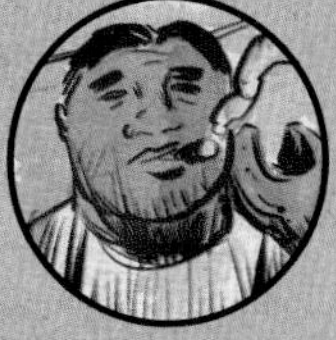

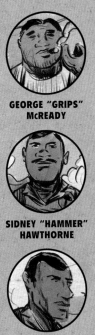

GEORGE "GRIPS" McREADY

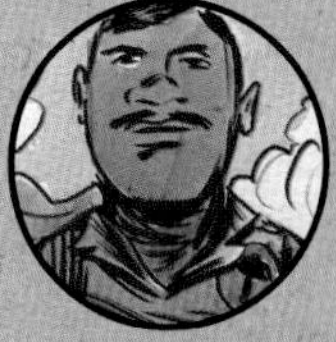

SIDNEY "HAMMER" HAWTHORNE

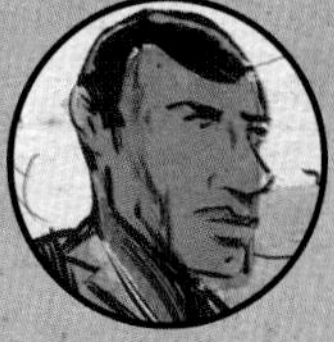

JOHN PAUL "JP" DESJARDINS

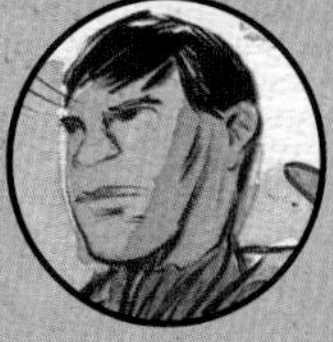

LI ZHANG YONG

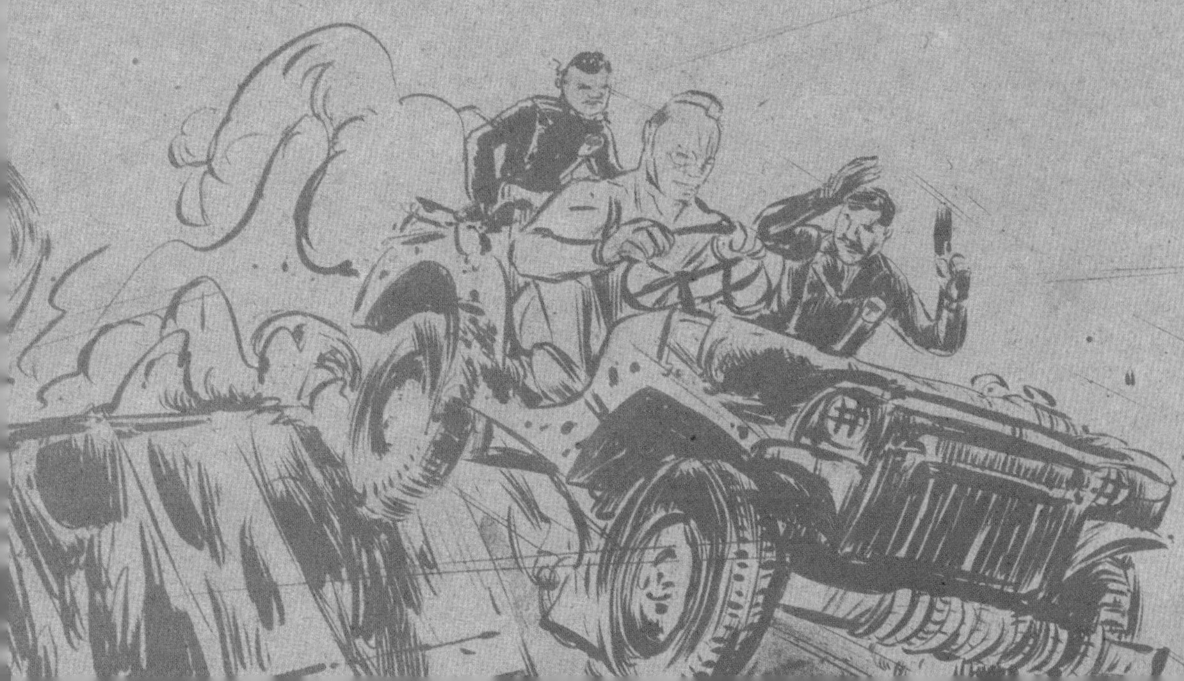

Art by Ray Fawkes

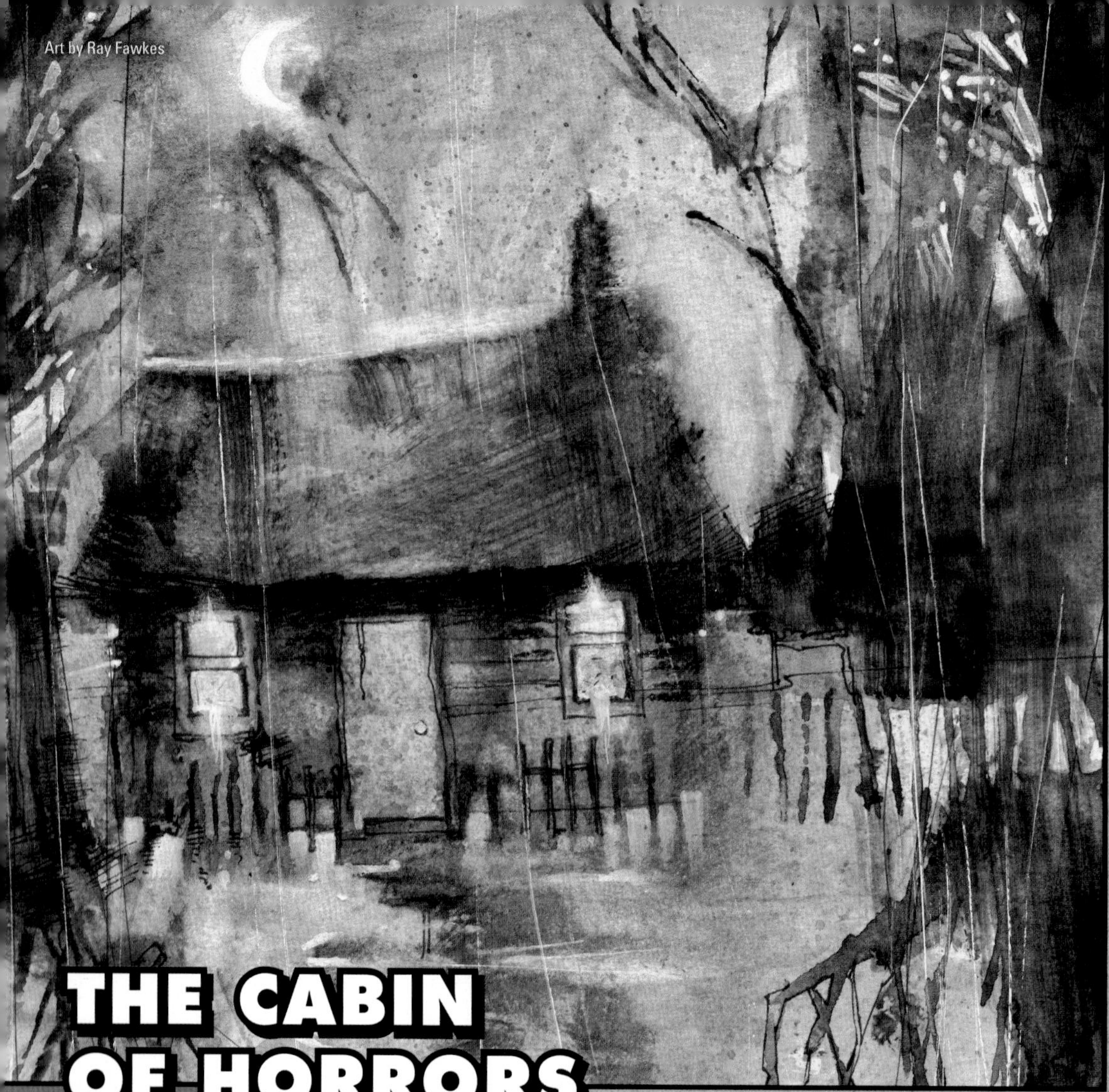

THE CABIN OF HORRORS

First Appearance: Black Hammer *#1*

HISTORY

QUICK! TURN THE PAGE! I beg of you, dear reader . . . don't allow your eyes to lag. Control your urge! Colonel Weird's entry is much more palatable than this vile abode's. But if you must read on, earnest traveler, there will be nothing I can do to save your tainted soul. Once you discover this **wretched womb of wood**, its very image will light fire to your dreams! Your life will continue on, never satisfied. Your heart will thump with hollow, unfulfilled echoes. Your mind will scritch centipedes that—! Still here? Very well . . . Don't say I didn't warn you . . .

Not so far away that you can't reach it, the Cabin of Horrors awaits all who seek dark answers and harbor forgotten secrets. What lurks behind its groaning doors? What ghoulish beast holds key to both your demise and your rebirth? Its thirst, unquenchable. Its desires, undying. Feed it your stories, feed it your mysteries, and perhaps it will **spare** you. And, if you're unlucky enough, it will bargain your life for another's . . . bestowing you the Cabin's burden . . . Now, don't be afraid. Step up! You've come this far. Embrace the termites and daemons that lurk deep within its bowels . . . Wrap your little fingers between their many legs and howl until you croak!

Oh dear. What's this? Are those **wings** sprouting on your back? HA HA! They suit you well . . . Enjoy the cabin, my dear. You're its guardian now. If you hope to pass on this burden, I suppose you will need to tempt someone else into reading this page, won't you? **HAHAHAHA!**

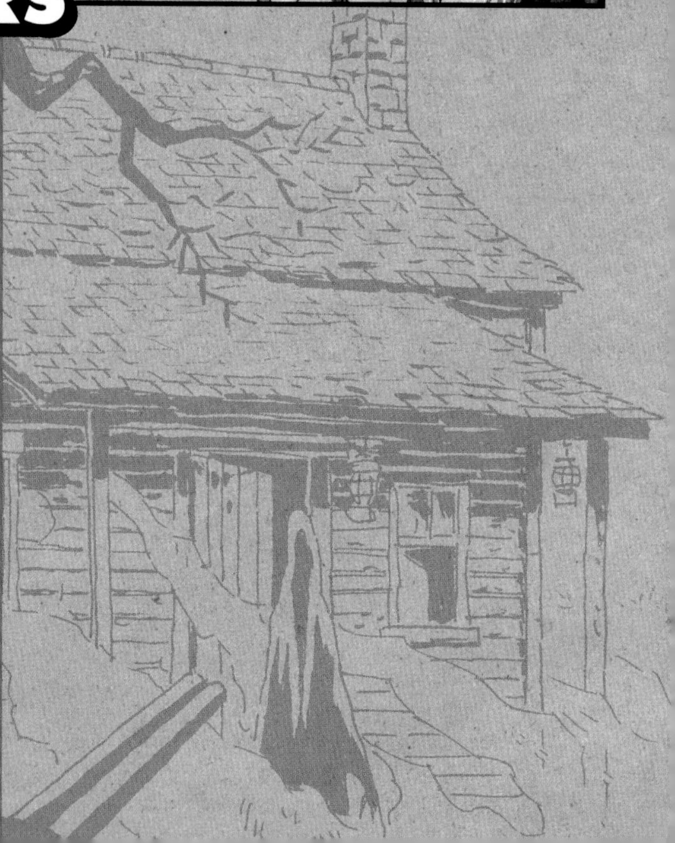

COLONEL WEIRD

PERSONAL DATA
Alter Ego: *Randall Weird*
Notable Aliases: *Chronokus*
Occupation: *Astronaut; Interstellar Adventurer*
Marital Status: *Single*
Known Relatives: *Unknown*
Group Affiliation: *None*
Base of Operations: *Moonbase 12; Para-zone*
First Appearance: Black Hammer *#1*
Height: *5'8"* ***Weight:*** *150 lbs.*
Eyes: *Brown* ***Hair:*** *White (originally blonde)*

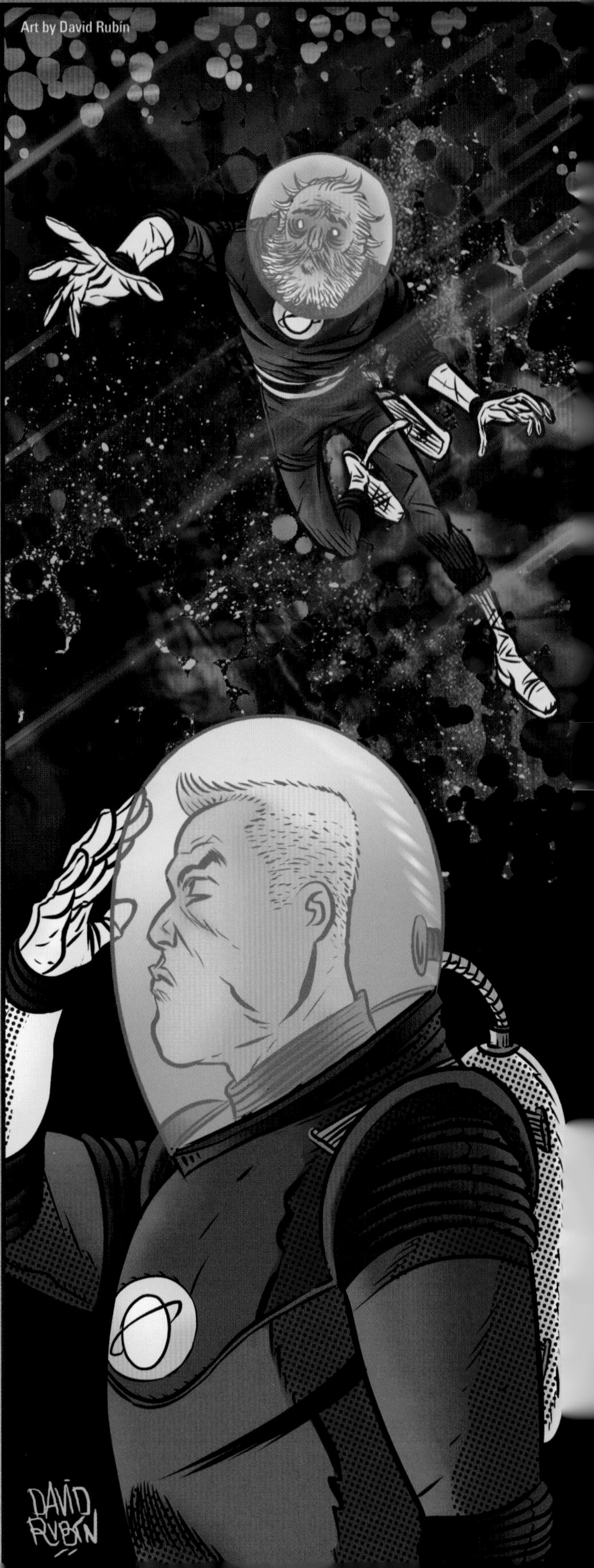

Art by David Rubín
DAVID RUBÍN

HISTORY
During a mission through the Osler star system, Randall Weird was directed to an uncharted planet in response to a distress signal. After arriving, Weird soon found **himself** in distress as he was chased across the planet by its flesh-hating, robotic inhabitants. He was rescued by the source of the planet's signal, a robot named TLK-E WLK-E (see "Talky-Walky"). The two escaped the planet together and eventually formed the universe's greatest interstellar partnership.

During one fateful mission for NASA, the duo explored the planet Virius-6. After promising his Earth-bound girlfriend, Eve, that he'd return in time for the New Year, Weird stumbled upon cave drawings of what appeared to be an ancient galactic map. Upon further investigation, Weird and Talky followed the map to its coordinates, only to discover a strange cosmic doorway. Against Talky's better judgment, Weird entered the portal and found himself transported to the Para-zone! Even worse, he was trapped!!

Nine years passed as Weird traveled through the timeless and spaceless interdimensional void of the Para-zone—until finally he found his way back to Earth and his beloved Eve. However, he had aged rapidly and had lost his sanity in the process. Eve begged Weird to take her into the Para-zone with him, even though he warned her of its risks. When they entered the Para-zone's cosmic doorway, those risks proved true, and Eve was torn apart layer-by-layer before Weird's very eyes.

With his interstellar adventures behind him, Weird began aimlessly floating between the Para-zone and Earth dimensions, constantly reliving past and future events. During the first Cataclysm after Anti-God's (see "Anti-God") arrival on Earth, Colonel Weird was one of the few costumed heroes left to aid in his defeat. He, too, went missing after Black Hammer's fatal strike against Anti-God and hasn't been seen since . . .

One hundred years in the future, Colonel Weird becomes Chronokus—one of the Quantum League's greatest foes (see "The Quantum League")!

POWERS & WEAPONS
Though the full extent of Weird's powers is unknown, he can apparently teleport incredible distances through space and time, phase through solid objects, float by seemingly defying gravity, and tap into the Para-zone's cosmic energies. In addition, Weird's NASA and Air Force training makes him an excellent hand-to-hand combatant and an accomplished pilot. He is often in the use of a flying rocket pack and a plasma blaster.

CTHU-LOU

Art by David Rubin

PERSONAL DATA

Alter Ego: Louis Kaminski
Occupation: Plumber
Marital Status: Married
Known Relatives: Elaine Kaminski (wife); Louise Kaminski (daughter)
Group Affiliation: The Legion of Evil
Base of Operations: Spiral City
First Appearance: Sherlock Frankenstein and the Legion of Evil #2
Height: 5'10" **Weight:** 333 lbs.
Eyes: Green **Hair:** Green Tentacles

HISTORY

Not to be mistaken for the Cthu-Lou of the 1970s, Louis Kaminski was a humble plumber before he was summoned down into the Spiral City sewers. He was greeted by a talking, green-eyed rat and a giant, floating squid simply referred to as "the Great One." The rat explained that the Great One was in need of a new emissary on Earth. A new Lou was needed to become the Many-Angled One's Cthu-Lou, and that Lou was Louis Kaminski. Kaminski attempted to escape the Dark Lord's green tentacles but was promptly captured and swallowed whole. He returned home gaseous, covered in green ooze, and speaking in strange tongues. Suddenly, Kaminski even began sprouting tentacles of his very own. He transformed into a humanoid squid—the new Cthu-Lou.

Kaminski unwillingly began a life of villainy as Cthu-Lou and begrudgingly did the Dark Lord's evil bidding on Earth. While he avoided hurting civilians, Cthu-Lou faced off against Black Hammer and many other heroes across his villainous years. With his heart simply not in the villainy game, however, Kaminski retired before the first Cataclysm, which spared him of that commotion.

Kaminski has since returned his focus to his once-illustrious plumbing career. Most people, however, don't seem to be interested in hiring the Dark Lord's squid emissary to fix their pipes. He spends most of his time with his daughter, Louise (see "Cthu-Louise"), and arguing with his wife, Elaine.

POWERS & WEAPONS

As the Dark Lord's squid emissary on Earth, Cthu-Lou is a humanoid squid. He has eight eyes and many tentacles, each with superhuman strength. He also has superior plumbing skills, and was once featured on a Global Planet listicle titled "10 Plumbers You Have to Hire Before You Die (During the Next Cataclysm)."

CTHU-LOUISE

Art by Emi Lenox

PERSONAL DATA

Alter Ego: Louise Kaminski
Occupation: High School Student
Marital Status: Single
Known Relatives: Louis Kaminski (father); Elaine Kaminski (mother)
Group Affiliation: N/A
Base of Operations: Spiral City
First Appearance: Sherlock Frankenstein and the Legion of Evil #2
Height: 5'4" **Weight:** 120 lbs.
Eyes: Green **Hair:** Green Tentacles

HISTORY

Louise Kaminski is the naturally born child of Louis (see "Cthu-Lou") and Elaine Kaminski. Being the daughter of a former supervillain wasn't easy growing up. Louise often found herself in the crossfires of her parents' strained relationship and was treated poorly by both. She first found hope when she met Lucy Weber (see "Black Hammer II"), while Lucy was interviewing her father during her search for Sherlock Frankenstein (see "Sherlock Frankenstein"). Louise and Lucy quickly bonded, but Lucy left to resume her search for her missing father (see "Black Hammer I"). Louise was all alone, once again.

Years later, Louise was attending elementary school when she was visited in her dreams by her "grandfather"—the Many-Angled One—who had transformed her father into Cthu-Lou. Louise ignored his calls and is trying to be a normal, good girl despite her monstrous appearance. However, her classmates won't allow her to forget what she is: a green, tentacled freak. Louise must make a choice: Will she give into her Many-Angled tendencies and seek vengeance, or will she rise above them and become Spiral City's first tentacled hero? Either way, Louise just hopes to one day be considered "normal."

POWERS & WEAPONS

Louise took on the likeness of her father rather than her mother. This means that she is also green and tentacled but has four eyes instead of eight. She is in the top of her class in every subject and is especially skilled at *Mortal Kombat*. Louise is also possibly able to summon the almighty wrath and destruction of the Great One through chthonic chants and portals.

GHOST HUNTER

PERSONAL DATA
Alter Ego: *Oberst Klaus von Löwe*
Occupation: *Pilot*
Marital Status: *Single*
Known Relatives: *Father (deceased)*
Group Affiliation: *Nazis*
Base of Operations: *Germany*
First Appearance: Black Hammer '45 *#1*
Height: *5'11"* ***Weight:*** *175 lbs.*
Eyes: *Gray* ***Hair:*** *White*

HISTORY
Born into Austrian royalty, von Löwe was the son of an esteemed, record-setting fighter pilot from World War I. Von Löwe followed in his father's footsteps and eventually surpassed him. He became the deadliest pilot in the history of the world—with 850 kills to his name, including Captain Jack Flag, Bulldog, the Atlantic King, and two members of the Black Hammer Squadron (see "Black Hammer Squadron"). Coined der Jägergeist or "the Ghost Hunter," von Löwe became a legend and was feared by many.

He continued to cross paths with the Black Hammer Squadron throughout World War II; however, no moment is more infamous than the battle for the Greenbaums between the Ghost Hunter, the Black Hammer Squadron, and the Russian mecha unit—the Red Tide.

POWERS & WEAPONS
Von Löwe has no known superhuman abilities, but his skills in the cockpit are unparalleled. He also has the innate ability to send a shiver up every spine in any room that he walks into. Besides his Stuka's artillery, von Löwe is never seen without his handy Luger pistols.

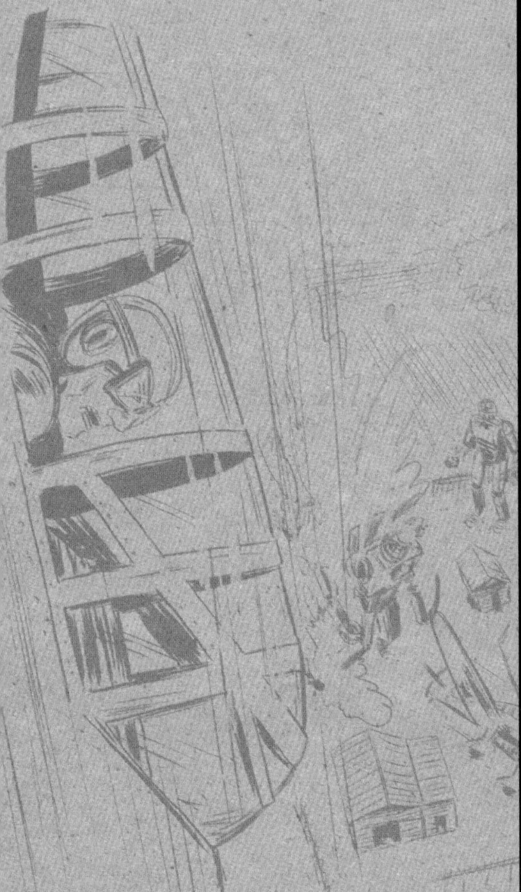

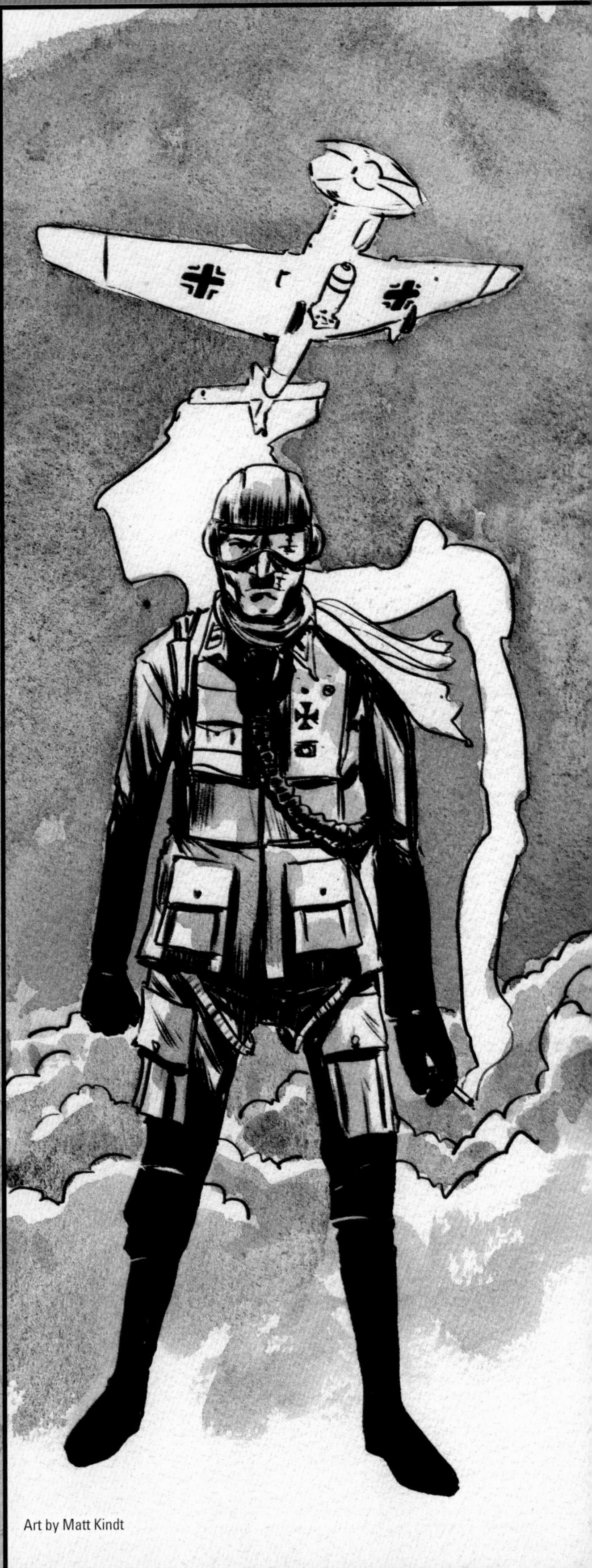

Art by Matt Kindt

Art by Emi Lenox

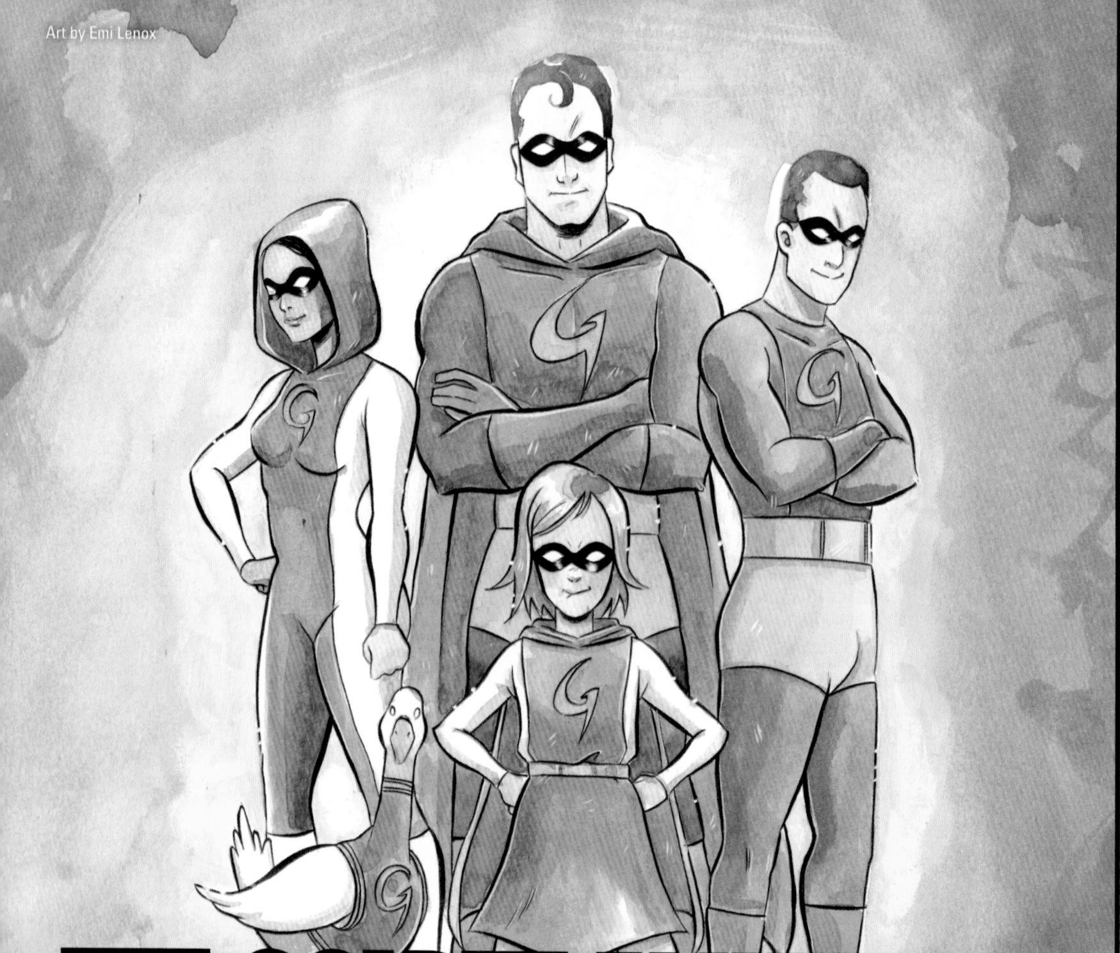

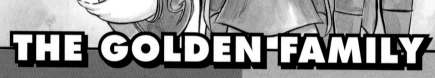

THE GOLDEN FAMILY

First Appearance: Black Hammer *#8*

HISTORY

The Golden Family consists of five individuals who have been granted special powers by the ancient wizard Zafram and, by proxy, Golden Gail. Zafram himself wielded his Golden powers for eons while trapped on Earth between worlds. He determined to seek out a worthy heir and fulfill a prophecy: that someone pure of heart would one day inherit his powers.

When his death loomed close, Zafram had a mysterious figure hand orphan Gail Gibbons a movie ticket and lure her into a dark theater. There, Zafram struck Gail with mystical lightning and granted her powers, which Gail gained by saying the wizard's name. She transformed into Golden Gail, America's Super Sweetheart (see "Golden Gail"). Zafram had at last found a worthy successor and died shortly thereafter.

The next additions to the Golden Family came when Gail, after fifty years of superheroics, wanted to retire and pass on the Golden torch. She granted a portion of Zafram's powers to Captain Golden, Golden Gary, Golden Gwen, and Golden Goose and formed the Golden Family. Together, the Golden Family protected Spiral City and planet Earth from the threats once faced by Gail alone. Golden Gwen also eventually joined the teen-superhero squad, Y-Force.

When Anti-God set his sights on Earth during the first Cataclysm (see "Anti-God"), the Golden Family members were some of the first superhuman responders to arrive. They were easily defeated, murdered, and cast aside. Golden Gail came out of retirement and joined the last remnants of Earth's heroes against Anti-God. She, along with the others, disappeared after Black Hammer's killing blow and hasn't been seen since . . .

MEMBERS

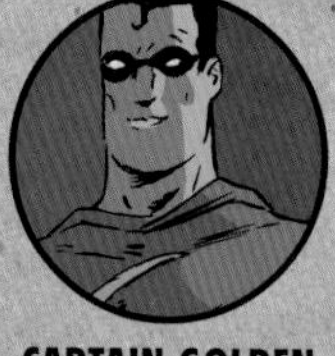

CAPTAIN GOLDEN

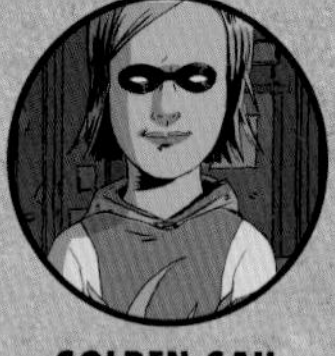

GOLDEN GAIL

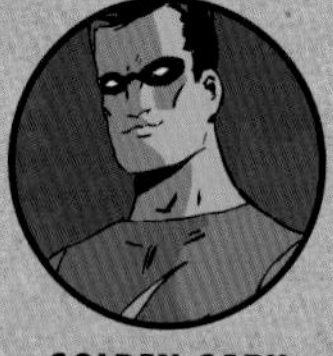

GOLDEN GARY

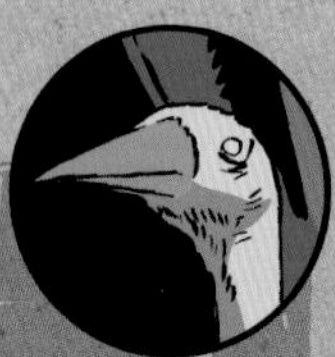

GOLDEN GOOSE

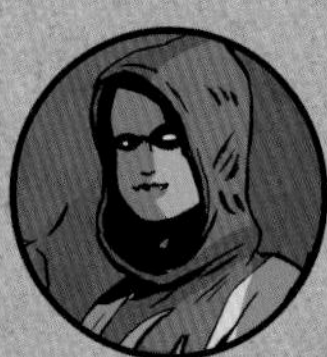

GOLDEN GWEN

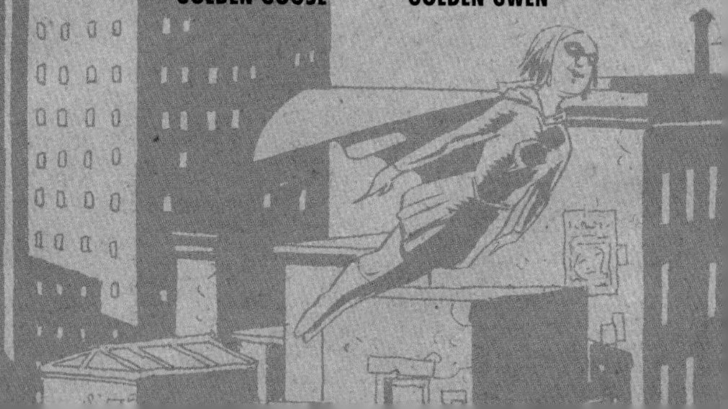

GOLDEN GAIL

PERSONAL DATA
Alter Ego: *Gail Gibbons*
Occupation: *Retired Superhero*
Marital Status: *Single*
Known Relatives: *Unknown (orphaned)*
Group Affiliation: *The Liberty Squadron; The Golden Family*
Base of Operations: *Spiral City*
First Appearance: Black Hammer *#1*
Height: *4'1" (5'5" as Gibbons)*
Weight: *62 lbs. (151 lbs. as Gibbons)*
Eyes: *Blue (brown as Gibbons)*
Hair: *Blonde (brown as Gibbons)*

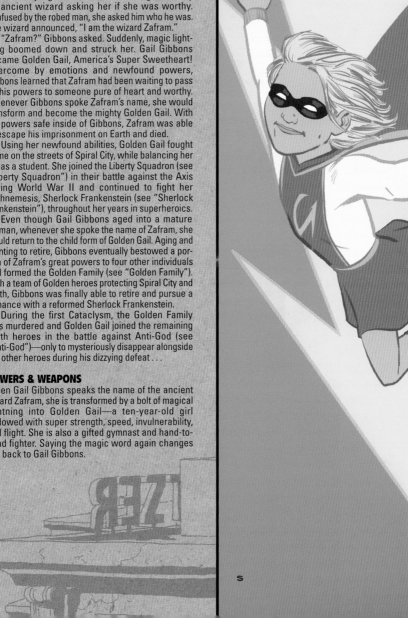

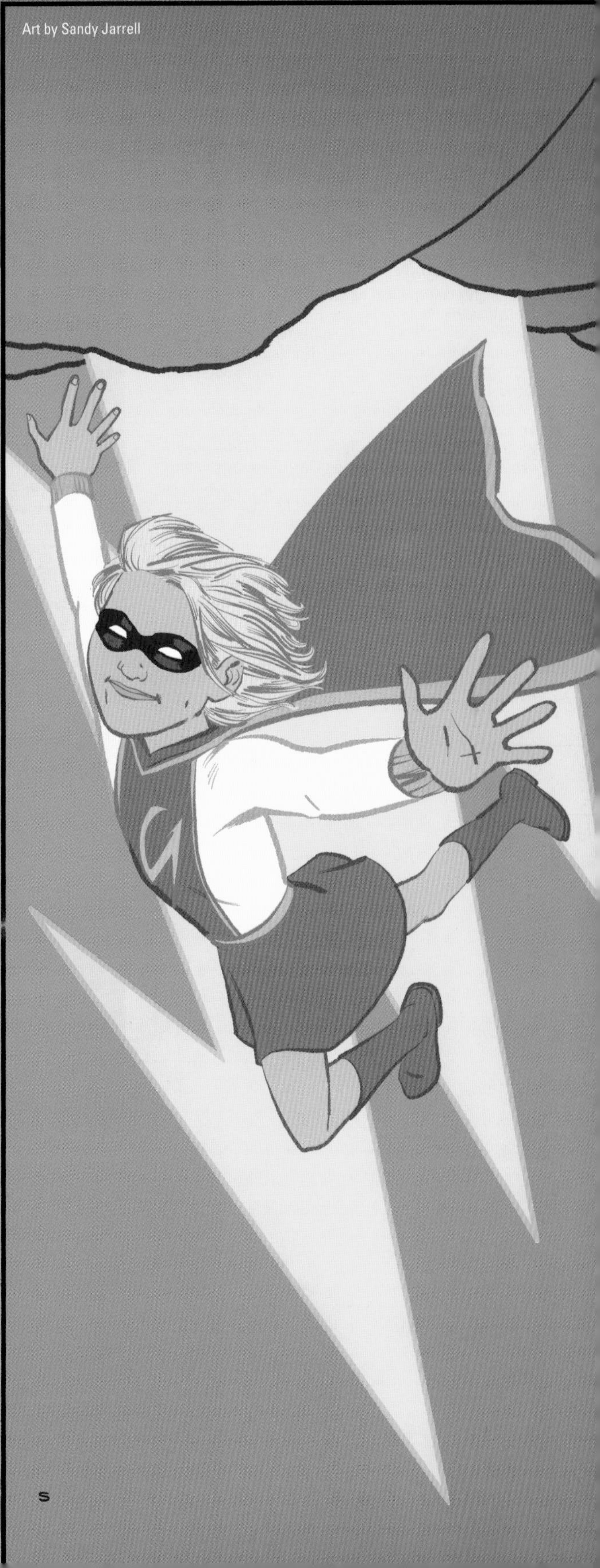
Art by Sandy Jarrell

HISTORY
Orphaned as an infant, Gail Gibbons was left to be raised by the Spiral City Orphanage. Growing up within horrible conditions, Gibbons finally experienced enough torment and ran away one stormy night. She hid from the rain at an abandoned theater only to be offered a movie ticket by a mysterious shadowed figure. Upon entering the theater against her better judgement, Gibbons was greeted by an ancient wizard asking her if she was worthy. Confused by the robed man, she asked him who he was. The wizard announced, "I am the wizard Zafram."

"Zafram?" Gibbons asked. Suddenly, magic lightning boomed down and struck her. Gail Gibbons became Golden Gail, America's Super Sweetheart! Overcome by emotions and newfound powers, Gibbons learned that Zafram had been waiting to pass on his powers to someone pure of heart and worthy. Whenever Gibbons spoke Zafram's name, she would transform and become the mighty Golden Gail. With his powers safe inside of Gibbons, Zafram was able to escape his imprisonment on Earth and died.

Using her newfound abilities, Golden Gail fought crime on the streets of Spiral City, while balancing her life as a student. She joined the Liberty Squadron (see "Liberty Squadron") in their battle against the Axis during World War II and continued to fight her archnemesis, Sherlock Frankenstein (see "Sherlock Frankenstein"), throughout her years in superheroics.

Even though Gail Gibbons aged into a mature woman, whenever she spoke the name of Zafram, she would return to the child form of Golden Gail. Aging and wanting to retire, Gibbons eventually bestowed a portion of Zafram's great powers to four other individuals and formed the Golden Family (see "Golden Family"). With a team of Golden heroes protecting Spiral City and Earth, Gibbons was finally able to retire and pursue a romance with a reformed Sherlock Frankenstein.

During the first Cataclysm, the Golden Family was murdered and Golden Gail joined the remaining Earth heroes in the battle against Anti-God (see "Anti-God")—only to mysteriously disappear alongside the other heroes during his dizzying defeat . . .

POWERS & WEAPONS
When Gail Gibbons speaks the name of the ancient wizard Zafram, she is transformed by a bolt of magical lightning into Golden Gail—a ten-year-old girl endowed with super strength, speed, invulnerability, and flight. She is also a gifted gymnast and hand-to-hand fighter. Saying the magic word again changes her back to Gail Gibbons.

GRIMJIM

PERSONAL DATA
Alter Ego: *Unknown*
Occupation: *Crime Boss*
Marital Status: *Unknown*
Known Relatives: *Unknown*
Group Affiliation: *N/A*
Base of Operations: *Spiral City*
First Appearance: Sherlock Frankenstein and the Legion of Evil *#1*
Height: *6'5"* ***Weight:*** *189 lbs.*
Eyes: *Red* ***Hair:*** *Bald*

HISTORY
Not much is known about the gruesome Grimjim. He is seemingly immortal and has been active in Spiral City for at least one hundred years. He is also in a constant state of evolution, as he reinvents himself with each new decade. As the years pass, Grimjim only seems to get grimmer and grimmer. He is a sadist through and through.

Grimjim has murdered thousands of people (and animals and plants too!) over his wretched life, and—were he not unkillable—he surely would have been executed for his crimes long ago. No one knows where he came from, what created him, or why his mind is warped so terribly. Although, some believe Grimjim to be the devil himself . . .

POWERS & WEAPONS
Grimjim is seemingly immortal and unkillable. He quickly heals and regenerates from even the most serious of injuries. Grimjim also has super senses that predominantly grant him heightened hearing and sight. He is usually seen alongside his crew of skull-wearing cronies and wielding his signature handguns.

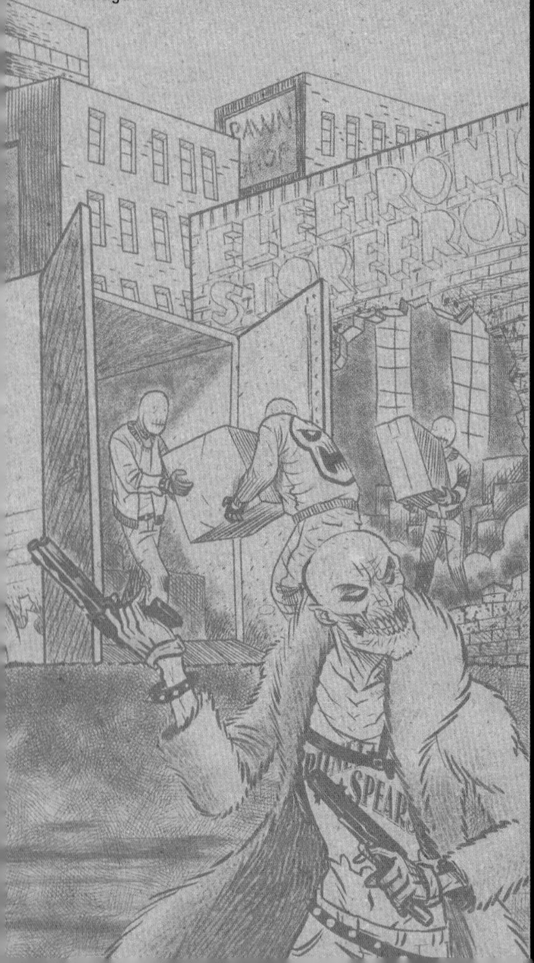

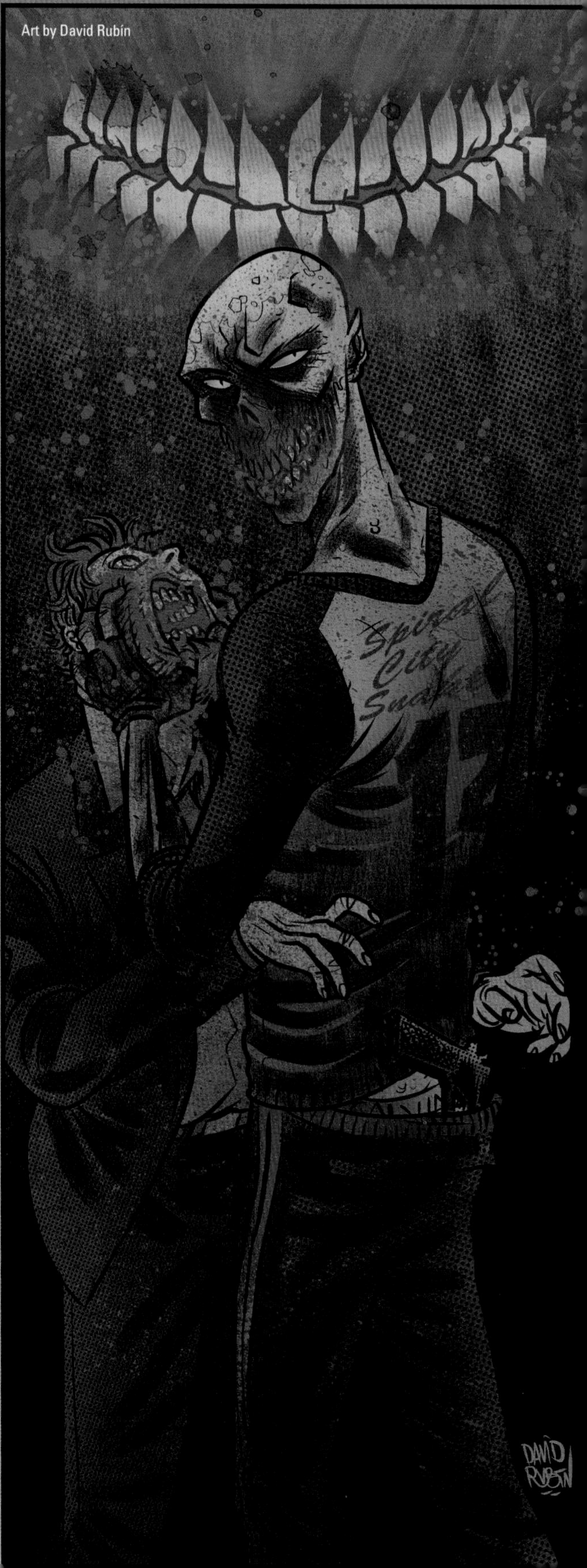

Art by David Rubín

THE HORSELESS RIDER

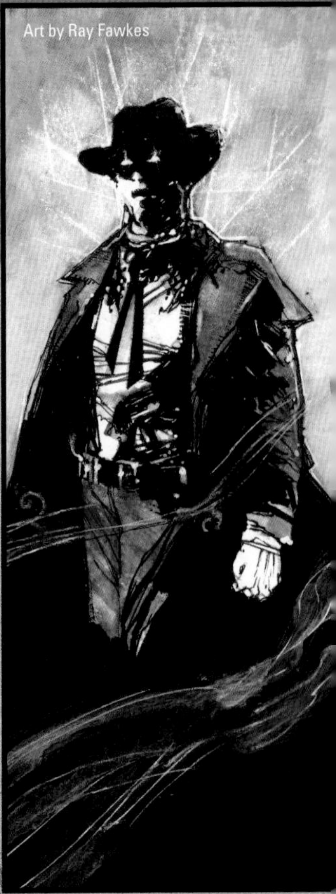
Art by Ray Fawkes

PERSONAL DATA
Alter Ego: *Jacob Tex*
Occupation: *Gambler; Gunslinger*
Marital Status: *Single*
Known Relatives: *None*
Group Affiliation: *The Liberty Squadron*
Base of Operations: *The Wild West*
First Appearance: Sherlock Frankenstein and the Legion of Evil *#4*
Height: *6'2"* ***Weight:*** *185 lbs.*
Eyes: *White* ***Hair:*** *White*

HISTORY
After murdering and cheating his way across the Old West, gambler Jacob Tex was eventually killed in a drunken saloon brawl. However, his life wasn't over yet, and his death had just begun. God enlisted Tex to exact vengeance on the evil men of the Wild West. He became the haunting "Specter of the Prairies," the Horseless Rider.

In cases where a supernatural threat is involved, the Horseless Rider has been known to appear in the present day, particularly in Spiral City, where he shares an uneasy alliance with many modern superheroes.

POWERS & WEAPONS
The Horseless Rider's abilities defy all attempts at classification. He seems to be able to appear and vanish at will. At times he has shown the ability to control supernatural energies. He can become intangible and is impervious to harm. He often uses his mystical six-shooters to exact vengeance.

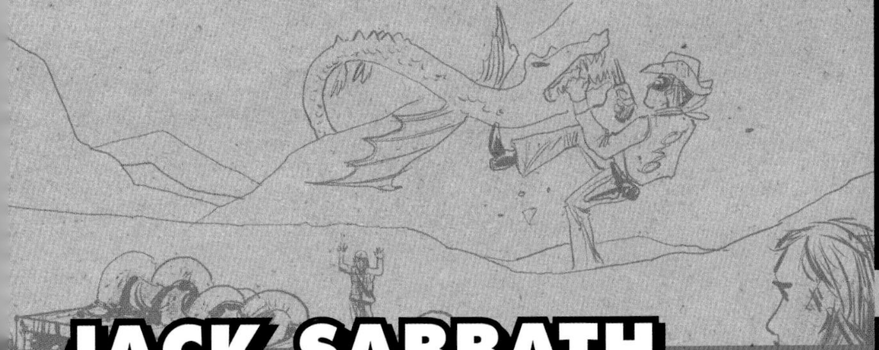

JACK SABBATH

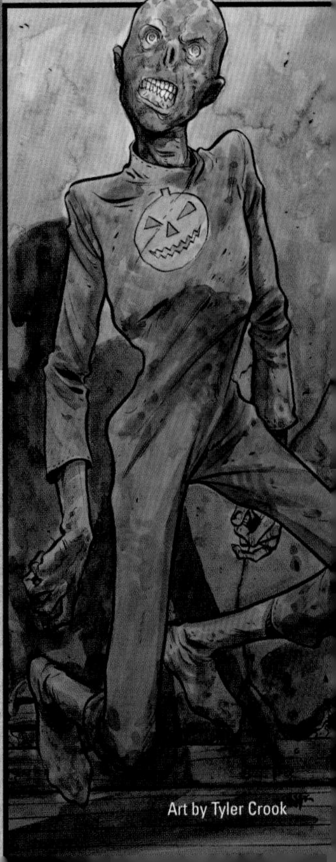
Art by Tyler Crook

PERSONAL DATA
Alter Ego: *N/A*
Occupation: *Ghostly Guide*
Marital Status: *Single*
Known Relatives: *Rusty Sabbath (father); Goldie Sabbath (mother)*
Group Affiliation: *The Unbelievable Unteens*
Base of Operations: *The Cabin of Horrors*
First Appearance: Black Hammer: Age of Doom *#2*
Height: *5'9"* ***Weight:*** *123 lbs.*
Eyes: *White* ***Hair:*** *Decomposed*

HISTORY
Jack Sabbath grew up in Spiral City. His father was a postman and his mother a nurse. Even as a baby, strange things tended to happen around Jack, but his parents were too frightened to tell anyone. As Jack grew into adolescence, the strange phenomena that followed him grew more extreme, and they could no longer ignore the fact that young Jack was different. Jack's parents were very religious people, and they worried that their son may be some sort of demon. The truth was that Jack was born with superhuman abilities that destined him for both greatness and tragedy (see "The Unbelievable Unteens")...

Years later, after his death, Jack Sabbath is condemned to act as a ghostly guide to the recently deceased. He has been roaming the interconnected supernatural realms of the afterlife for three decades. But Jack only wants one thing: to be alive again.

POWERS & WEAPONS
Jack was born with a superhuman ability that allows him to channel and harness paranormal energies from the ethereal planes. This grants him magical talents that involve chaos- and reality-warping abilities. He is also able to open portals and travel across different supernatural realms.

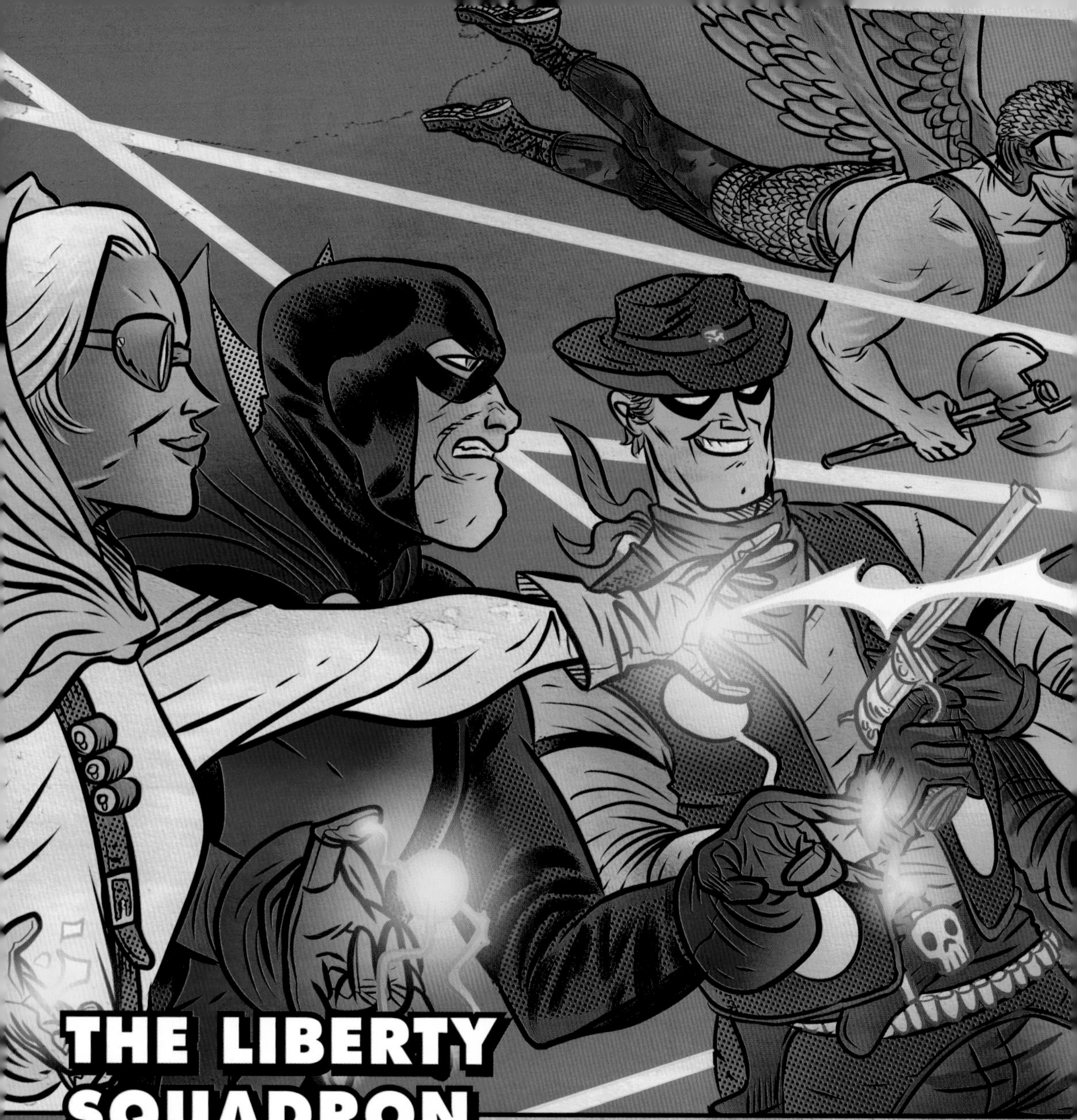

THE LIBERTY SQUADRON

First Appearance: Sherlock Frankenstein and the Legion of Evil *#4*

HISTORY

The Liberty Squadron is the oldest organization of superheroes in history and also one of the greatest. As war broke out across Europe, Spiral City's heroes came together to debate the actions necessary. Should they join the fight overseas or stay in America and secure their border? A vote commenced to determine the outcome, and it was a draw! However, just then, Dr. Jimmy Robinson arrived on the scene and announced his debut as Doctor Andromeda! Robinson became the deciding vote, and the Liberty Squadron was born! The Squadron took the battle to Europe and faced the Axis head-on. They played a key role during World War II and returned war heroes.

The Liberty Squadron eventually disbanded in the aftermath of the war.

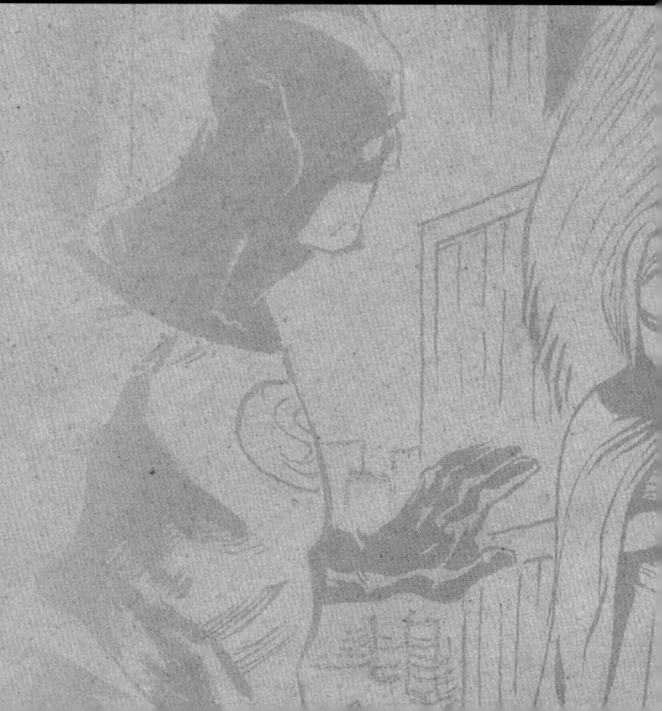

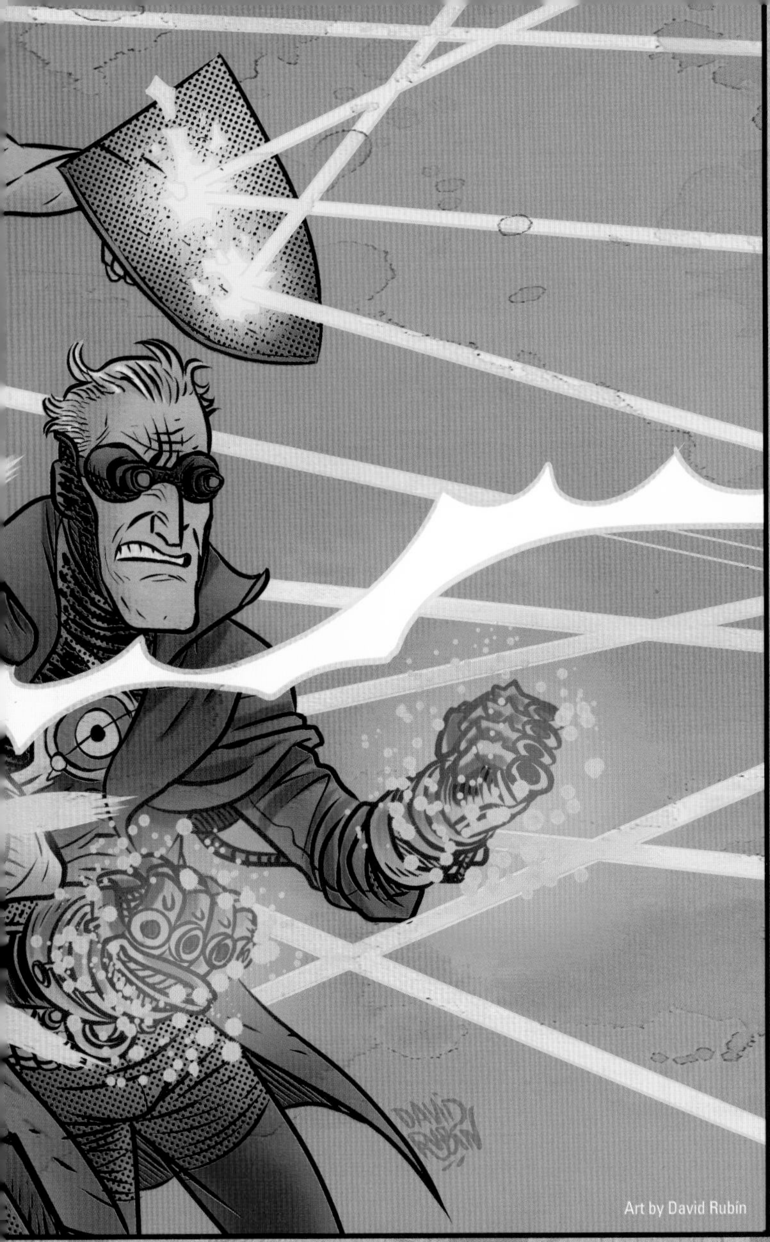

Art by David Rubin

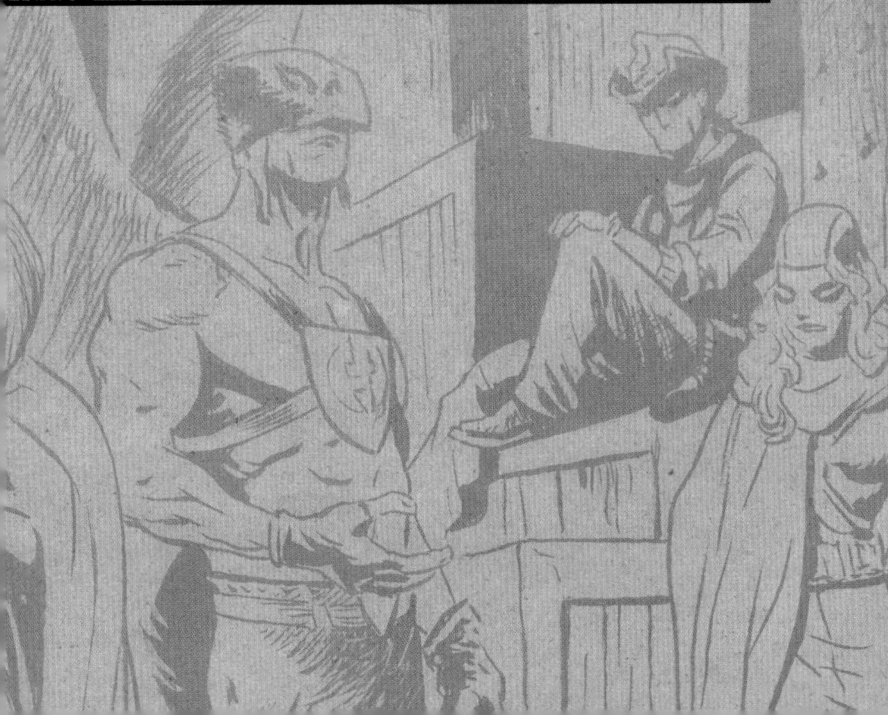

MEMBERS

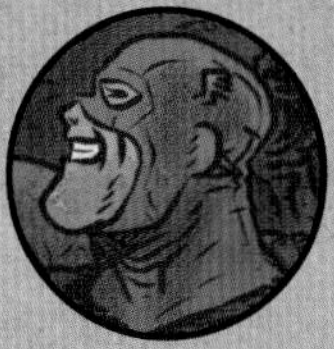

ABRAHAM SLAM

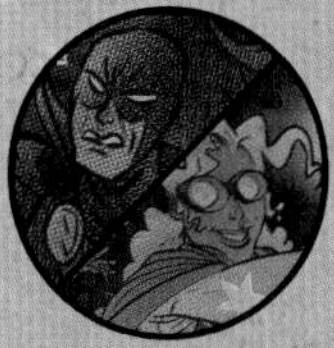

CAPTAIN NIGHT & DR. DAY

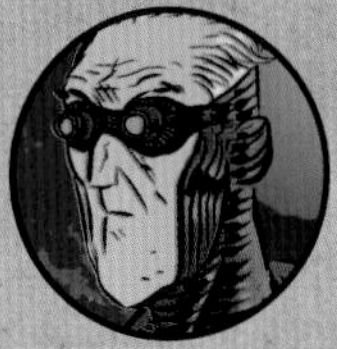

DOCTOR ANDROMEDA

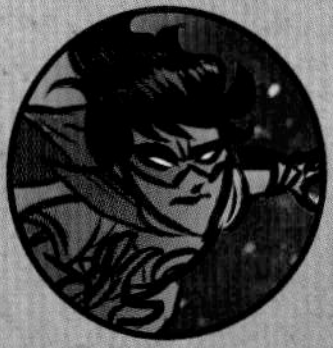

GOLDEN GAIL

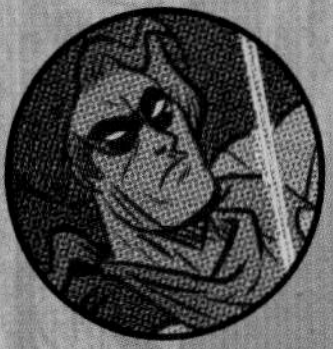

THE HORSELESS RIDER

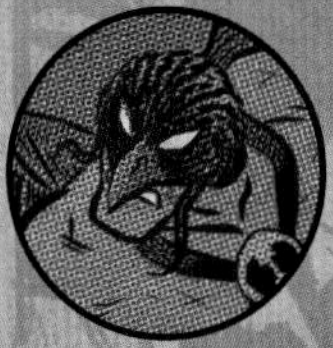

WINGMAN

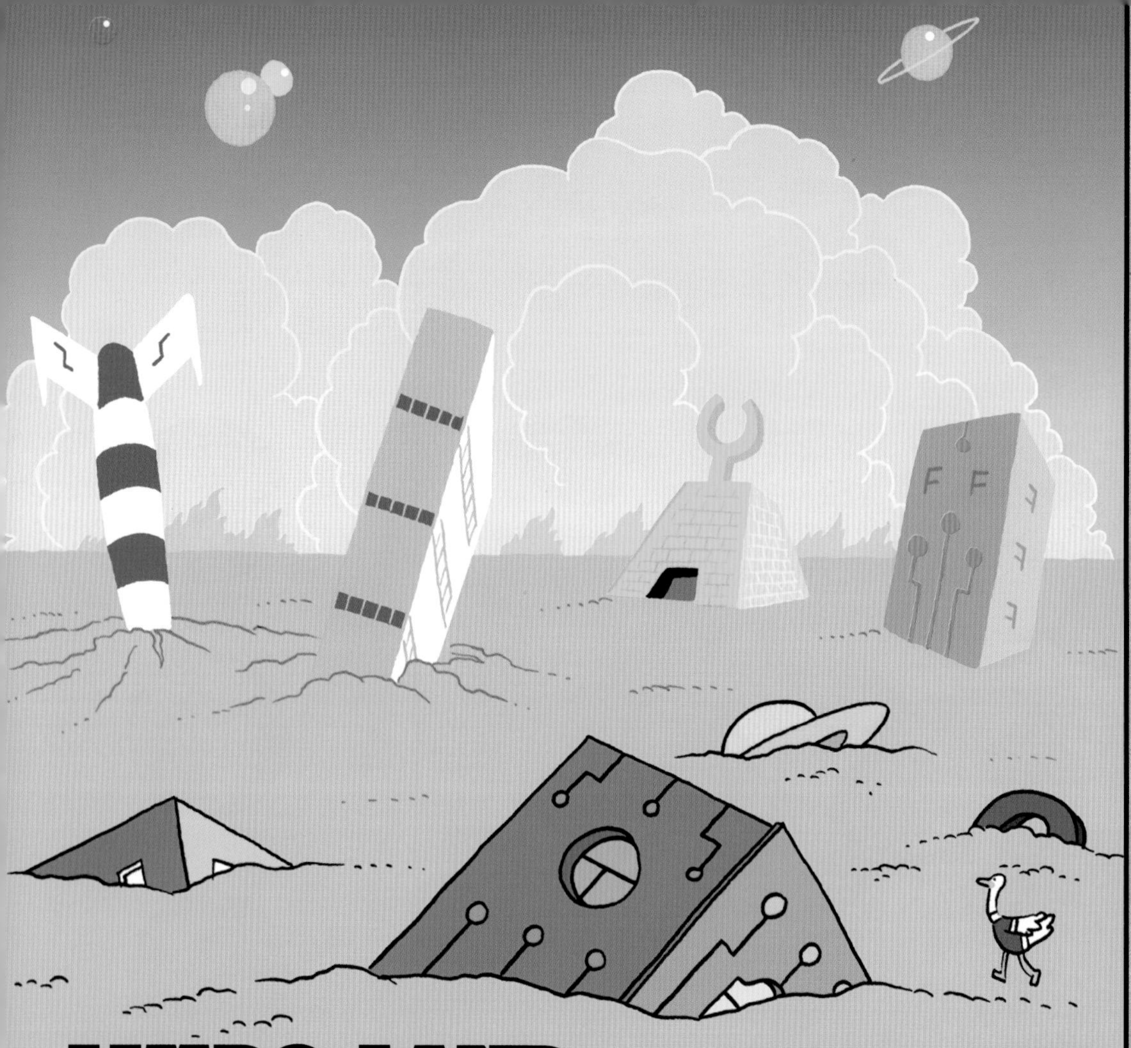

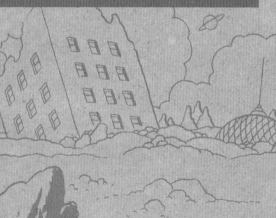

Art by Rich Tommaso

LIMBO LAND

First Appearance: Black Hammer: Age of Doom *#6*

HISTORY

Limbo Land is filled with the unrealized characters from unfinished stories that the Creator has either forgotten about or disposed of. This is a dimension constantly shifting and changing shape, seemingly at random but much more likely due to the nefarious whims of some scatterbrain despot. It's hard to make it to the page. It's even harder to make it to a page that matters. Only Golden Goose has ever managed to slip through the cracks of the Creator's subconscious and make it into three official panels and one variant cover!

MEMBERS

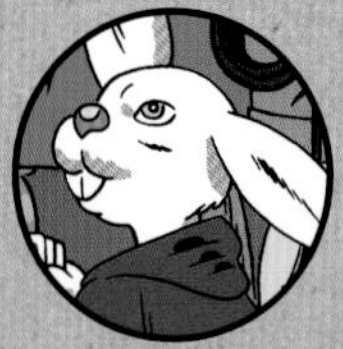

BARBALI-BUNNY

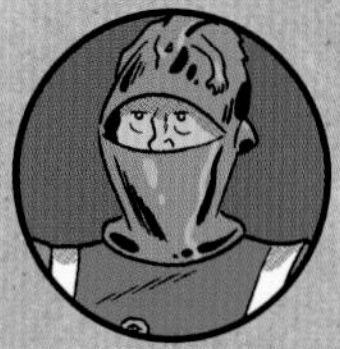

BURT LANCELOT

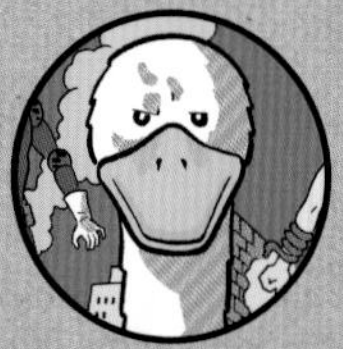

GOLDEN GOOSE

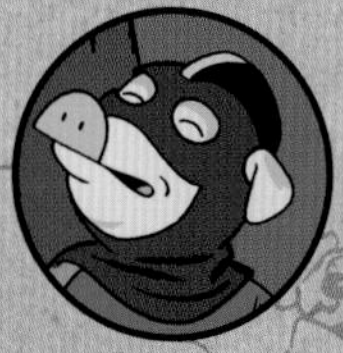

HAM SLAMWICH

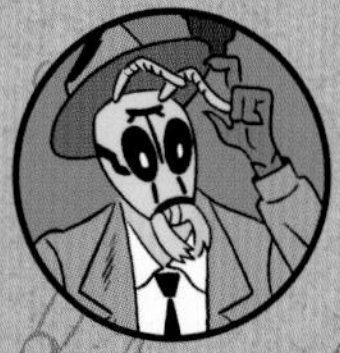

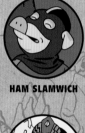

INSPECTOR INSECTOR

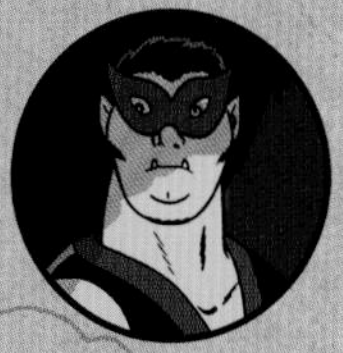

MISTER GRIZZLY

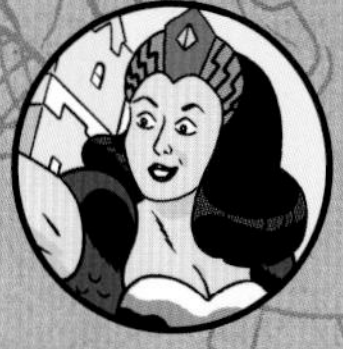

MS. MOONBEAM

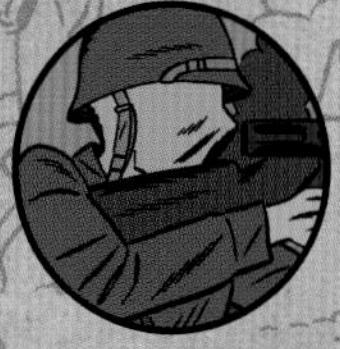

SOLDIER X

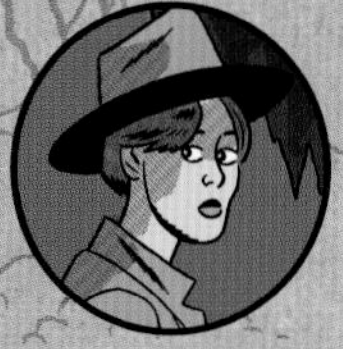

STELLA STEELE

LONNIE JAMES

PERSONAL DATA
Alter Ego: *N/A*
Occupation: *Bartender*
Marital Status: *Unknown*
Known Relatives: *Unknown*
Group Affiliation: *N/A*
Base of Operations: *The Anteroom*
First Appearance: Black Hammer: Age of Doom *#1*
Height: *6'5"* ***Weight:*** *247 lbs.*
Eyes: *Blue* ***Hair:*** *Bald; Red Beard*

HISTORY
Lonnie James runs the dodgiest pub in existence: the Anteroom. It's a meeting place of sorts for all the misfits and monsters of the omniverse to come together for a couple o' drinks and to rock out **hard**. It's the spot where stories go to wait and pace the dance floor. James runs the joint, keeping the band list moving and the attendees happy—just make sure not to trust the guy. When Lucy Weber (see "Black Hammer II") arrived on his scene, he led her along with false pretenses and then abandoned her in Hell. So, yeah, he's a grade-A bastard.

POWERS & WEAPONS
Talking. It's what he does best.

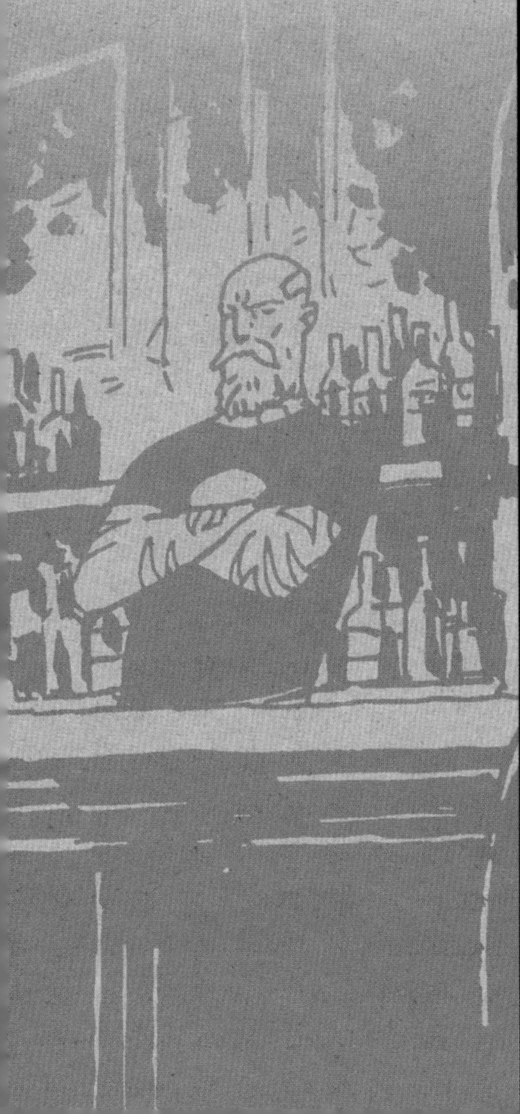

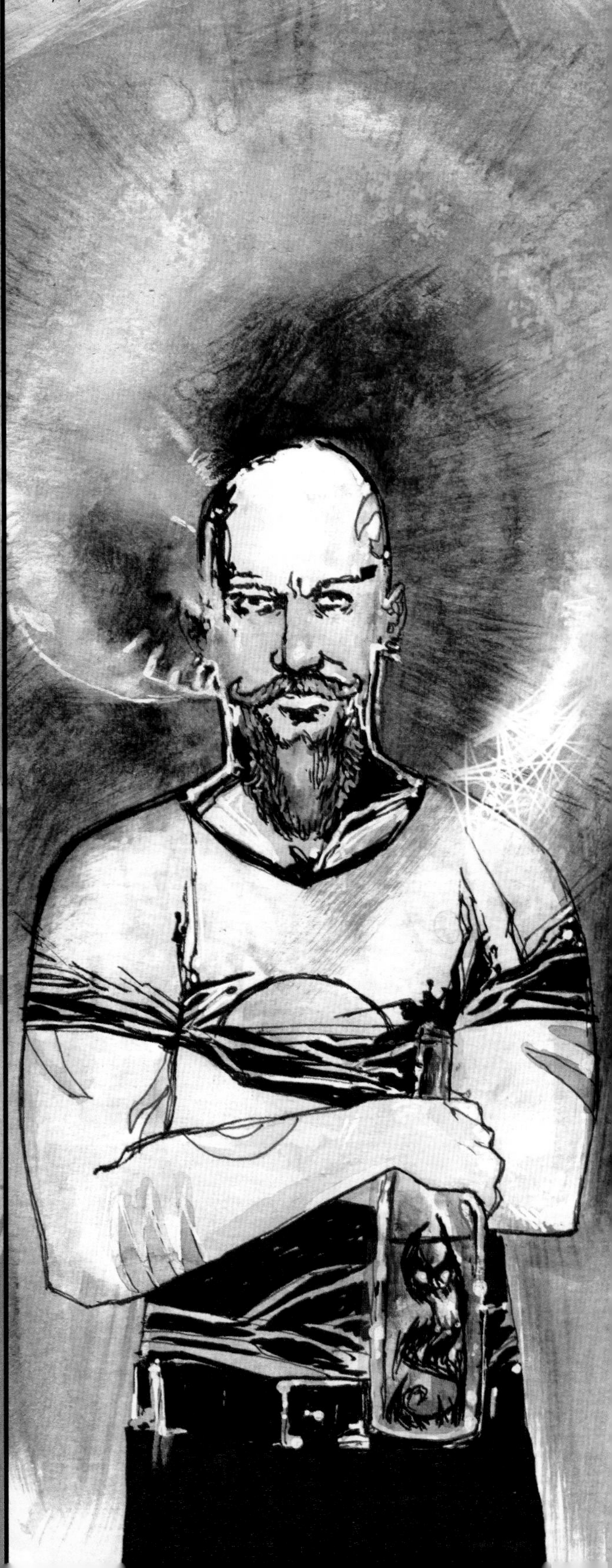

Art by Ray Fawkes

MADAME DRAGONFLY

PERSONAL DATA
Alter Ego: Unknown
Notable Aliases: Madame Butterfly
Occupation: Guardian of the Cabin of Horrors
Marital Status: Widowed
Known Relatives: Jacob (son; deceased)
Group Affiliation: None
Base of Operations: The Cabin of Horrors
First Appearance: Black Hammer #1
Height: 5'9"   *Weight:* 126 lbs.
Eyes: Green   *Hair:* Black

HISTORY

There once was a cabin in the woods not too far off from a wayward town. This was a cabin that lied in wait for lost souls and searching travelers. Its windows appeared lit and welcoming as if to coax those troubled spirits toward its horrific womb . . . until they approached and knocked. The door would creak open and darkness would swiftly fall. The frightened travelers would then be greeted by a winged witch with questions—what do you want or what do you need—and even more answers. This was Madame Dragonfly. She offered great things and expected even greater things in return. Her cabin housed many doors with many horrors behind them, and they should never be opened at any time. The travelers' immortal souls depended on it.

Not much was known about Madame Dragonfly's origins, although it was rumored that she was once an inhabitant of that wayward town not too far off. She too sought help from a winged witch. She, too, was made an offer in exchange for a granted wish. She, too, fell victim to a terrible curse. Dragonfly appeared to be a guardian of many horrors, but whether she was keeping those horrors at bay or simply awaiting her chance to unleash them is still unknown.

But, alas, decades seemed to pass and Madame Dragonfly remained. In her later years, she was rumored to have been seen with a swamp monster in a deranged romance of sorts. Those sightings and rumors were just that, however, and it was not known whether her heart was even capable of something as innately human as love. Madame Dragonfly was the guardian of many horrors, the biggest horrors being the ones she hid within herself.

She was seen in battle aiding the heroes of Earth against Anti-God (see "Anti-God") during the first Cataclysm. She too disappeared and is yet to be found. Her cabin mysteriously vanished alongside her . . .

One hundred years in the future, Madame Dragonfly—now calling herself Madame Butterfly—lives blissfully on Spiral Swamp with a new swamp sweetheart. However, this doesn't last long as she is called back into action by the Quantum League (see "The Quantum League").

POWERS & WEAPONS

Madame Dragonfly's abilities are intrinsically linked to her Cabin of Horrors. She can channel the dark energies contained within it, summoning the beings and powers of a hundred dimensions. This also grants her manipulation of the mystic arts, often in the form of incredibly powerful illusions. She is also in possession of a number of occult artifacts which lend her a variety of magical abilities.

Art by Lucy Sullivan

MECTOPLASM

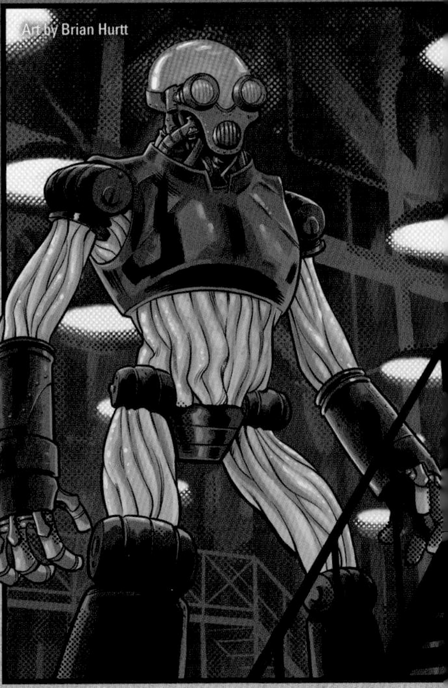

Art by Brian Hurtt

PERSONAL DATA
Alter Ego: *Eugene Tremblay*
Occupation: *Unwilling Criminal*
Marital Status: *Single*
Known Relatives: *Parents (deceased)*
Group Affiliation: *None*
Base of Operations: *Spiral Asylum*
First Appearance: Sherlock Frankenstein and the Legion of Evil *#1*
Height: *30′* ***Weight:*** *20 tons*
Eyes: *Pink* ***Hair:*** *None*

HISTORY
Little is known about Eugene Tremblay's past, but what is known is that he was only a child when he died in a freak accident. He was a small boy taken away from his parents too soon. Sherlock Frankenstein (see "Sherlock Frankenstein"), during his days of villainy, captured the boy's ghost and imprisoned it in an indestructible metal body, transferring his soul and consciousness into a powerful mechanical goliath.

Frankenstein then controlled Tremblay's metallic body for his own nefarious agenda. He brought the boy back from death and into a life of pain and forced servitude. Mectoplasm soon became a chief foe for Black Hammer, Madame Dragonfly, and Abraham Slam—with none of them knowing his true history. Tremblay wanted nothing to do with evil, for he was just an innocent child. He eventually broke free of Frankenstein's control and ran. He tried to escape his past and refused future offers of villainy, but blood was already on his hands. Tremblay was captured and imprisoned for the crimes he was forced to commit. He spends his days in a prison cell at Spiral Asylum.

POWERS & WEAPONS
Mectoplasm's body is nearly indestructible and is equipped with numerous weapons. Eugene's favorite device is the teddy launcher, but Sherlock rarely ever allowed him to use that one. He can also fire blasts of burning ectoplasm from his gauntlets.

METAL MINOTAUR

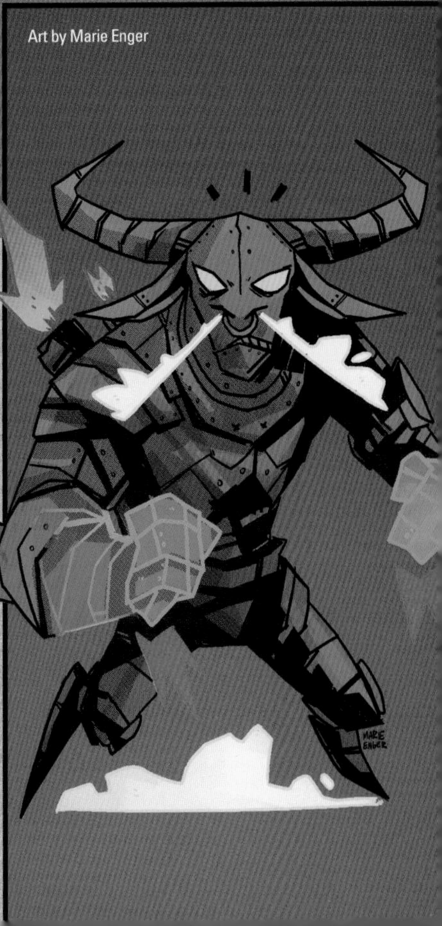

Art by Marie Enger

PERSONAL DATA
Alter Ego: *N. Parker*
Occupation: *Engineer; Inventor*
Marital Status: *Married*
Known Relatives: *Geneviève Goupil (wife)*
Group Affiliation: *N/A*
Base of Operations: *Spiral City*
First Appearance: Sherlock Frankenstein and the Legion of Evil *#3*
Height: *10′* ***Weight:*** *2.5 tons*
Eyes: *Brown* ***Hair:*** *Gray (formerly black)*

HISTORY
N. Parker was an incredibly gifted engineer and mechanic. She did the obvious and used these talents to build a massive suit of mythical battle armor. Parker soon began an illustrious career as the Metal Minotaur and became one of Black Hammer's greatest foes (see "Black Hammer I"). With each defeat, Parker improved her armor until she built her most powerful one yet. This armor acted like an exoskeleton by directly connecting to her spine, but hubris got the better of this brilliant engineer. She rushed her creation and never accounted for the shifts of mass the exoskeleton would take! When she attempted to walk in the armor, it snapped her back like a toothpick.

Black Hammer quickly rescued Parker from her bone-crushing Cretan cage and transported her to New World. Starlok (see "Starlok & the Lightriders") used his otherworldly magic and medicine to heal her as much as he could. While she would never walk again, Parker survived the experience and was able to bond with her former enemy, Black Hammer.

When Anti-God arrived on Earth during the first Cataclysm (see "Anti-God"), Parker responded to a call from Sherlock Frankenstein (see "Sherlock Frankenstein"). She donned her Metal Minotaur armor once more with the help of Manaconda and had plans to help Spiral City's heroes in their battle against Anti-God. However, before any of the villains could join the fight, the heroes disappeared in a flash of light after Anti-God's defeat.

Parker now lives in a long-term care facility on the East End of Spiral City, where she spends her time reading Motor magazine, playing Ms. Pac-Man, and chain-smoking.

POWERS & WEAPONS
The Metal Minotaur is a formidable achievement in engineering. Linked directly to Parker's brain, the powered suit operates in accordance with her movements. It grants superhuman strength and durability and an array of weaponry—including, but not limited to: sonic cannons, flamethrowers, buzz saws, quake hooves, and a laser bullwhip.

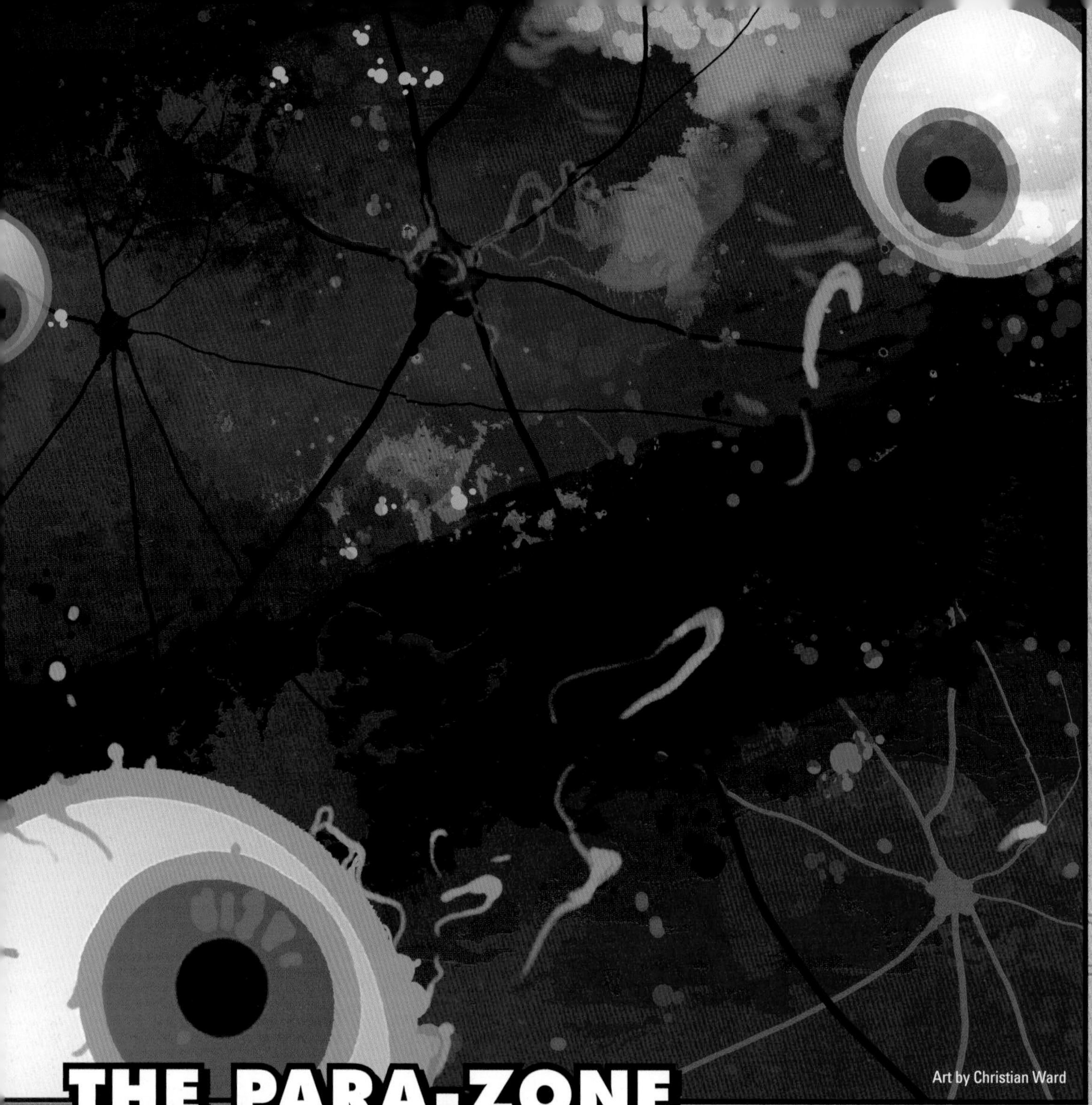

Art by Christian Ward

THE PARA-ZONE

First Appearance: Black Hammer *#5*

HISTORY

A place beyond places. A time beyond time. The Para-zone lies between dimensions, and only a few have managed to breach its membrane. Colonel Weird (see "Colonel Weird") is the only man to have entered the realm and survived. He gained incredible abilities and insight, but it was all at the expense of his mind. He now drifts between his reality and the Para-zone—lost within the curves and angles of its design.

Meanwhile, Jimmy Robinson, the costumed hero Doctor Andromeda, never visited the Para-zone but was able to invent a Para-Gauntlets that tapped into its para-radiation. He harnesses it as a weapon to fight evil across the universe with his squad of intergalactic para-wand wielders: the Star Sheriff Squadron.

The Para-zone is a dimension that sits just beyond ours. It is always watching. It is always knowing. If you ever happen to catch sight of one of its many eyes, do not stare and don't you dare make contact . . . You never know if it will take a liking to you. You never know if it will decide to pull you deep within its madness too . . .

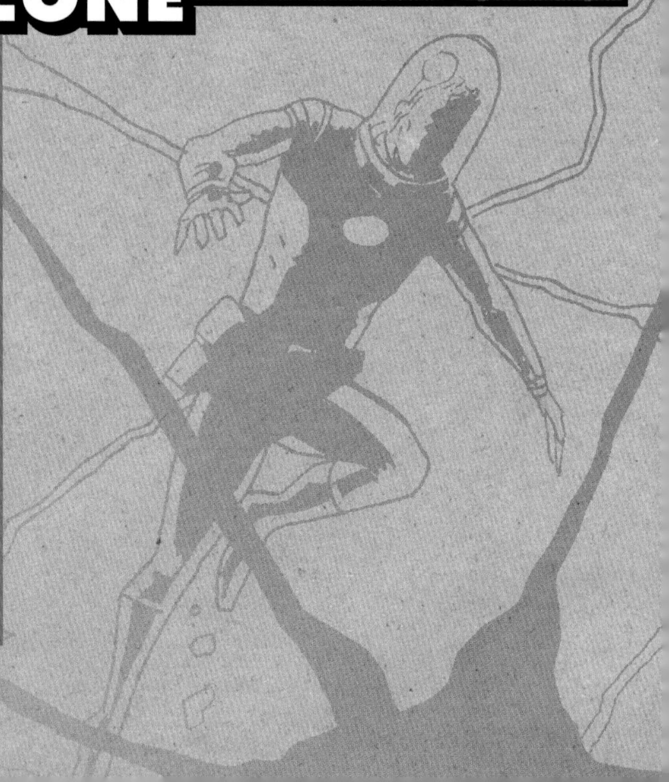

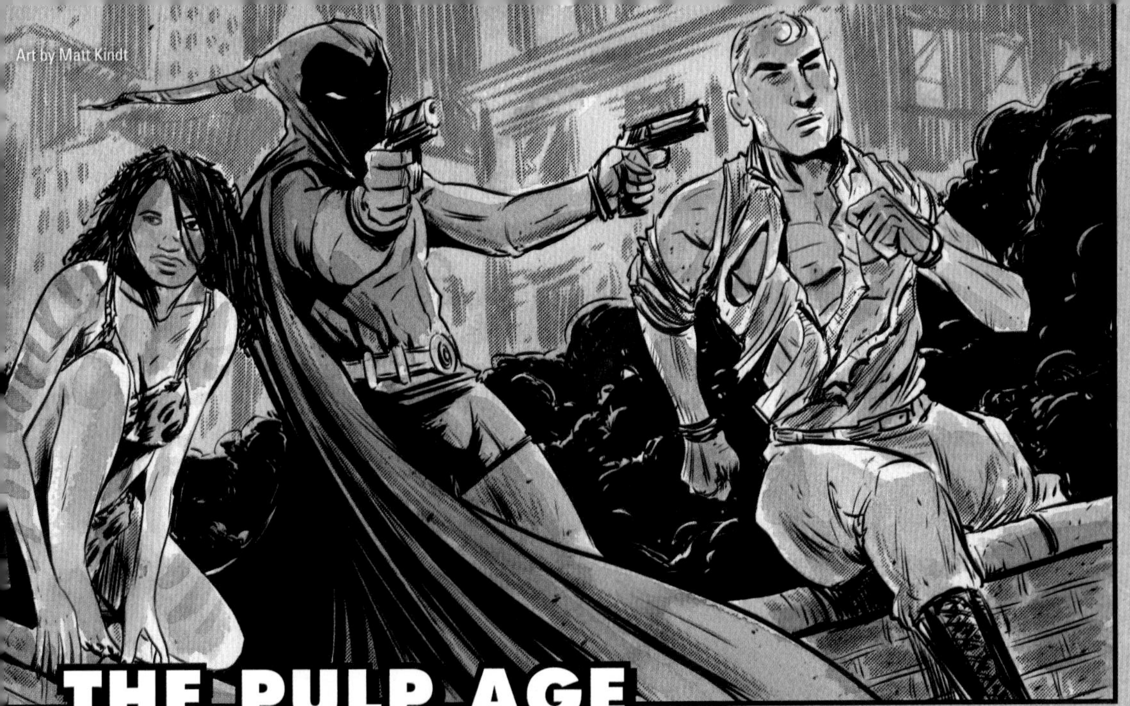
Art by Matt Kindt

THE PULP AGE

First Appearance: Sherlock Frankenstein and the Legion of Evil *#4*

MEMBERS

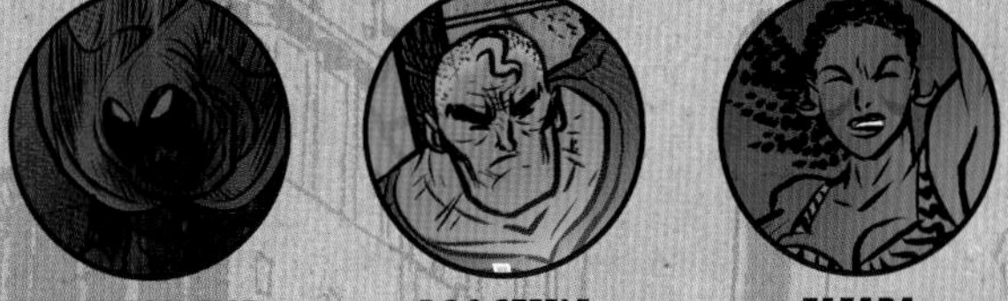
CRIMSON FIST
DOC STEELE
TAZARA

HISTORY

The 1930s saw the dawn of the superheroes. As Sherlock Frankenstein (see "Sherlock Frankenstein") set up shop in Spiral City as the world's first super villain, a trinity of heroic individuals rose up to meet him.

The first of these heroes was the adventurer, detective, researcher, physician, inventor, veterinarian, scientist, industrialist, master of disguise, and, as was eventually revealed, world-renowned violist, Doctor Nathan Steele. Raised by his Tibetan mother and a team of rogue international scientists assembled by his dead father, Steele was trained from birth through a series of rigorous experiments. This resulted in Steele acquiring peak human strength and agility, mastery of all martial arts, a brilliant scientific mind, and a "just okay" understanding of the occult. Steele eventually found himself returning to his father's homeland, America, where he became known as Doc Steele. He spent his days thwarting evildoers, rehabilitating criminals, and skiing the Himalayas.

Who sees what hate warps the minds of humankind? The Crimson Fist sees! Soon after Doc Steele's emergence, FBI agent Anthony Carcone went rogue and abandoned Hoover's bureau. He decided to take the war against organized crime into his own hands and became the first vigilante known as the Crimson Fist. The horror of crime taints the American dream. Crime cannot hide . . . The Crimson Fist sees!

Daughter to Congolese survivors escaping the tyranny of colonial rule, Tazara was snatched from her parents' cold, dead fingers after their pursuers cornered them deep within the Congo Basin. What these pursuers didn't realize, however, is that the jungle is always watching. A giant leopard sprang from the bushes and slashed their throats, rescuing Tazara and deciding to raise her as her own. Years passed and Tazara became revered as a goddess of the jungle—a warrior unlike any the world had ever known. She stands up for the oppressed and against those who seek to do them harm. In 1932 she eventually found herself in a foreign land . . . Spiral City!

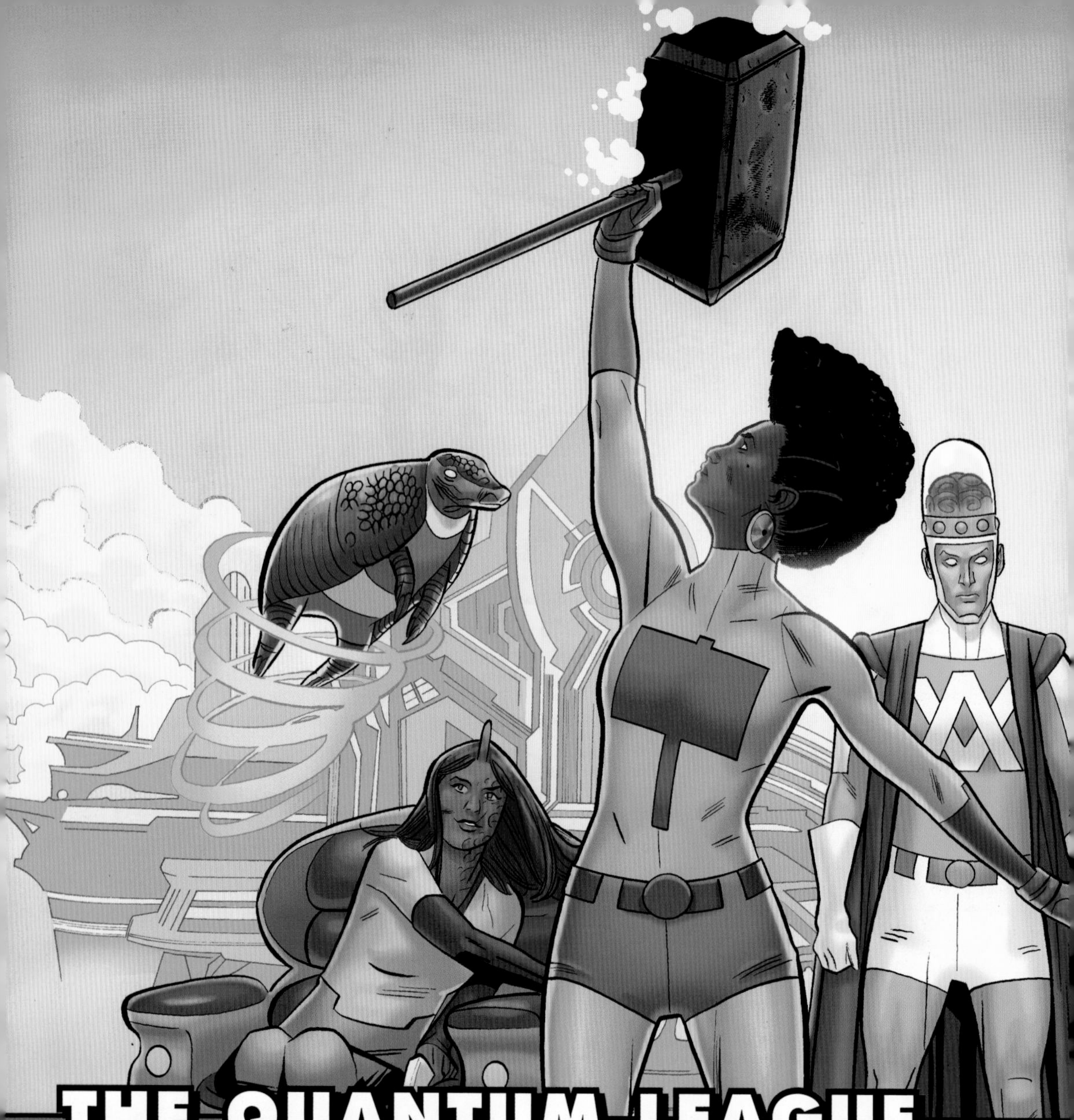

THE QUANTUM LEAGUE

First Appearance: *"The Quantum Age" from* Free Comic Book Day 2018

HISTORY

One hundred years in the future, the Quantum League acts as the first line of defense in the known universe. Archive, Modula, and Gravitus initially teamed up in response to a Charnian terrorist attack during the first intergalactic gravity-ball tournament. As they stood victorious before a cheering crowd, the trio decided it was necessary to form an interplanetary league of the greatest super beings in existence. Together, they brought peace to the galaxies that had hitherto never been achieved before, and they accomplished it together. Archive acted as the main leader and soon began an illicit affair with Hammer Lass—a descendant of Black Hammer (see "Black Hammer I & II"). However, Archive's commitment to his lover and team was challenged when a Martian horde arrived on Earth and the planet appeared doomed. In the aftermath of this cataclysmic event, the Quantum League disbanded, never to be formed again.

Until years later, a Martian codenamed Barbaliteen sought to reassemble the Quantum League in order to save the universe once more . . .

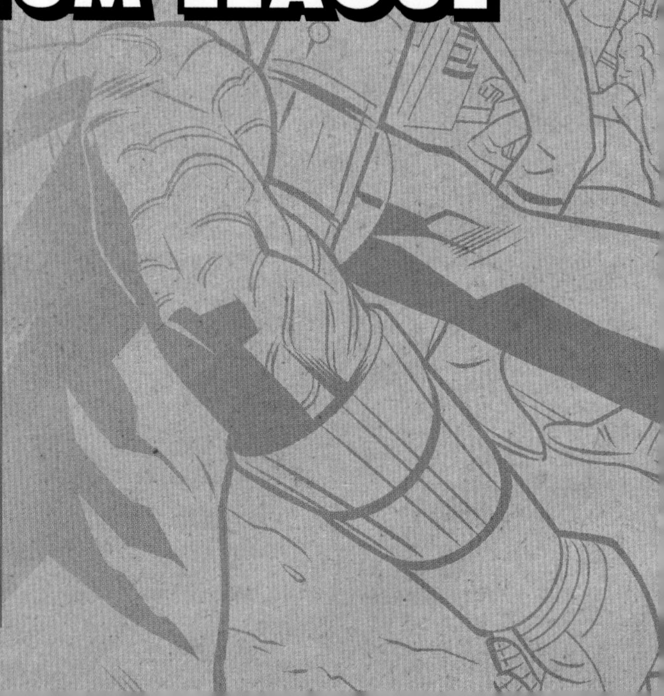

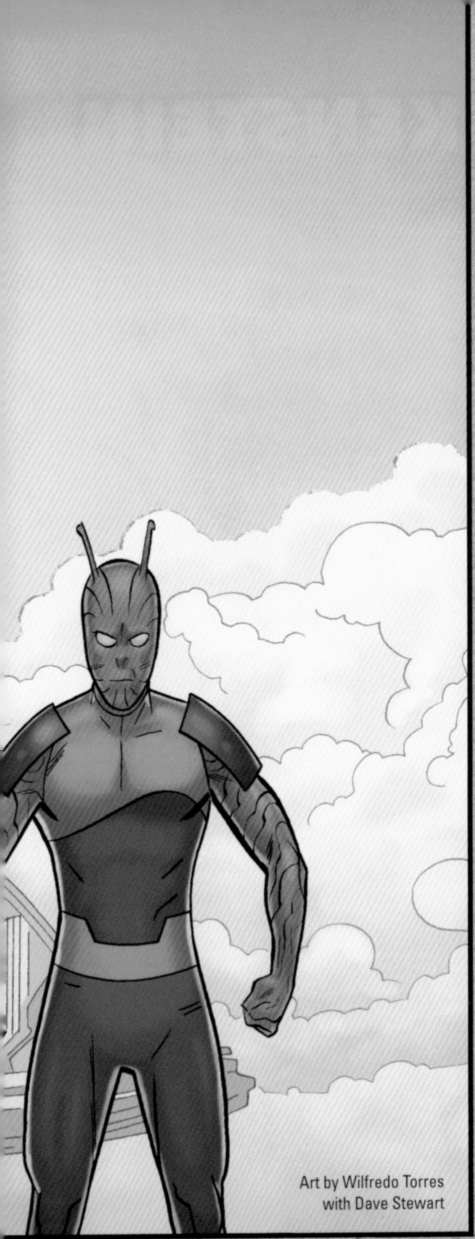

Art by Wilfredo Torres
with Dave Stewart

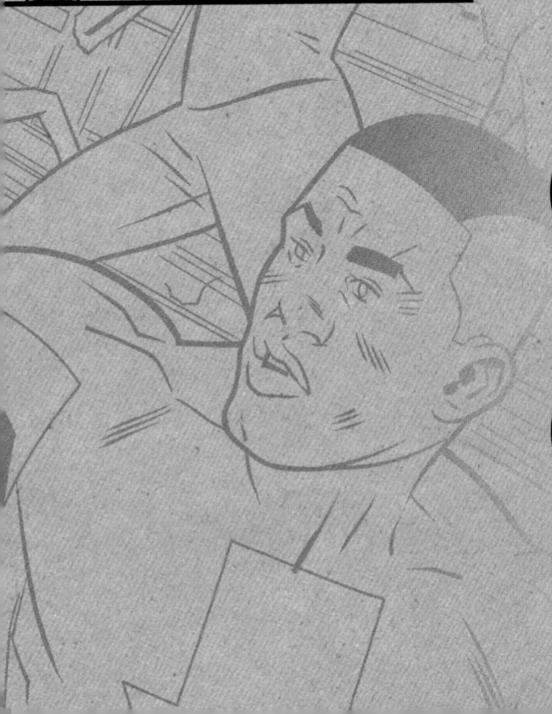

MEMBERS

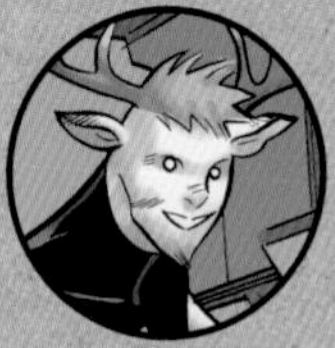
ANTLER BOY

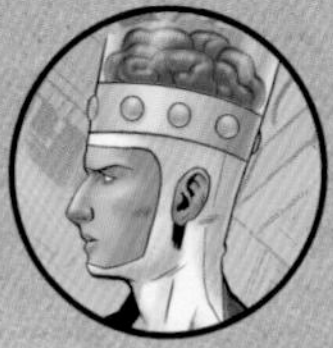
ARCHIVE

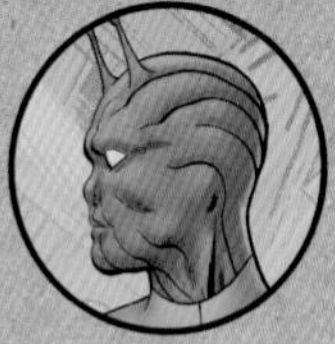
BARBALITEEN

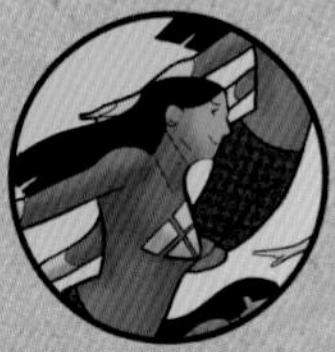
DOPPLER DIVA

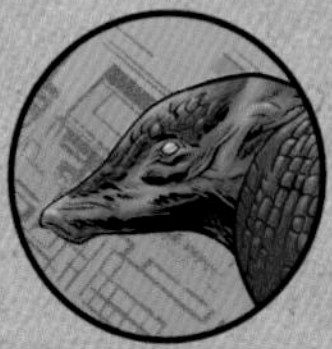
ERB

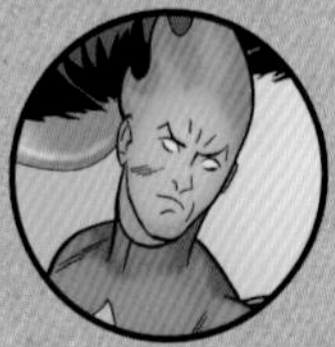
FIREBALL

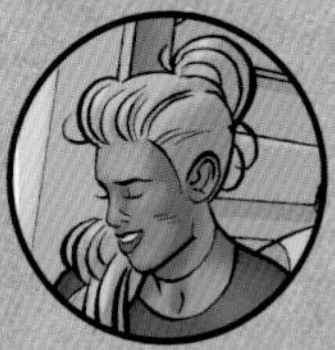
GLUE GIRL

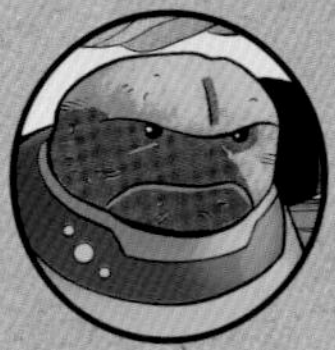
GOLIATHAN

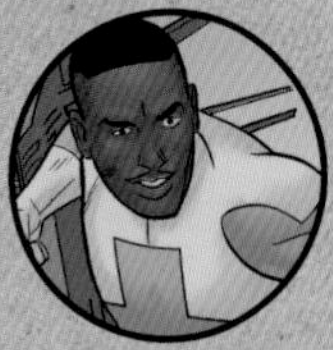
GRAVITUS

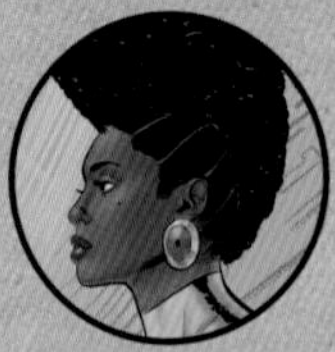
HAMMER LASS

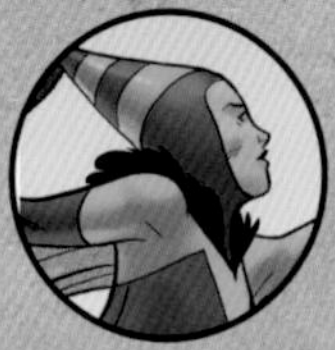
HORNET GIRL

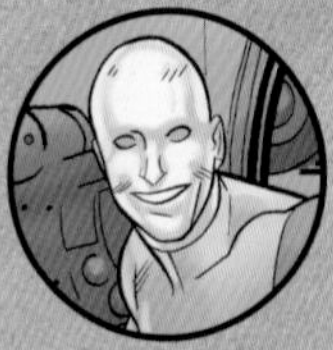
ICE BOY

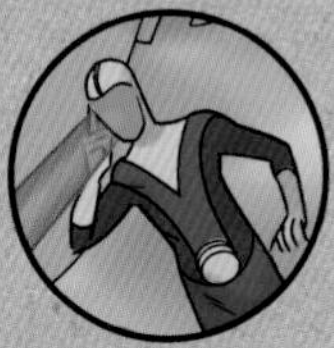
LASAR PHASAR

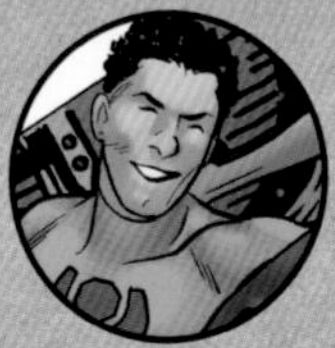
MECHANOS

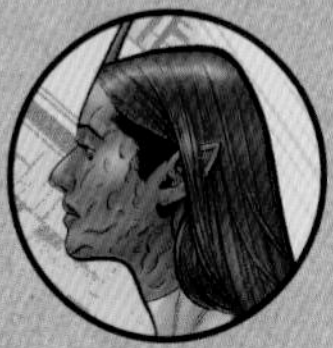
MODULA

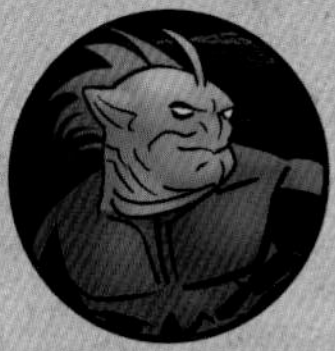
MONSTER BOY

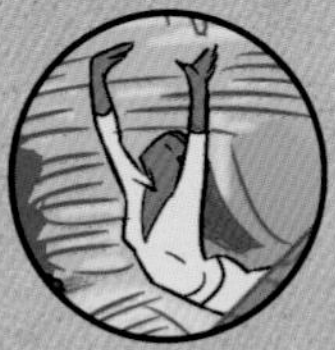
STORMA

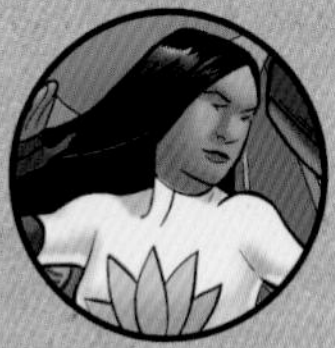
STRATUM

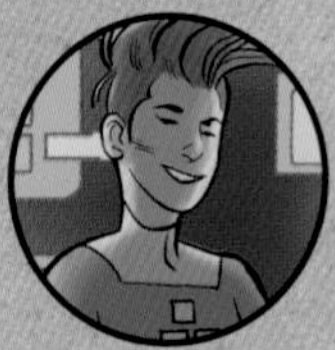
TRIONIC

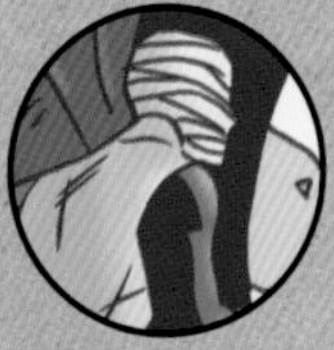
UNKNOWN BOY

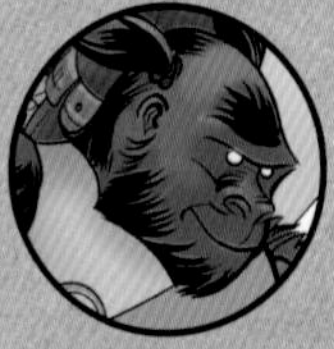
WARILLA

SHERLOCK FRANKENSTEIN

PERSONAL DATA
Full Name: Sherlock Frankenstein
Occupation: CEO of Frankenlock Worldwide
Marital Status: Widowed
Known Relatives: Unknown
Group Affiliation: N/A
Base of Operations: Spiral City Asylum
First Appearance: Black Hammer #2
Height: 6'3"   **Weight:** 170 lbs.
Eyes: Red   **Hair:** Bald

Art by David Rubín

HISTORY

In 1893, a man named Sherlock Frankenstein lay dying in a hospital bed. Left to rot in the care of a kindred nurse, Frankenstein determined to take his life and recovery into his own hands. Through the use of his brilliant intellect, Frankenstein invented a series of machines that cured his disease and granted him immortality. Reborn and undead with an ingenious mind, Sherlock turned his sights on bettering the world around him through the use of his inventions. What began was an illustrious career as Victorian London's—and possibly the world's—first superhero. He solved the crimes and thwarted the evildoers that no one else could. He became a legend.

Even after he achieved notoriety, Frankenstein never forgot the one person that ever showed him kindness. He returned to the nurse that once cared for him and soon the two were wed. Frankenstein's unbeating heart found love that day. Sadly, this new-found bliss and jubilation for life was not to last. Frankenstein's wife fell ill to the same disease that had ailed him. When he attempted to save his bride with the same machines that granted him immortality, they failed, and she died. Heartbroken and bitter toward a world that only caused him pain, Franken-stein abandoned his superhero career and pursued villainy instead. However, London held too many painful memories. Frankenstein left for the New World, the United States of America, and set his villainous gaze upon Spiral City.

There he has reigned as the supreme supervillain, battling heroes from the Pulp Age (see "The Pulp Age") to the modern age. His archnemesis is Golden Gail (see "Golden Gail"); however, there may be more to their relationship than it appears! He eventually retired from villainy and founded Frankenlock World-wide—a global leader in medicinal research and clean, renewable energy. Frankenstein rebranded once again. He was now the world's premiere, inter-national philanthropist.

He supposedly now spends his days locked in Spiral Asylum (see "Spiral Asylum"), where Lucy Weber (see "Black Hammer II") heads off to find him in search of her missing father . . .

POWERS & WEAPONS

Sherlock Frankenstein is immortal with a super-genius-level intellect. He has a myriad of inventions and weapons that he has created and enlists when necessary. These mostly include giant robots, death rays, and mammoth defrosters.

SKULLDIGGER & SKELETON BOY

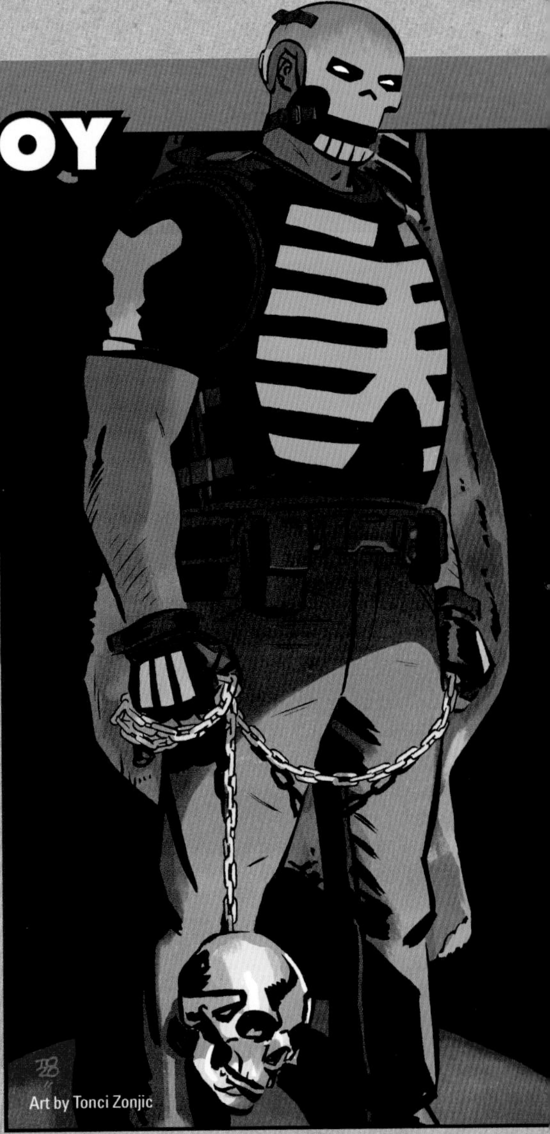

Art by Tonci Zonjic

PERSONAL DATA
Alter Ego: *Unknown*
Occupation: *Unknown*
Marital Status: *Unknown*
Known Relatives: *Unknown*
Group Affiliation: *N/A*
Base of Operations: *Spiral City*
First Appearance: Skulldigger *#1*
Height: *5'10"* ***Weight:*** *234 lbs.*
Eyes: *Brown* ***Hair:*** *Black*

Alter Ego: *Unknown*
Occupation: *Schoolboy*
Known Relatives: *Father (deceased); Mother (deceased)*
Group Affiliation: *N/A*
Base of Operations: *Spiral City*
First Appearance: Skulldigger *#1*
Height: *4'7"* ***Weight:*** *76.5 lbs.*
Eyes: *Hazel* ***Hair:*** *Red*

HISTORY
Very little is known about the masked vigilante known as Skulldigger, though there are persistent rumors that he was once Alley Rat, the child sidekick of the second iteration of the Crimson Fist. Whoever he is behind the skull mask, Skulldigger has been waging a brutal war against crime in Spiral City since the mideighties. His murderous ways have been condemned by the Spiral City Police Department and by most other costumed heroes, yet Skulldigger has never been brought to justice himself.

Recently Skulldigger has been seen operating with a sidekick of his own, known as Skeleton Boy.

POWERS & WEAPONS
As far as anyone knows, Skulldigger has no superhuman abilities, but he is a superb hand-to-hand combatant. He never uses firearms, and instead employs a metallic skull on a chain to bludgeon his opponents.

Little is known about Skeleton Boy or his abilities.

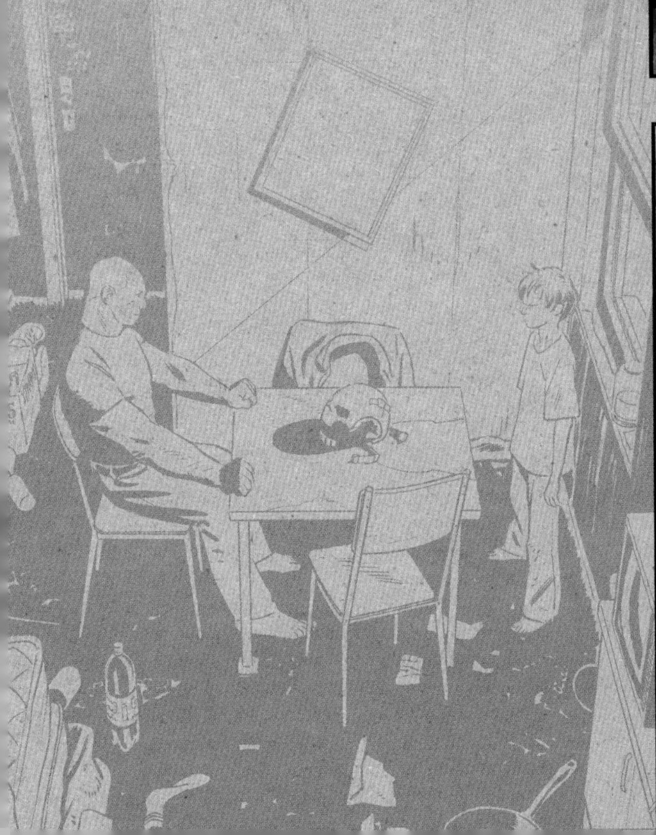

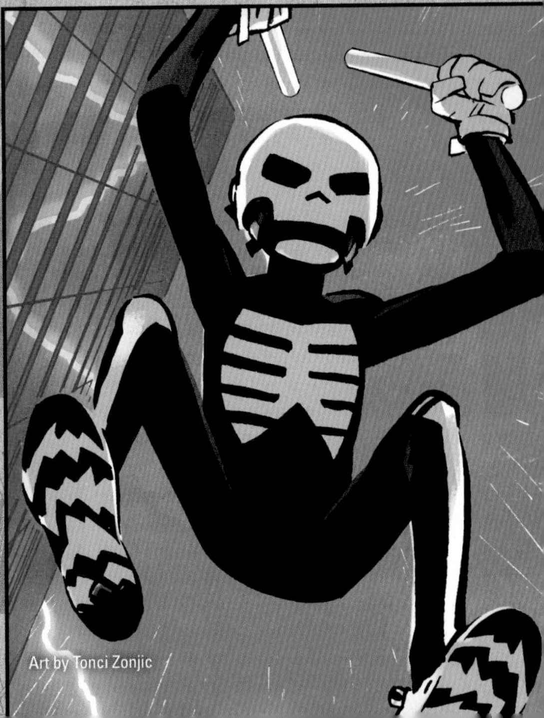

Art by Tonci Zonjic

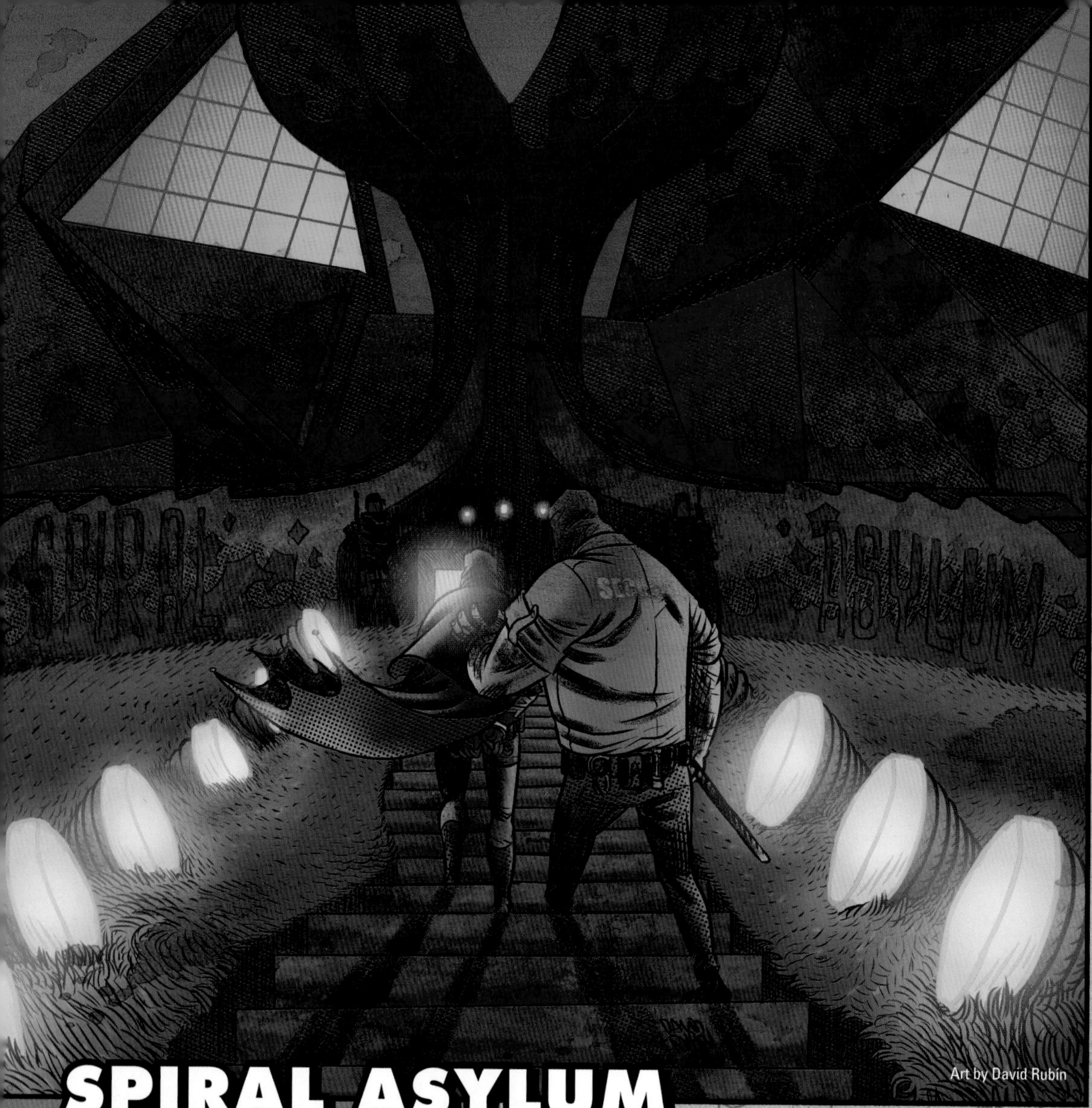
SPIRAL
ASYLUM

Art by David Rubin

SPIRAL ASYLUM

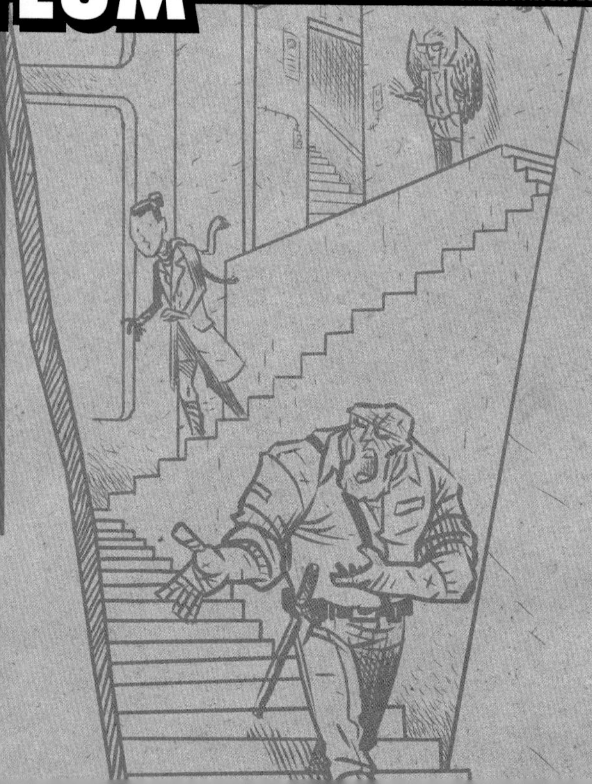

First Appearance: Sherlock Frankenstein and the Legion of Evil *#1*

HISTORY

Located in Spiral City, Spiral Asylum is the super-security prison for superpowered criminals. It's where the worst of the worst villains get locked away and forgotten about—until they escape and destroy the city's water main system again. (Editor's Note: Some-body has to keep Cthu-Lou in business!) Some of its illustrious prisoners include Sherlock Frankenstein (see "Sherlock Frankenstein"), Mectoplasm (see "Mectoplasm"), Grimjim (see "Grimjim"), Sultrix, Manaconda, and Devil's Ivy. The asylum is privately funded and run by a mysterious benefactor, so pretty much anything goes! If you want some advice, kid, don't f*ck up and find yourself at the mercy of the Wingman and the Concretestador. Their wounded egos can't handle much more than a mere mention of the good ol' days.

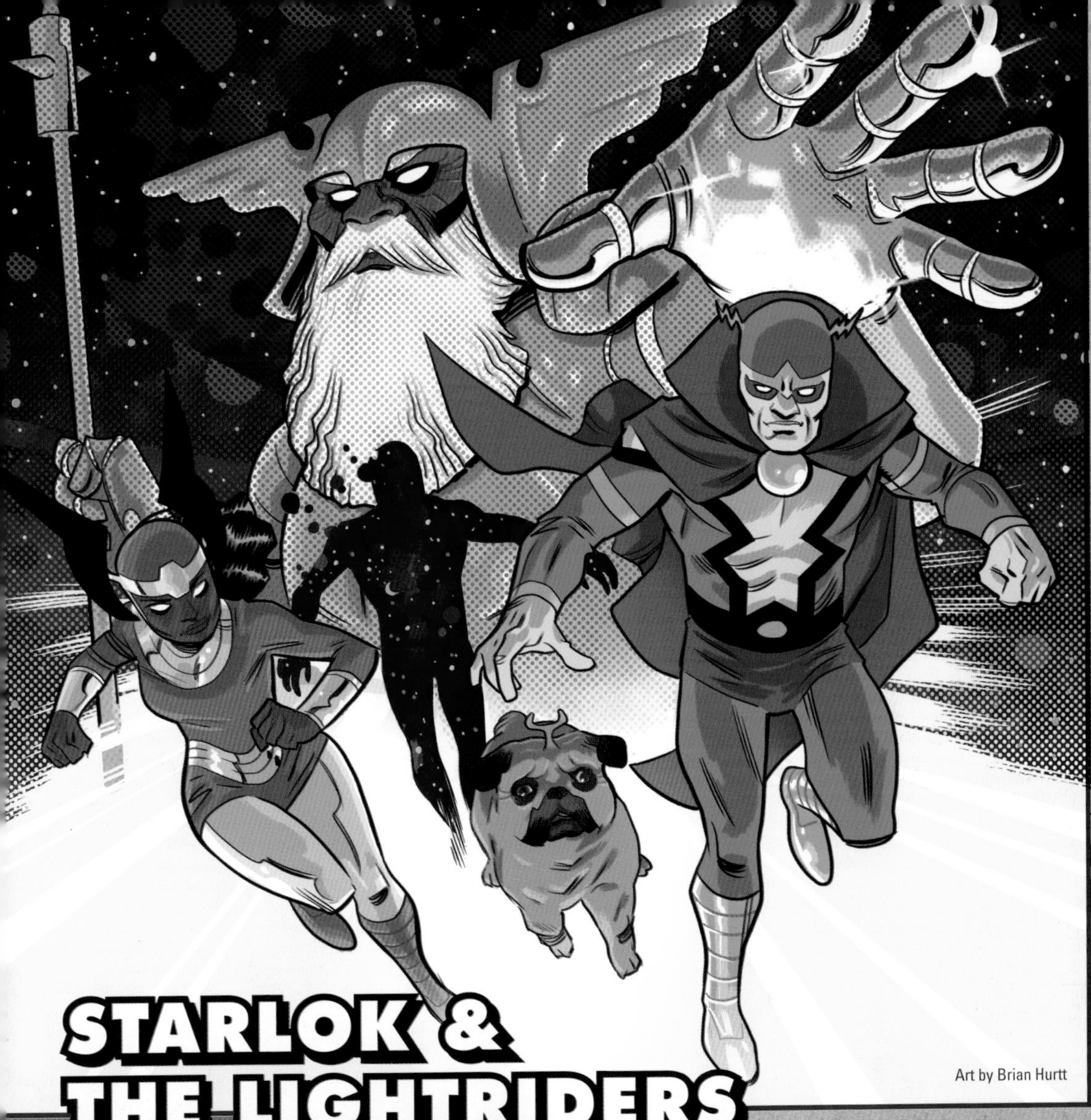

STARLOK & THE LIGHTRIDERS

Art by Brian Hurtt

First Appearance: Black Hammer *#1*
Headquarters: *New World*

HISTORY
Since the beginning of time, Starlok has led the cosmic battle against evil incarnate—his dark twin, Anti-God (see "Anti-God")—holding a delicate balance within the multiverse. The Lightriders are his first line of defense: an esteemed, powerful collection of individuals with cosmic abilities. The Escaper! No prison or snare can contain him! Whiptara! The warrior priestess with an unwavering crew of wham-tastic Whamazons! The youngest Lightrider, Time-Boy, and his loyal pet, Warpie the Chrono-Pup! And the most powerful Lightrider of them all . . . Black Hammer (see "Black Hammer I")! Each member fills a role and a title that must always be upheld. The multiverse depends on it!

The Lightriders (sans Black Hammer) were the first to fall at Anti-God's all-powerful anti-feet. Their doom opened the gates for the first Cataclysm.

MEMBERS

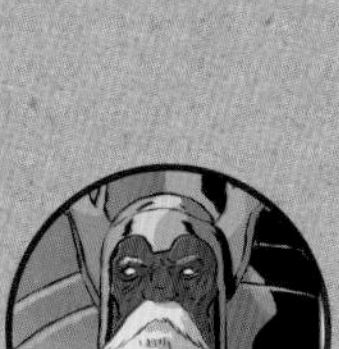

STARLOK

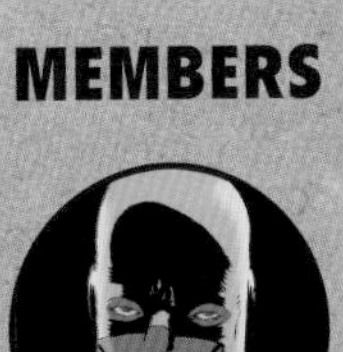

BLACK HAMMER I

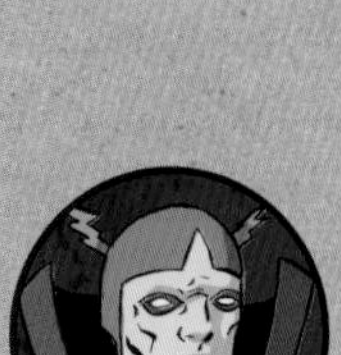

THE ESCAPER

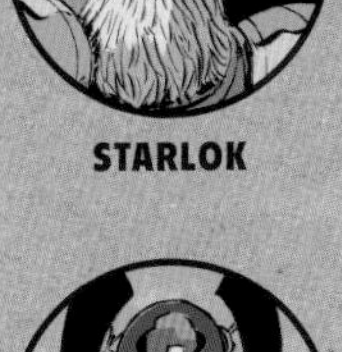

WHIPTARA & THE WHAMAZONS

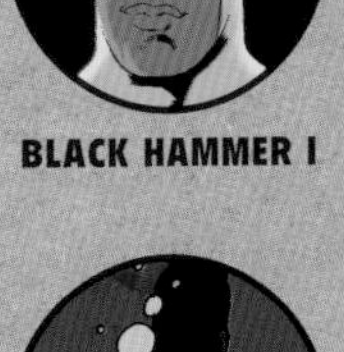

TIME-BOY

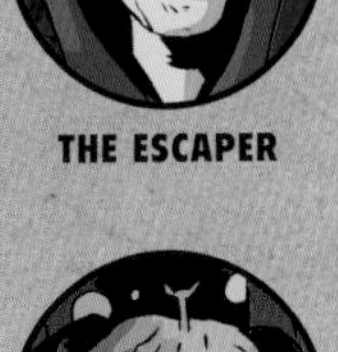

WARPIE THE CHRONO-PUP

TALKY-WALKY

PERSONAL DATA
Alter Ego: *TLK-E WLK-E*
Occupation: *Interstellar Adventurer; Inventor*
Marital Status: *Single*
Known Relatives: *Archive (son)*
Group Affiliation: *None*
Base of Operations: *Moonbase 12*
First Appearance: Black Hammer *#1*
Height: *6'0"* ***Weight:*** *301 lbs.*
Eyes: *None* ***Hair:*** *None*

HISTORY
Talky-Walky never fit in on her robot planet deep within the Osler star system. She grew up in New Technopolis and was a very inquisitive robot. She spent most of her time sending space probe satellites deep into orbit in hopes of discovering other signs of life. Instead of finding life, however, Talky began channeling television signals from a faraway planet called Earth. While the other robots harbored extreme hatred for non-silicon-based lifeforms, Talky-Walky fell in love with the humans that she broadcasted in secret. She studied humankind and longed to escape the robo-dictatorship on her own planet.

Taking matters into her own robo-hands, she sent a distress call into space hoping an earthling would find her. Subsequently, Colonel Randall Weird (see "Colonel Weird") arrived on the robo-planet! He was immediately met with hostility, and Talky came to his rescue. It was the beginning of a beautiful partnership.

Talky-Walky went on to join Colonel Weird on his interstellar adventures. They discovered the Parazone together, but Talky was wise enough to never venture inside it herself. She fought alongside the other heroes to protect her beloved Earth from Anti-God (see "Anti-God") during the first Cataclysm. She joined the heroes in their disappearance, as well . . .

One hundred years in the future, Talky-Walky has given up all hope in humanity, especially since Colonel Weird abandoned her for a self-imposed exile at the end of time. In retaliation, she created her own sentient, mechanical planet, where she has spawned a family of her own that will never abandon her. Her son is Archive, one of the founding members of the Quantum League (see "The Quantum League")—and, while she won't admit it, she is **very** proud of him!

POWERS & WEAPONS
Talky's robotic body is capable of extreme strength and durability. Her AI is unparalleled in the universe, as she is in a constant state of updating her operating system. This grants her genius-level intellect and the most complex database of sourdough recipes ever assembled. She is extremely susceptible to electrolasers—a weakness only known by her fellow robots and her best friend, Colonel Weird.

While Talky is much more of a lover than a fighter, she's not afraid to handle an OB6000 Z-thermal plasma-torch gun in the blazing heat of battle.

Art by Emi Lenox

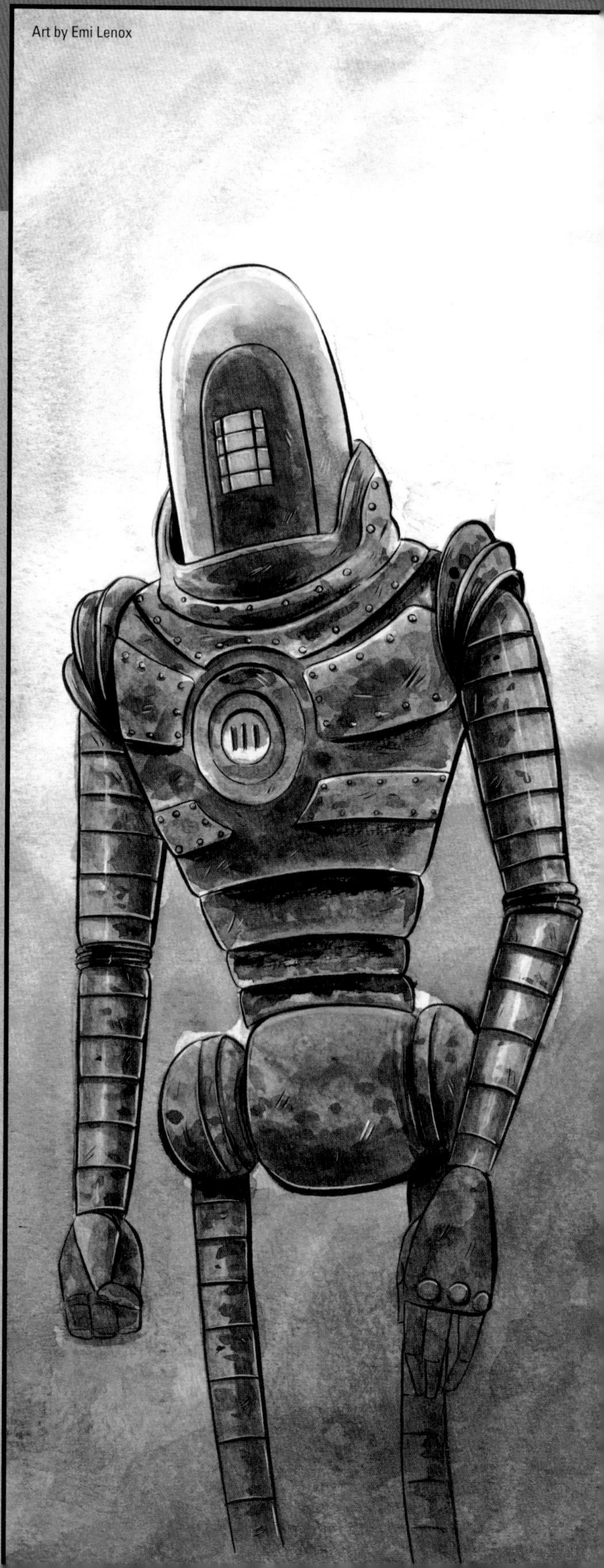

SHERIFF TRUEHEART

PERSONAL DATA
Alter Ego: *Earl Trueheart*
Occupation: *Police Officer*
Marital Status: *Divorced*
Known Relatives: *Tammy Trueheart (ex-wife)*
Group Affiliation: *Rockwood Bowling Club*
Base of Operations: *Rockwood*
First Appearance: Black Hammer *#1*
Height: *6'2"* ***Weight:*** *323 lbs.*
Eyes: *Blue* ***Hair:*** *White*

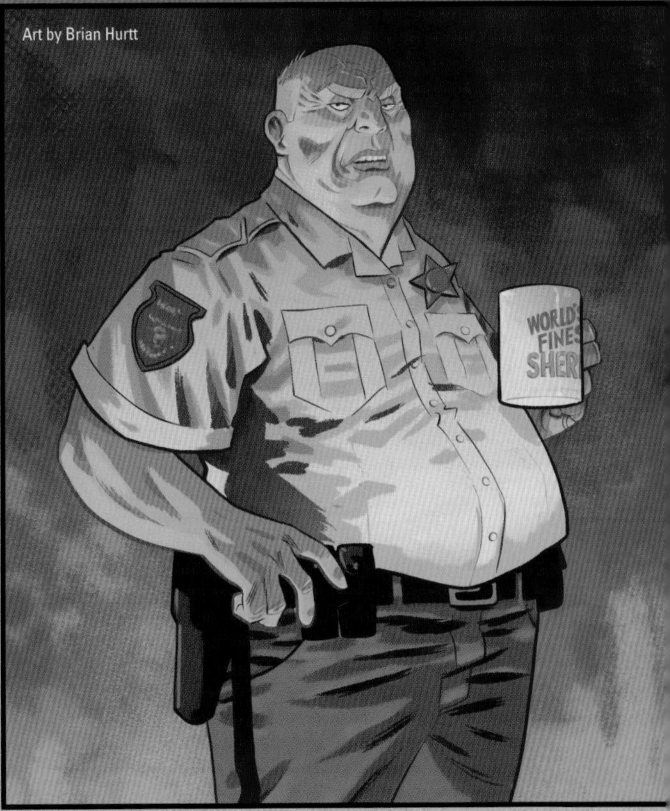
WORLD'S
FINES
SHER
Art by Brian Hurtt

HISTORY
Trueheart is Rockwood's town sheriff and also the soon-to-be ex-husband of Tammy Trueheart (See "Tammy Trueheart"). He's suspicious of Abraham (See "Abraham Slam") and his family, but that's mostly because of Abe's blossoming relationship with Tammy. His investigation into Black Hammer Farm and Abe's family eventually led to him crossing paths with Madame Dragonfly (see "Madame Dragonfly")—who proceeded to turn him into bubbling goo. Abe, Tammy, and the rest of Rockwood quickly noticed the disappearance of Trueheart. His absence remained a mystery until he showed up at Tammy's restaurant in a chipper and overly supportive mood. He now embraces Tammy and Abe's relationship and only wants the best for them! This stark change in character is unsettling to them both.

POWERS & WEAPONS
Sheriff Trueheart is a regular, zero-powers human. In fact, he's remarkably underwhelming in every way. That's why Tammy filed her divorce papers! He does have a handgun, though, so there's that.

TAMMY TRUEHEART

PERSONAL DATA
Alter Ego: *N/A*
Occupation: *Waitress*
Marital Status: *Divorced*
Known Relatives: *Earl Trueheart (ex-husband)*
Group Affiliation: *Patti's Angels*
Base of Operations: *Rockwood*
First Appearance: Black Hammer *#1*
Height: *5'4"* ***Weight:*** *185 lbs.*
Eyes: *Blue* ***Hair:*** *Brown*

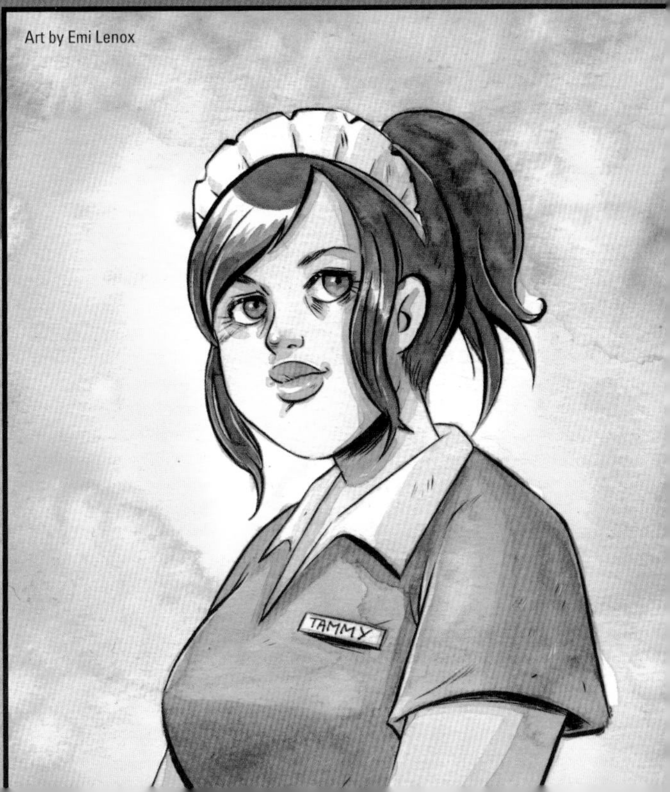
TAMMY
Art by Emi Lenox

HISTORY
Tammy is Rockwood's premier waitress working at the town's local diner. She was once married to the town sheriff (see "Sheriff Trueheart") but has since filed for divorce. Tammy also started a relationship with Abraham Slamkowski (see "Abraham Slam"). When Sheriff Trueheart was reported missing, Tammy became suspicious of Abe, since she knew that the two had recently come to blows. She called off the relationship with Abe, as she needed some time to think. The two reconciled, and, on the same morning, Sheriff Trueheart popped up outside of Tammy's workplace. He was in an especially good mood and confessed his support for Tammy and Abe's relationship. This act of goodwill was definitely out of place but seemed to put Tammy's heart at ease.

POWERS & WEAPONS
Tammy doesn't have any superhuman abilities, but she does flip a mean flapjack! She will beat your fine ass in checkers, too.

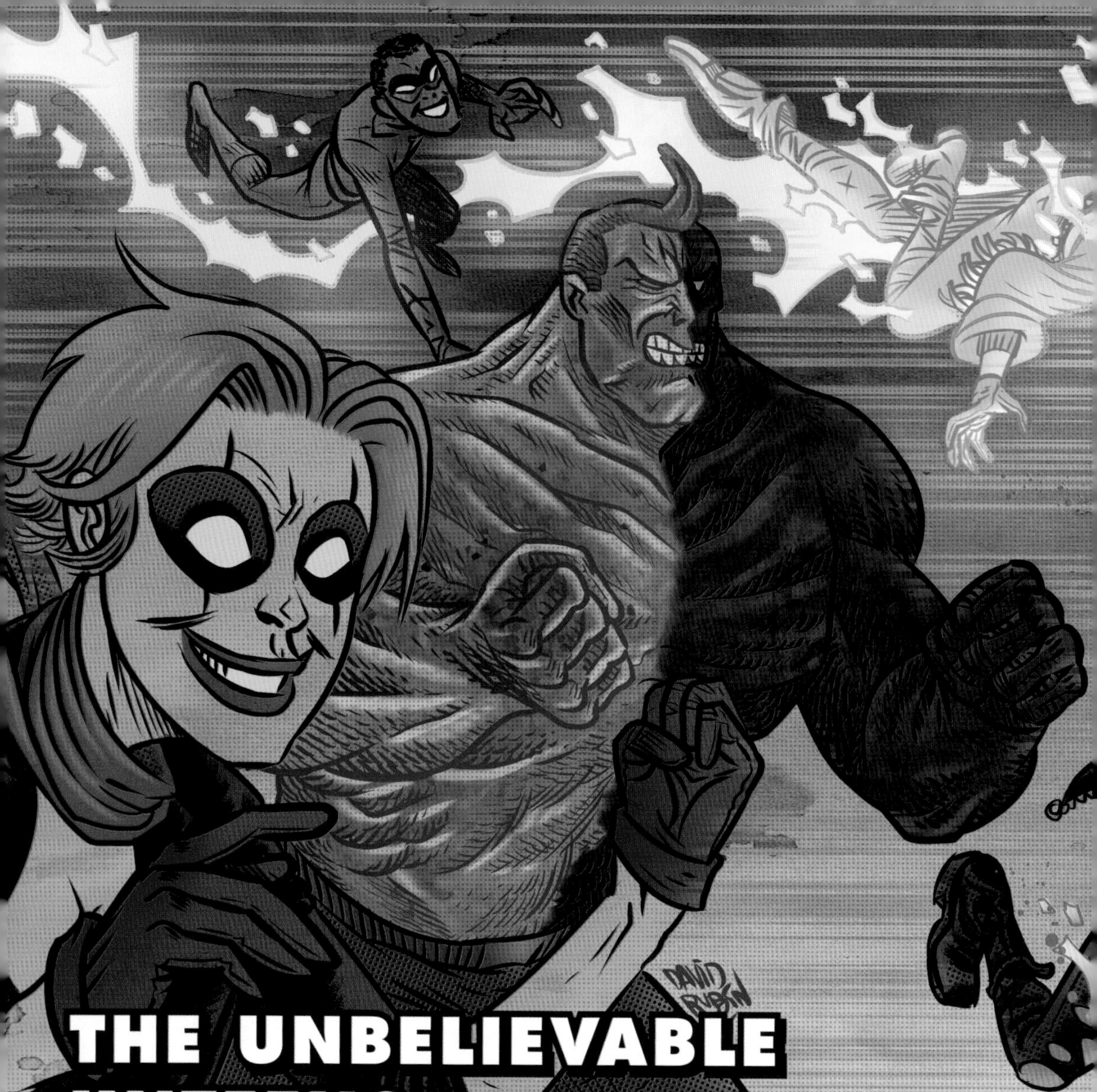
DAVID RUBIN

THE UNBELIEVABLE UNTEENS

First Appearance: *"Horrors to Come" from* Free Comic Book Day 2019

HISTORY

Dr. Miles Moniker was an eccentric billionaire who made his fortune in pharmaceuticals. Moniker's only child, a daughter named Alexis, was always a loner, and her social awkwardness became even more dramatic when she developed superpowers at puberty. Her psychic abilities made her a "freak" amongst her classmates. Moniker soon sold his company and invested his money into finding and training similarly superpowered children from across the globe with whom Alexis could feel at home. Over the coming years, as he helped Alexis gain control of her powers, Moniker brought together several ostracized super teens to live and study in his mansion.

They were: Jack Sabbath, the wise-cracking boy wizard; Straka, the Czechoslovakian powerhouse; Kid Boom, the highly combustible hothead; Strobe, the dazzling damsel of light; and Alexis became Snapdragon, the mysterious beauty with a thousand minds. Together they defeated evil time and time again, becoming the teenage super sensations known as the Unbelievable Unteens. They were best friends and, in the case of Jack Sabbath and Alexis, even lovers. But all good things must come to an end, and, for the Unbelievable Unteens, it **did not** end well . . .

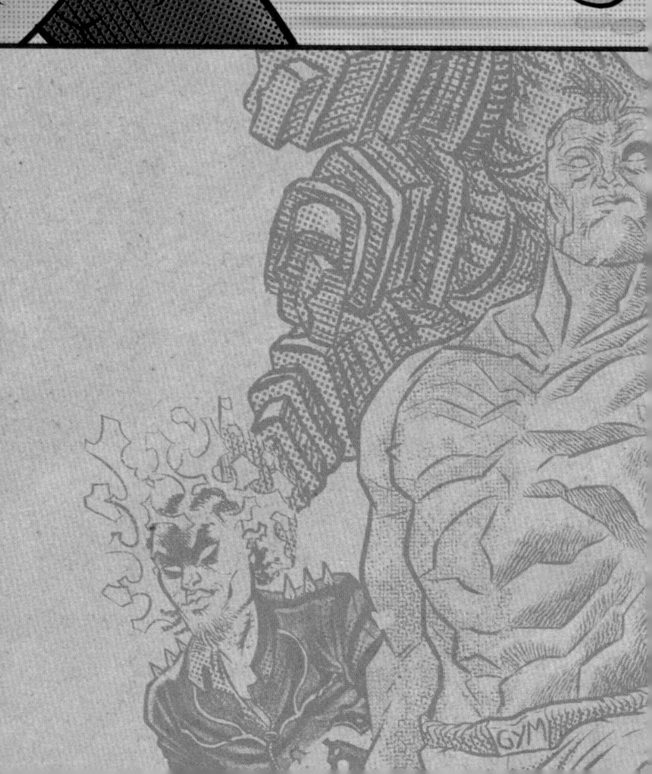
GYM

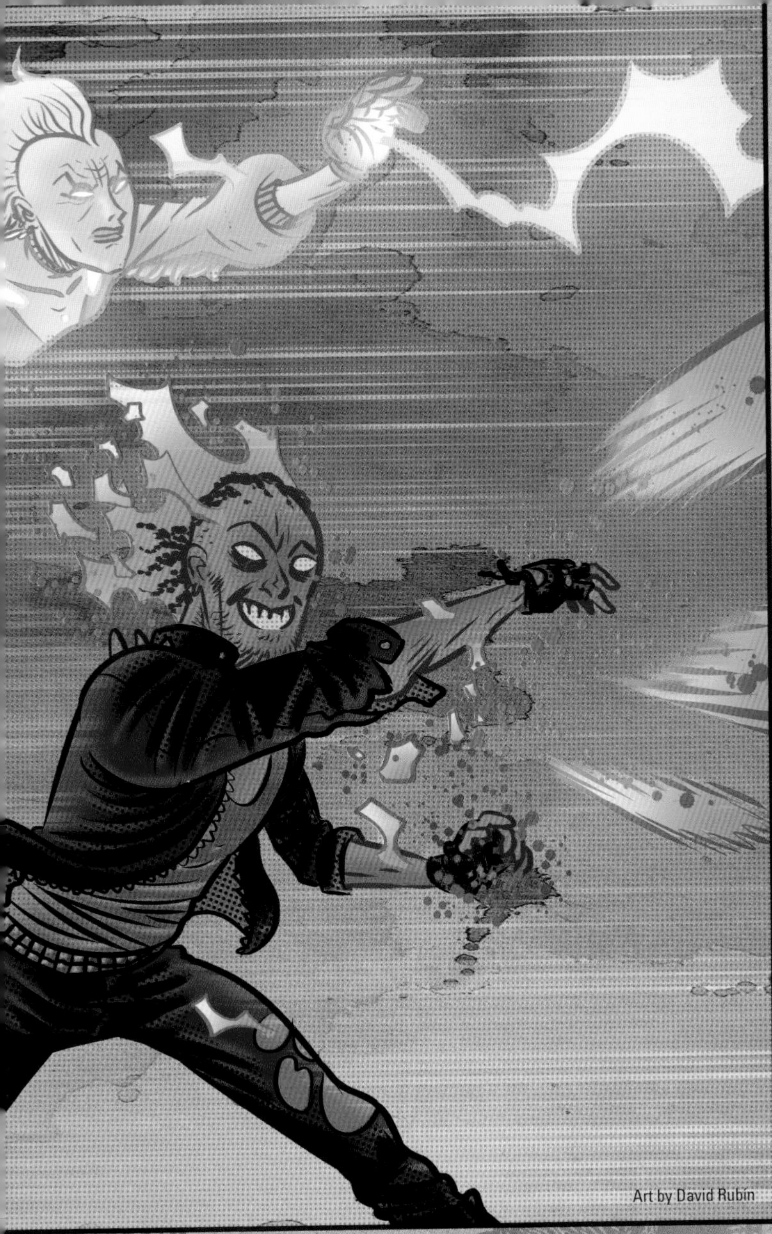

Art by David Rubín

MEMBERS

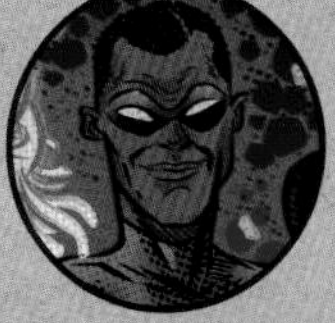

JACK SABBATH

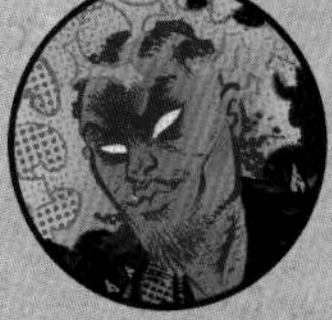

KID BOOM

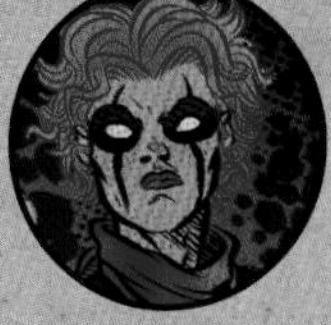

SNAPDRAGON

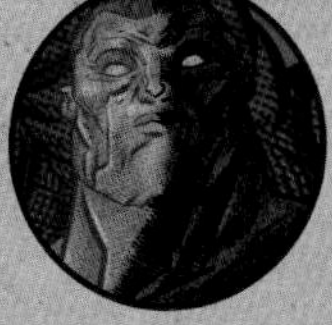

STRAKA

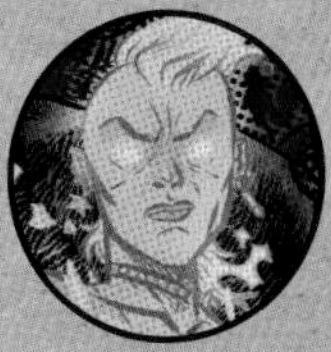

STROBE

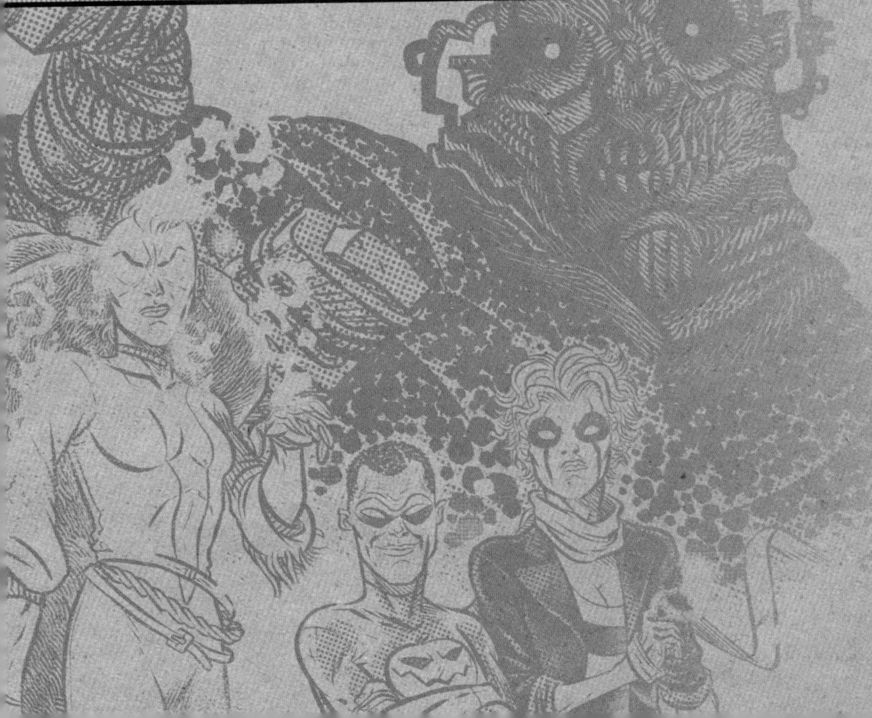

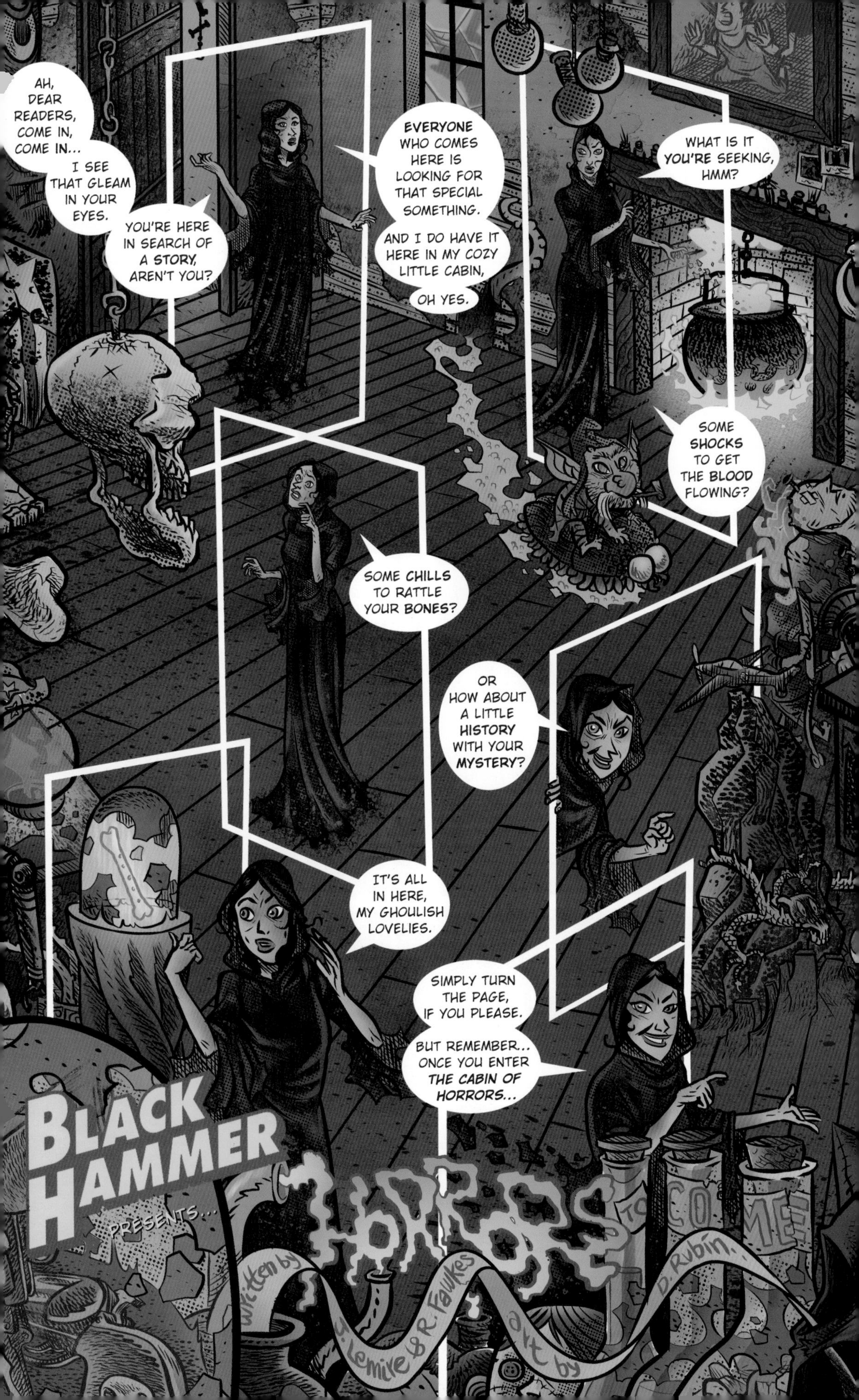
AH, DEAR READERS, COME IN, COME IN...
I SEE THAT GLEAM IN YOUR EYES.
YOU'RE HERE IN SEARCH OF A STORY, AREN'T YOU?
EVERYONE WHO COMES HERE IS LOOKING FOR THAT SPECIAL SOMETHING.
AND I DO HAVE IT HERE IN MY COZY LITTLE CABIN,
OH YES.
WHAT IS IT YOU'RE SEEKING, HMM?
SOME SHOCKS TO GET THE BLOOD FLOWING?
SOME CHILLS TO RATTLE YOUR BONES?
OR HOW ABOUT A LITTLE HISTORY WITH YOUR MYSTERY?
IT'S ALL IN HERE, MY GHOULISH LOVELIES.
SIMPLY TURN THE PAGE, IF YOU PLEASE.
BUT REMEMBER... ONCE YOU ENTER THE CABIN OF HORRORS...
BLACK HAMMER
PRESENTS...
HORRORS
TO COME
written by J. Lemire & R. Fawkes
art by D. Rubin

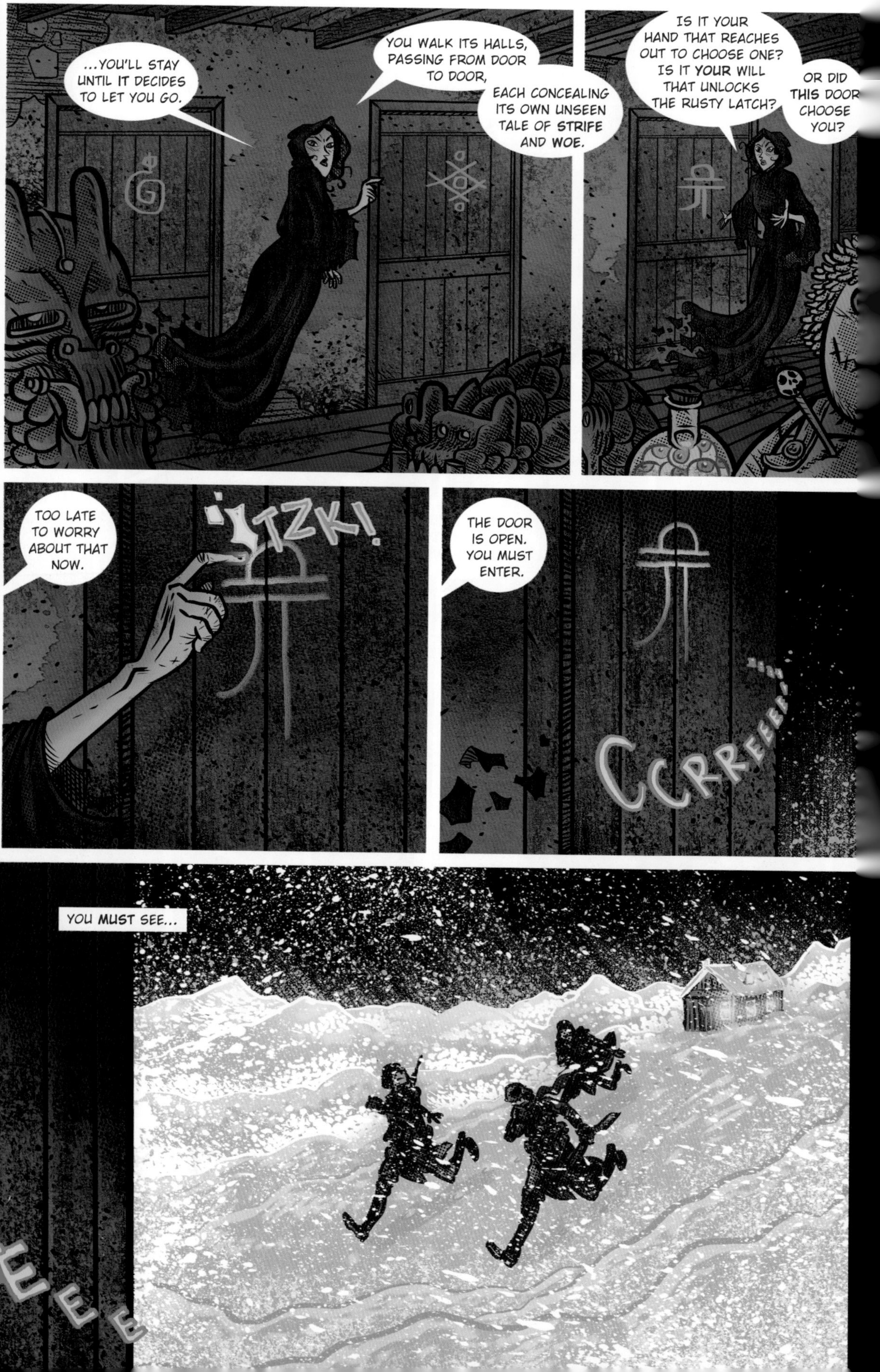
...YOU'LL STAY UNTIL IT DECIDES TO LET YOU GO.
YOU WALK ITS HALLS, PASSING FROM DOOR TO DOOR,
EACH CONCEALING ITS OWN UNSEEN TALE OF STRIFE AND WOE.
IS IT YOUR HAND THAT REACHES OUT TO CHOOSE ONE? IS IT YOUR WILL THAT UNLOCKS THE RUSTY LATCH?
OR DID THIS DOOR CHOOSE YOU?
TOO LATE TO WORRY ABOUT THAT NOW.
TZK!
THE DOOR IS OPEN. YOU MUST ENTER.
CCRREEEE
YOU MUST SEE...

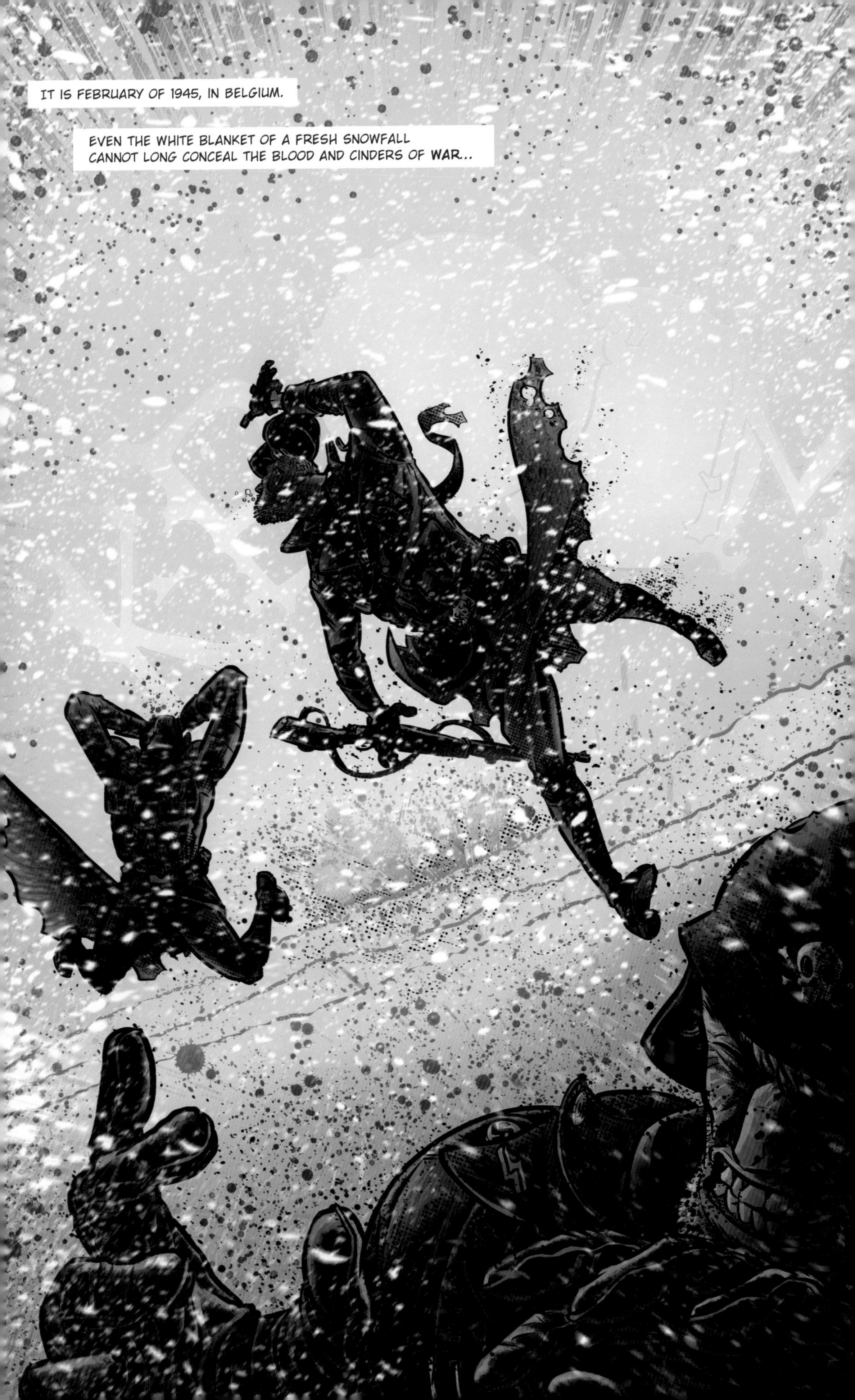
IT IS FEBRUARY OF 1945, IN BELGIUM.
EVEN THE WHITE BLANKET OF A FRESH SNOWFALL CANNOT LONG CONCEAL THE BLOOD AND CINDERS OF WAR...

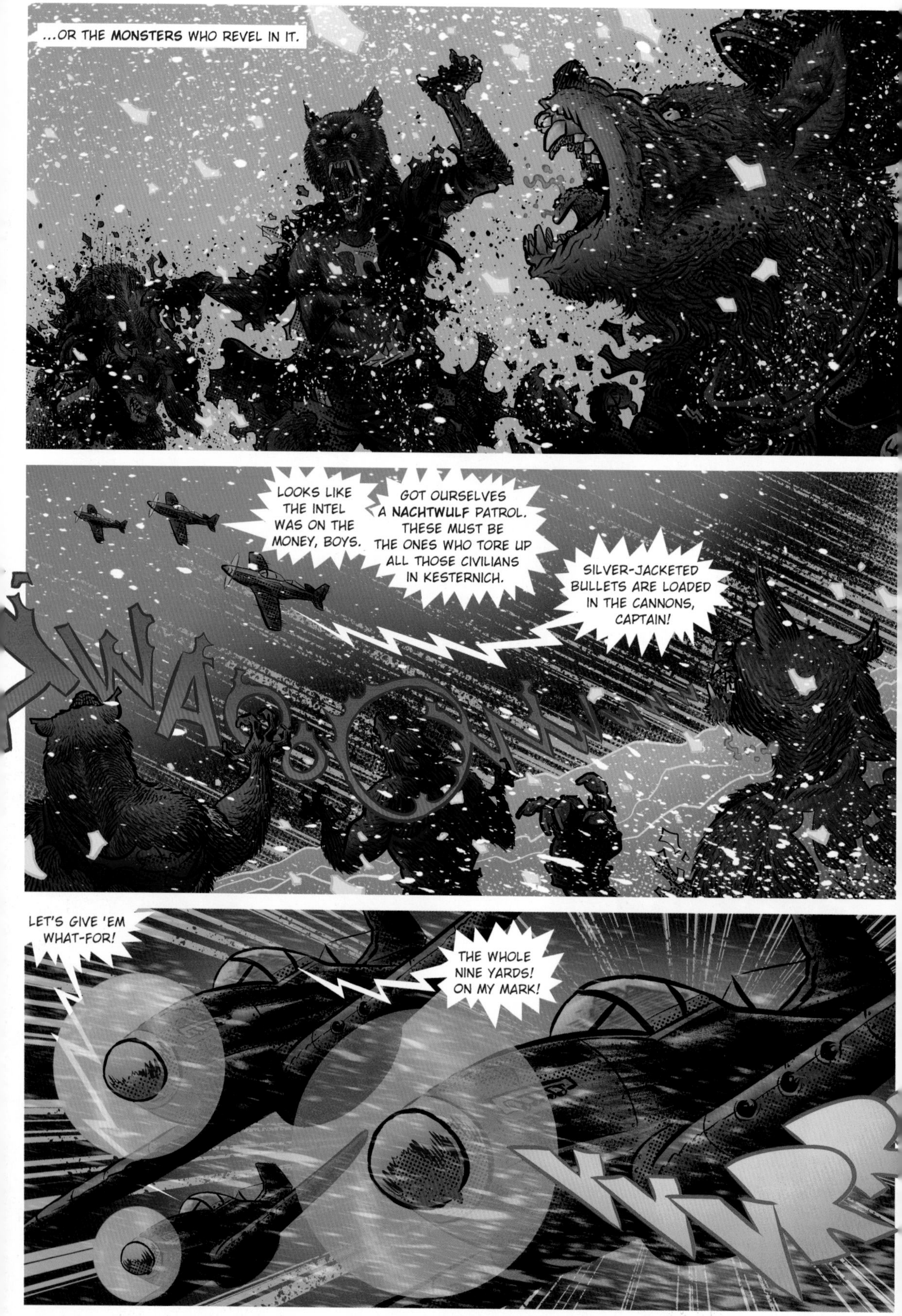
...OR THE MONSTERS WHO REVEL IN IT.
LOOKS LIKE THE INTEL WAS ON THE MONEY, BOYS.
GOT OURSELVES A NACHTWULF PATROL. THESE MUST BE THE ONES WHO TORE UP ALL THOSE CIVILIANS IN KESTERNICH.
SILVER-JACKETED BULLETS ARE LOADED IN THE CANNONS, CAPTAIN!
LET'S GIVE 'EM WHAT-FOR!
THE WHOLE NINE YARDS! ON MY MARK!

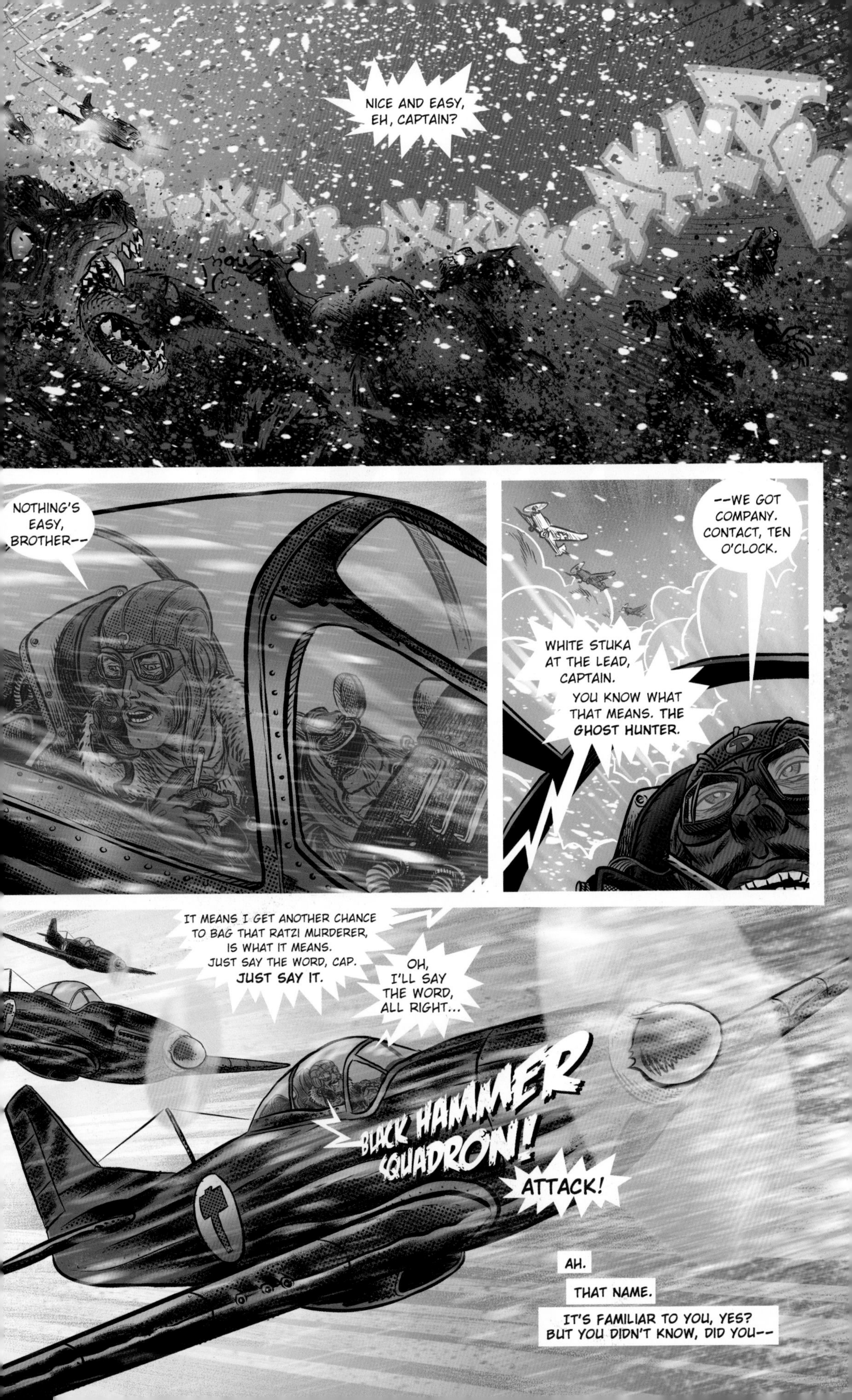
NICE AND EASY, EH, CAPTAIN?
NOTHING'S EASY, BROTHER--
--WE GOT COMPANY. CONTACT, TEN O'CLOCK.
WHITE STUKA AT THE LEAD, CAPTAIN.
YOU KNOW WHAT THAT MEANS. THE GHOST HUNTER.
IT MEANS I GET ANOTHER CHANCE TO BAG THAT RATZI MURDERER, IS WHAT IT MEANS. JUST SAY THE WORD, CAP. JUST SAY IT.
OH, I'LL SAY THE WORD, ALL RIGHT...
BLACK HAMMER SQUADRON!
ATTACK!
AH.
THAT NAME.
IT'S FAMILIAR TO YOU, YES? BUT YOU DIDN'T KNOW, DID YOU--

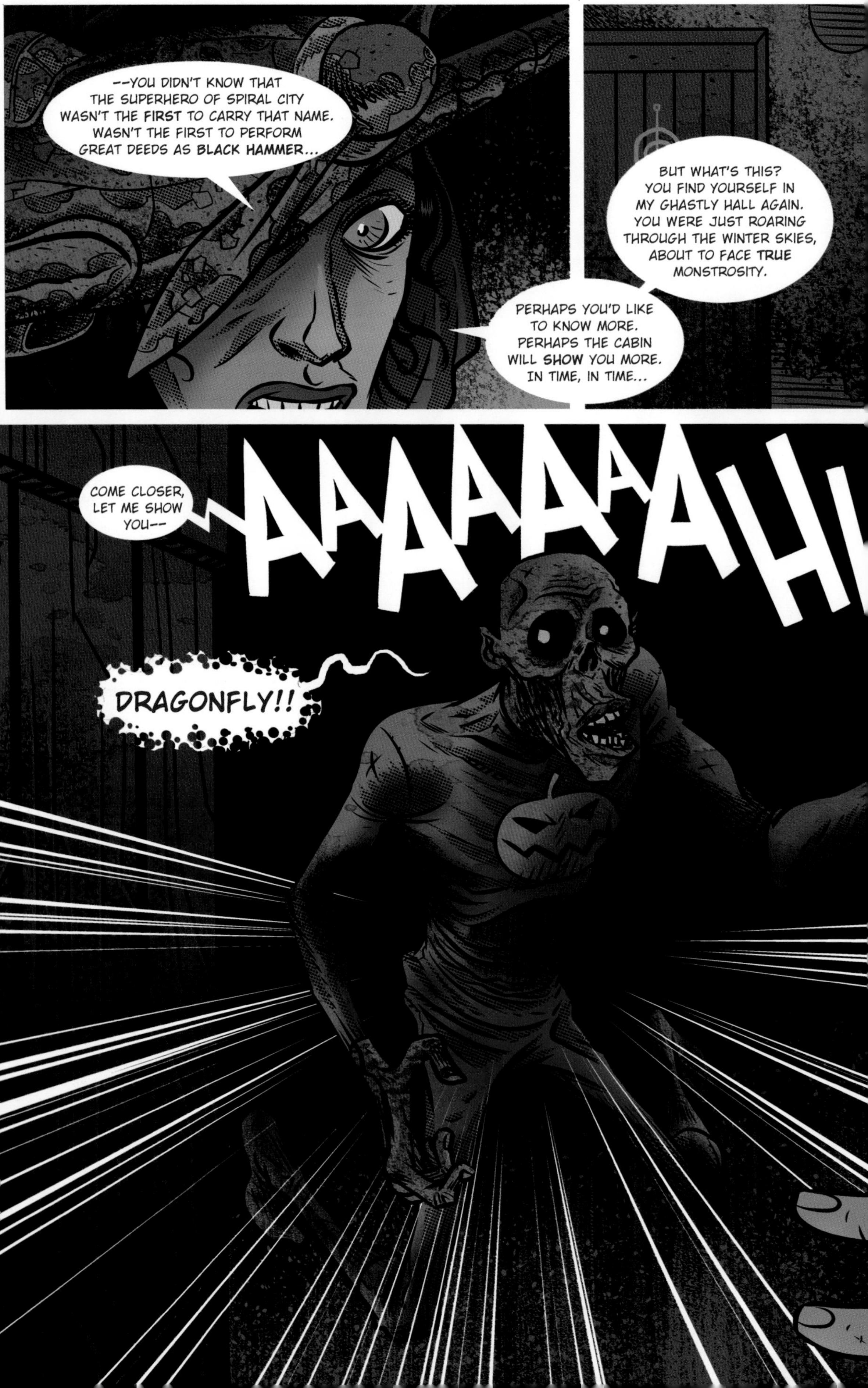
--YOU DIDN'T KNOW THAT THE SUPERHERO OF SPIRAL CITY WASN'T THE **FIRST** TO CARRY THAT NAME. WASN'T THE FIRST TO PERFORM GREAT DEEDS AS **BLACK HAMMER**...
BUT WHAT'S THIS? YOU FIND YOURSELF IN MY GHASTLY HALL AGAIN. YOU WERE JUST ROARING THROUGH THE WINTER SKIES, ABOUT TO FACE **TRUE** MONSTROSITY.
PERHAPS YOU'D LIKE TO KNOW MORE. PERHAPS THE CABIN WILL **SHOW** YOU MORE. IN TIME, IN TIME...
COME CLOSER, LET ME SHOW YOU--
AAAAAAAH
DRAGONFLY!!

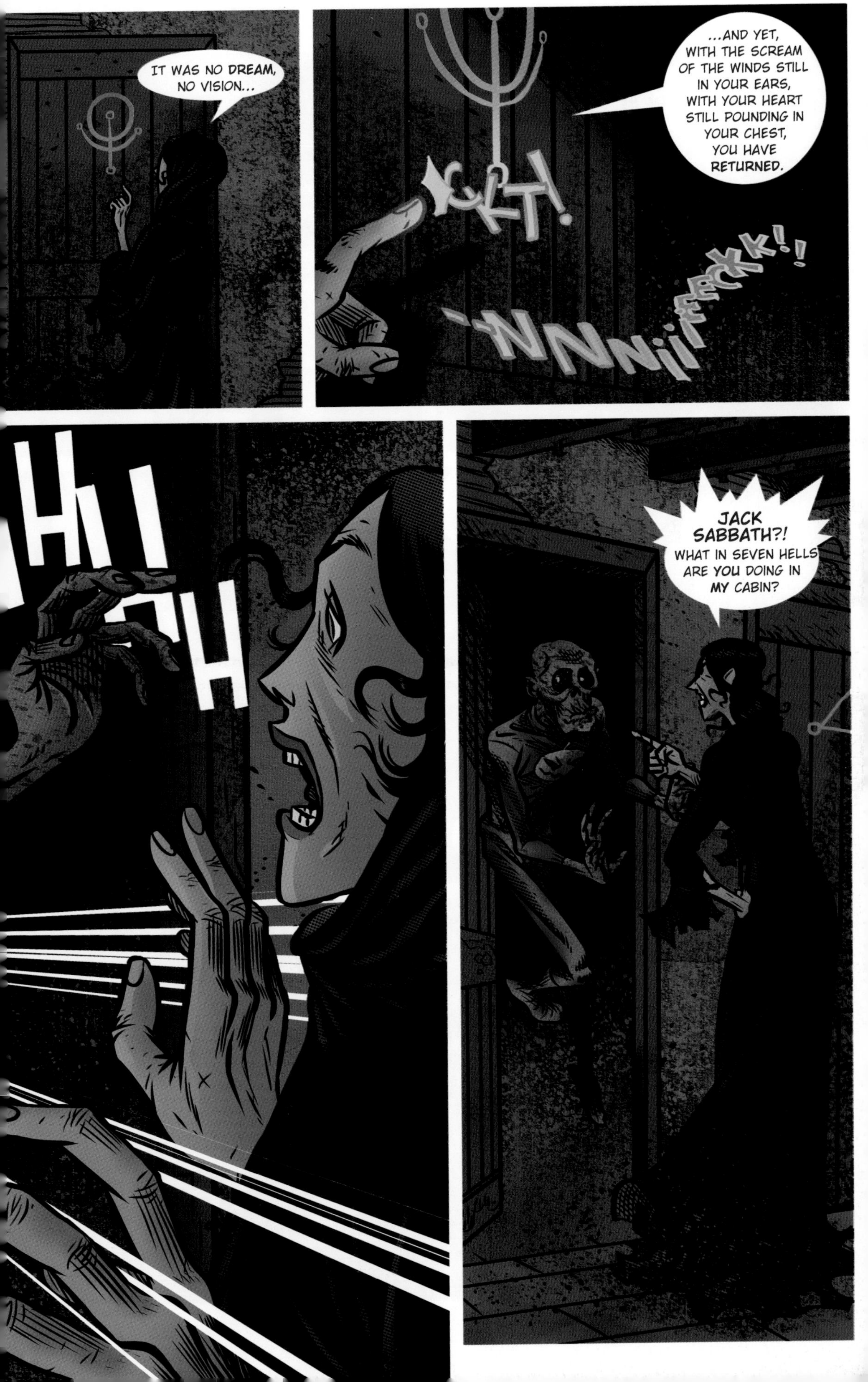

IT WAS NO DREAM, NO VISION...
...AND YET, WITH THE SCREAM OF THE WINDS STILL IN YOUR EARS, WITH YOUR HEART STILL POUNDING IN YOUR CHEST, YOU HAVE RETURNED.
CKLT!
NNNiiFECKK!!
JACK SABBATH?! WHAT IN SEVEN HELLS ARE YOU DOING IN MY CABIN?

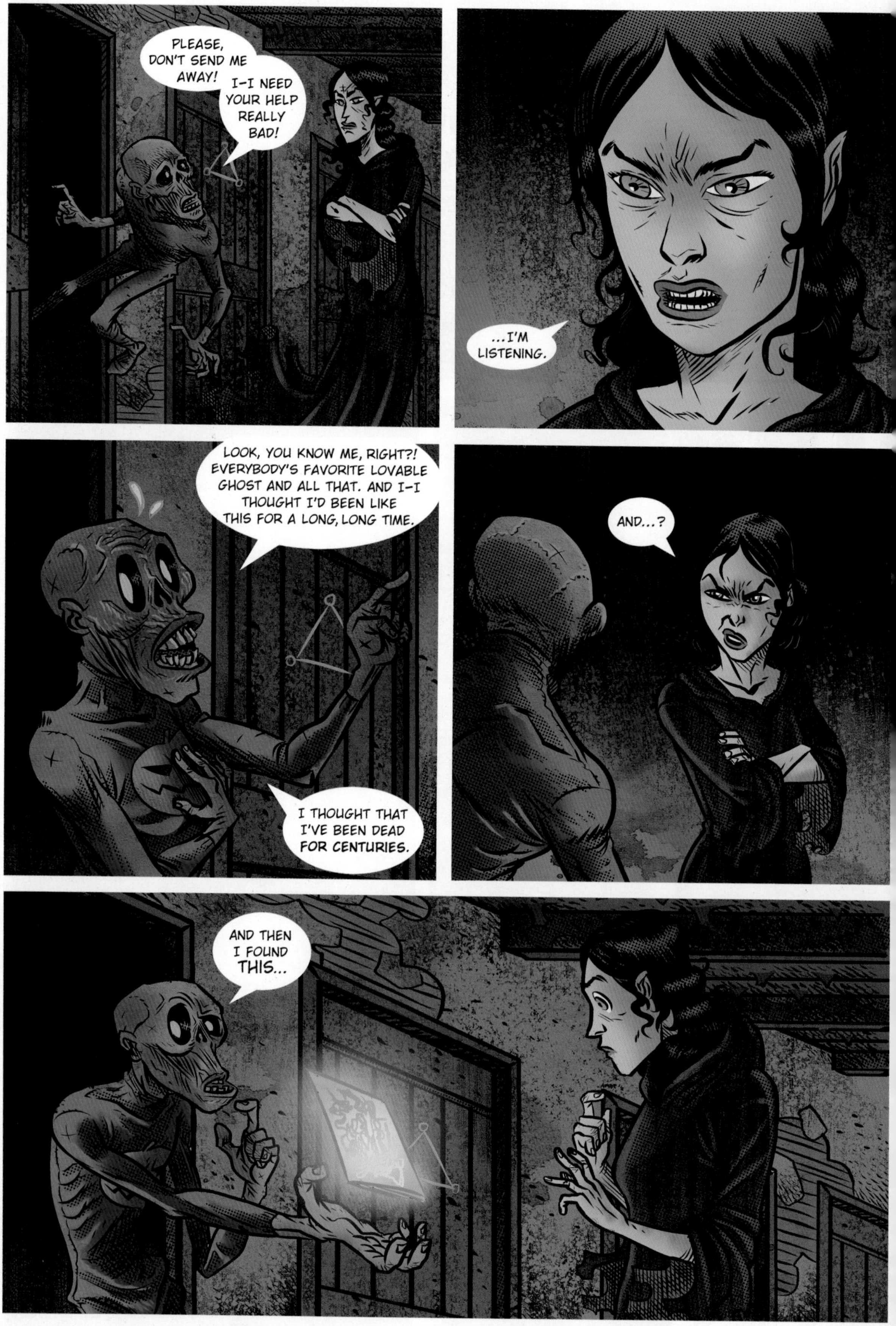
PLEASE, DON'T SEND ME AWAY!
I-I NEED YOUR HELP REALLY BAD!
...I'M LISTENING.
LOOK, YOU KNOW ME, RIGHT?! EVERYBODY'S FAVORITE LOVABLE GHOST AND ALL THAT. AND I-I THOUGHT I'D BEEN LIKE THIS FOR A LONG, LONG TIME.
I THOUGHT THAT I'VE BEEN DEAD FOR CENTURIES.
AND...?
AND THEN I FOUND THIS...

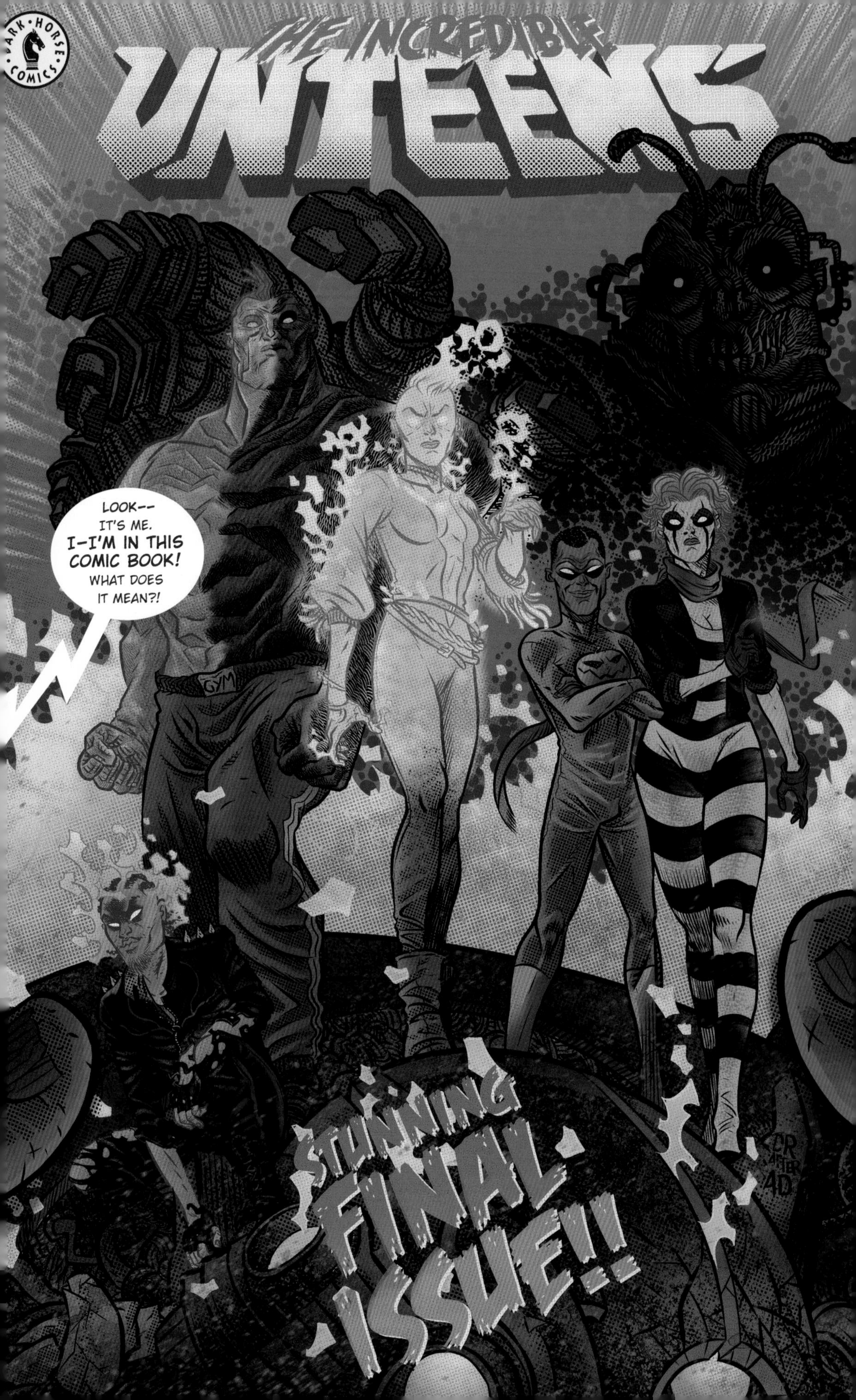
DARK HORSE COMICS
THE INCREDIBLE
UNTEENS
LOOK--
IT'S ME.
I-I'M IN THIS
COMIC BOOK!
WHAT DOES
IT MEAN?!
GYM
STUNNING
FINAL
ISSUE!!

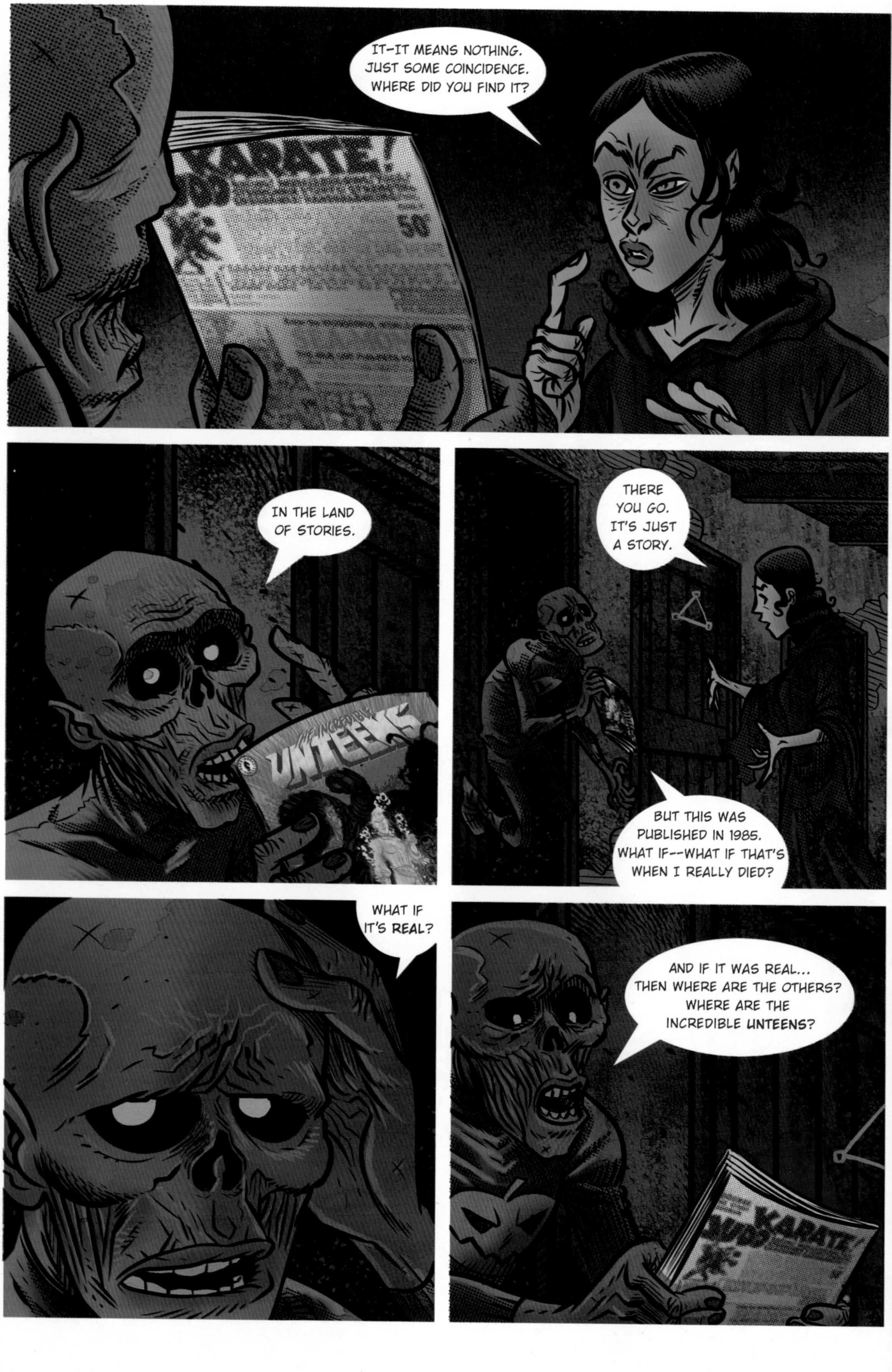

IT-IT MEANS NOTHING. JUST SOME COINCIDENCE. WHERE DID YOU FIND IT?
KARATE!
IN THE LAND OF STORIES.
THE INCREDIBLE UNTEENS
THERE YOU GO. IT'S JUST A STORY.
BUT THIS WAS PUBLISHED IN 1985. WHAT IF--WHAT IF THAT'S WHEN I REALLY DIED?
WHAT IF IT'S **REAL**?
AND IF IT WAS REAL... THEN WHERE ARE THE OTHERS? WHERE ARE THE INCREDIBLE **UNTEENS**?
KARATE

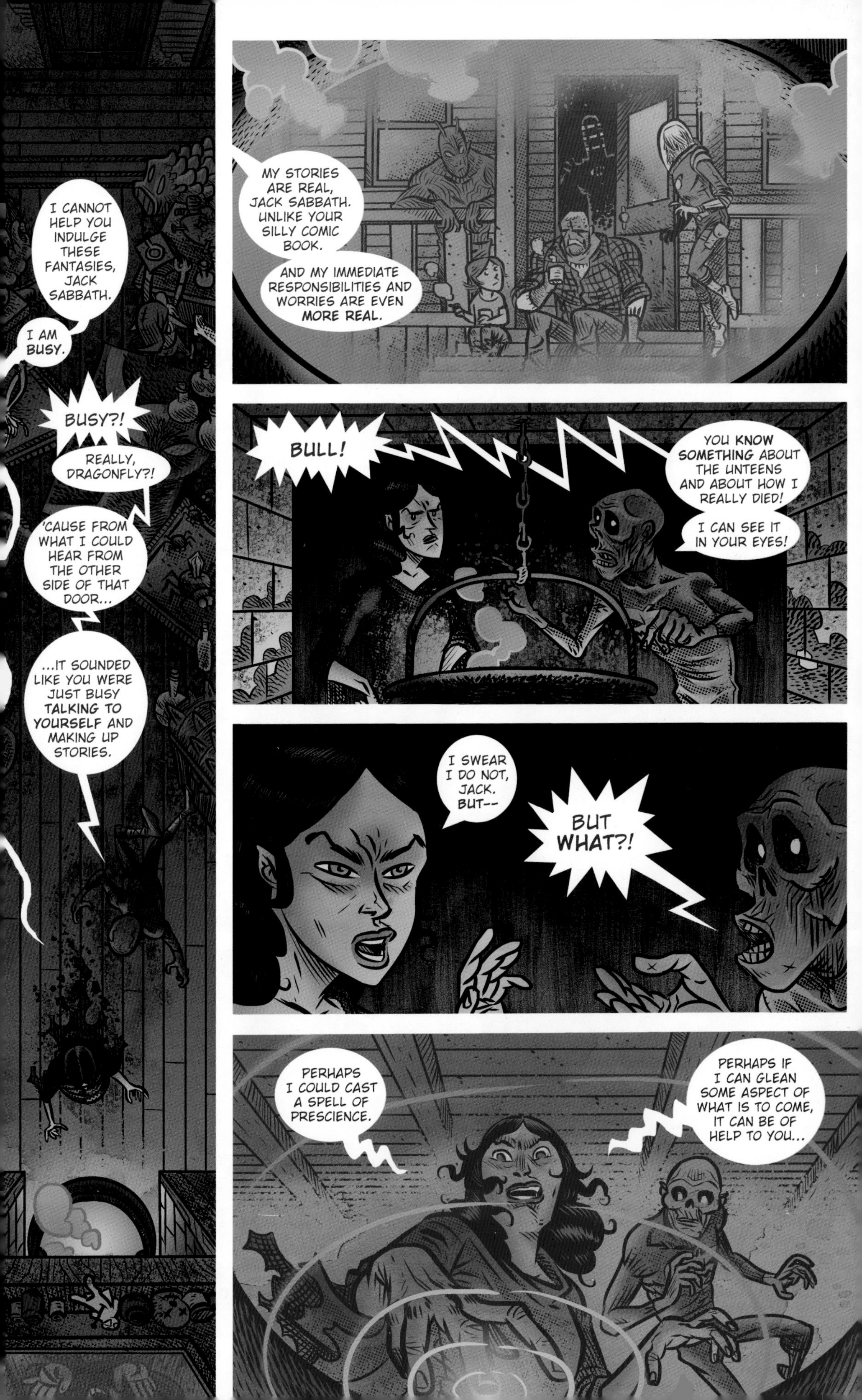

I CANNOT HELP YOU INDULGE THESE FANTASIES, JACK SABBATH.
I AM BUSY.
BUSY?!
REALLY, DRAGONFLY?!
'CAUSE FROM WHAT I COULD HEAR FROM THE OTHER SIDE OF THAT DOOR...
...IT SOUNDED LIKE YOU WERE JUST BUSY TALKING TO YOURSELF AND MAKING UP STORIES.
MY STORIES ARE REAL, JACK SABBATH. UNLIKE YOUR SILLY COMIC BOOK.
AND MY IMMEDIATE RESPONSIBILITIES AND WORRIES ARE EVEN MORE REAL.
BULL!
YOU KNOW SOMETHING ABOUT THE UNTEENS AND ABOUT HOW I REALLY DIED!
I CAN SEE IT IN YOUR EYES!
I SWEAR I DO NOT, JACK. BUT--
BUT WHAT?!
PERHAPS I COULD CAST A SPELL OF PRESCIENCE.
PERHAPS IF I CAN GLEAN SOME ASPECT OF WHAT IS TO COME, IT CAN BE OF HELP TO YOU...

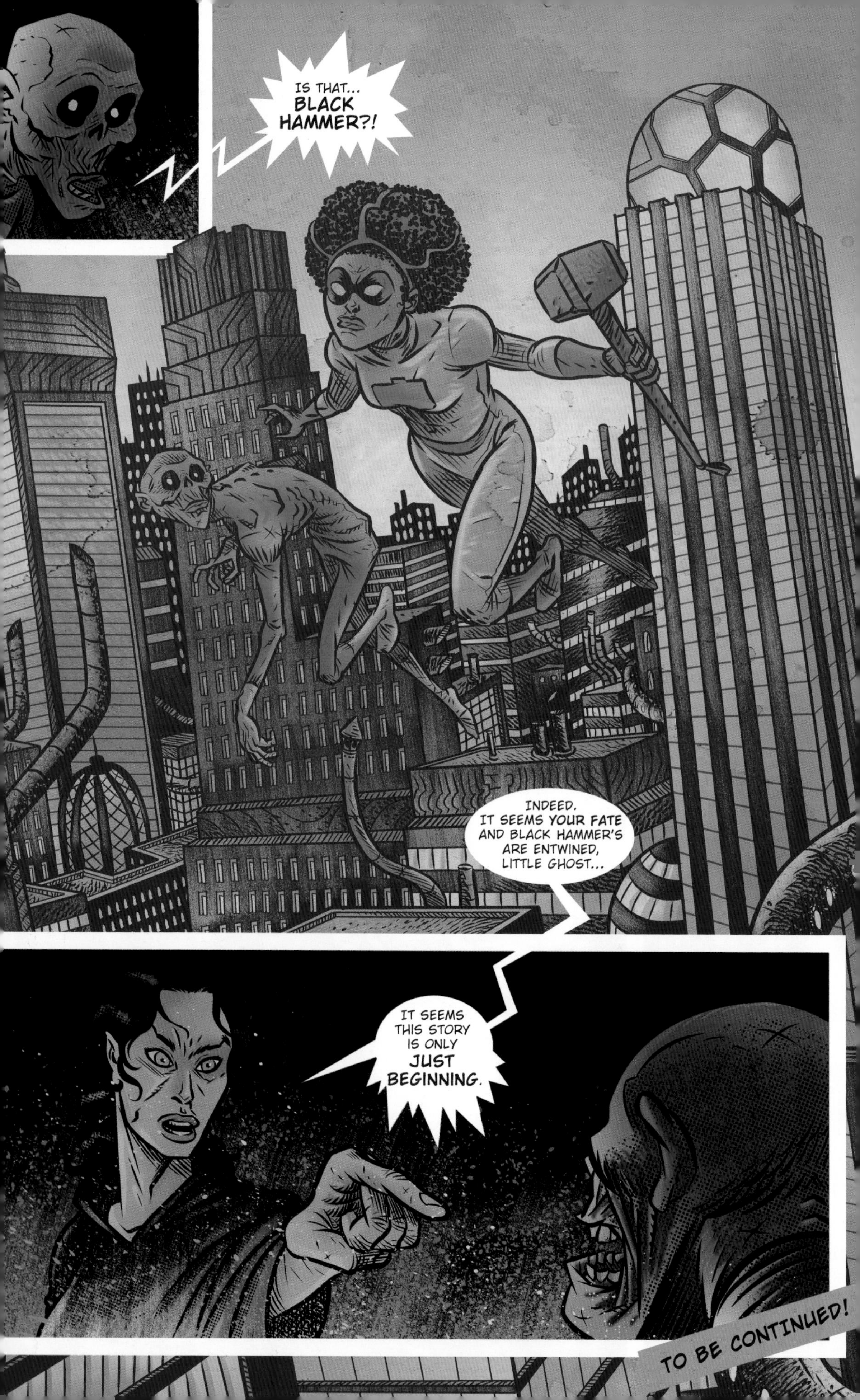
IS THAT... BLACK HAMMER?!
INDEED. IT SEEMS YOUR FATE AND BLACK HAMMER'S ARE ENTWINED, LITTLE GHOST...
IT SEEMS THIS STORY IS ONLY JUST BEGINNING.
TO BE CONTINUED!

BLACK HAMMER SKETCHBOOK

Here are Ray Fawkes' layouts for his short from the *Giant-Sized Annual.*

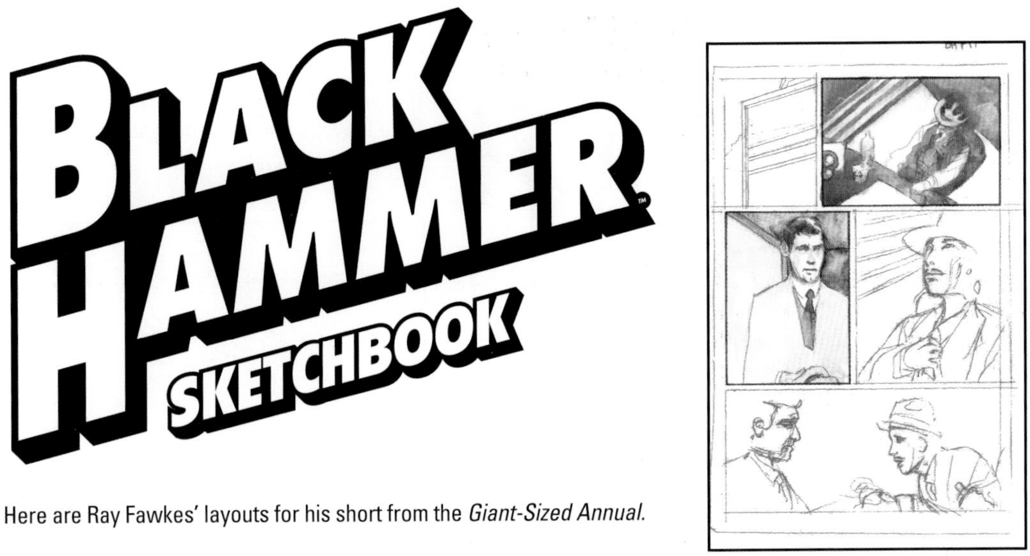

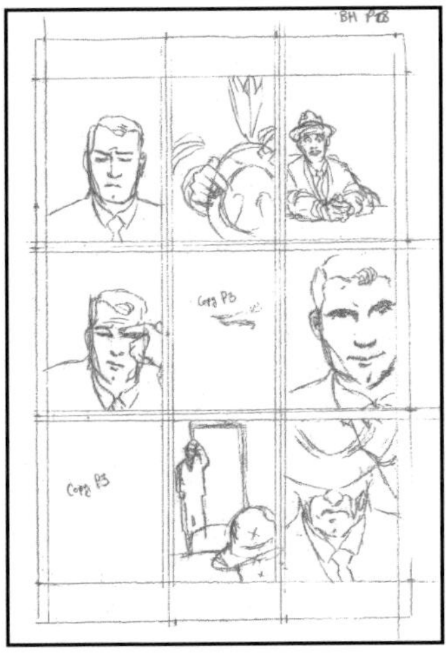

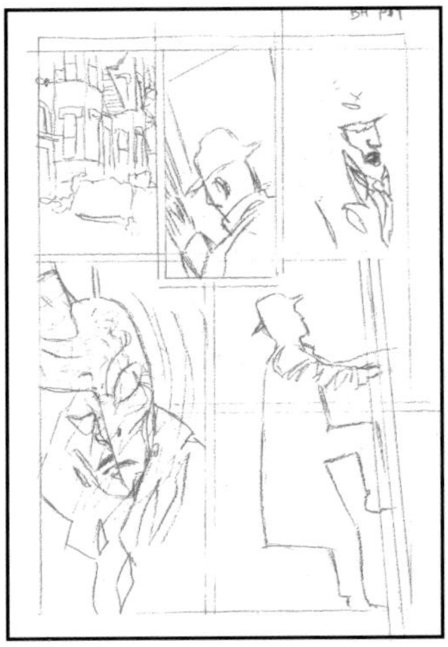

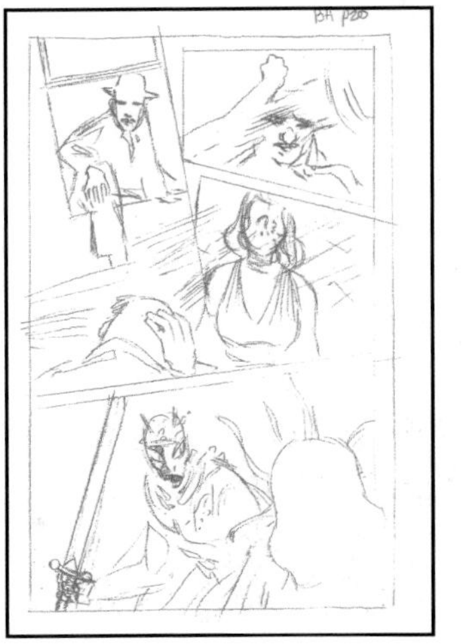

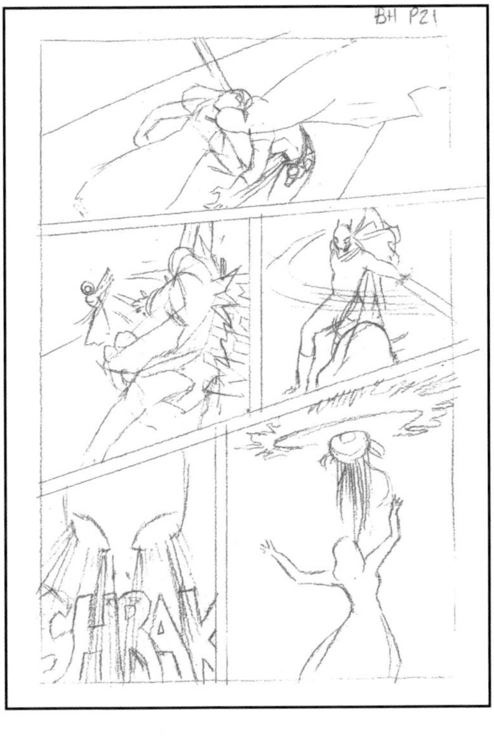
BH P21
SHRAK

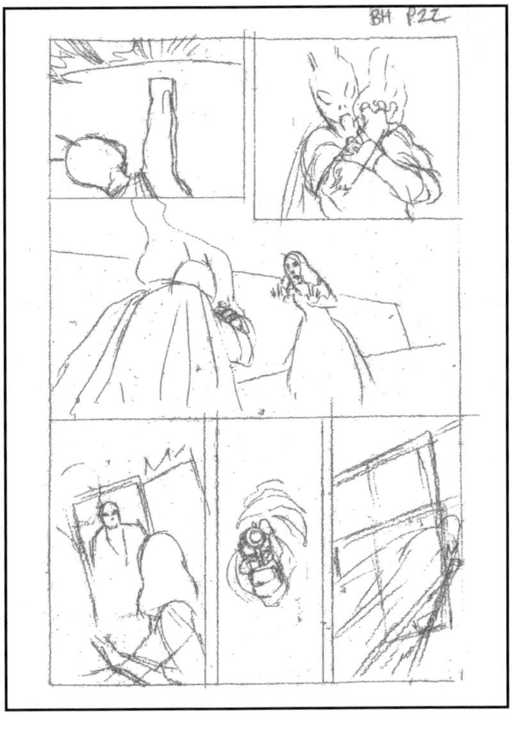
BH P.22

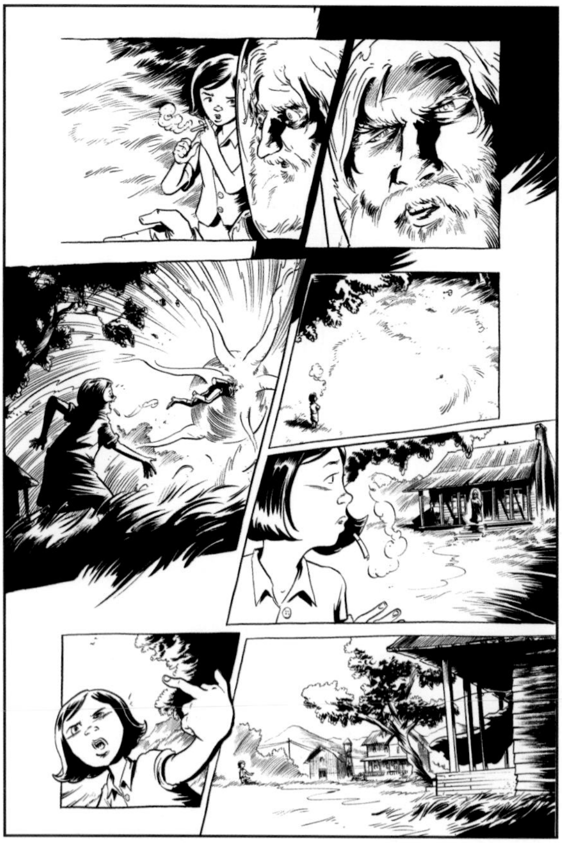

On these next four pages are Mike Allred and Nate Powell's original pencils and inks for the *Giant-Sized Annual*.

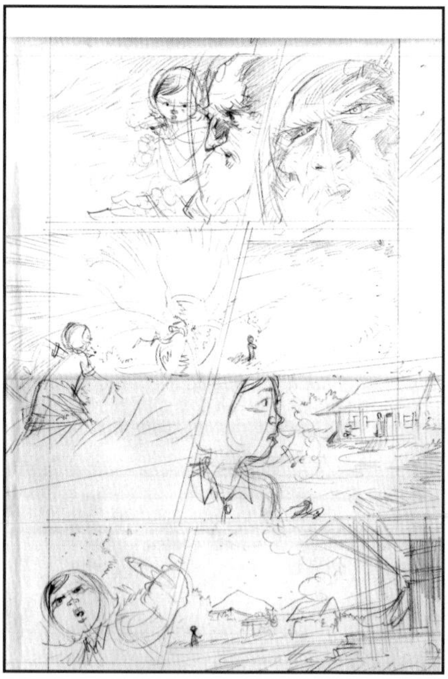

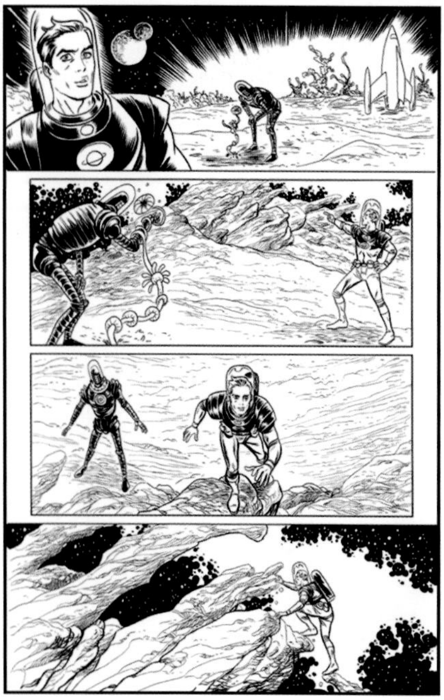

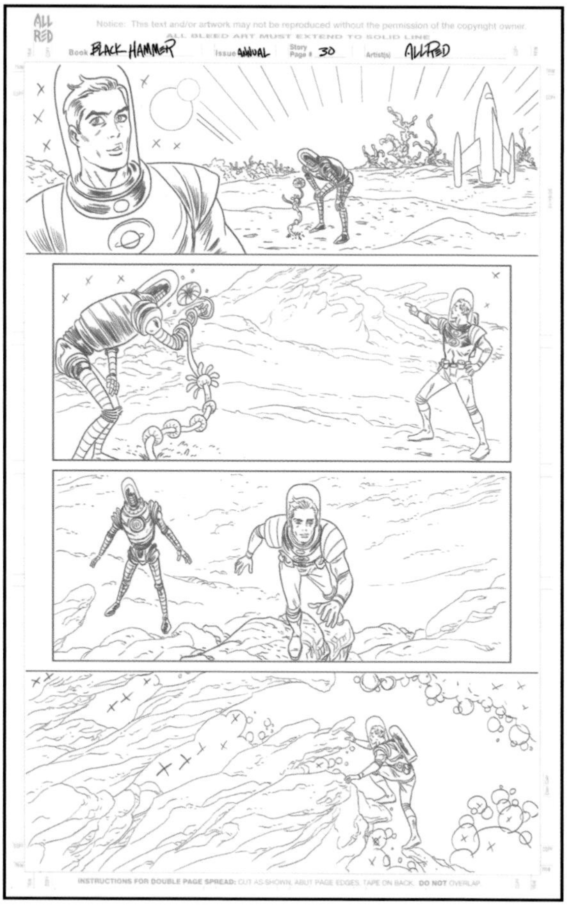
ALL RED
Notice: This text and/or artwork may not be reproduced without the permission of the copyright owner.
ALL BLEED ART MUST EXTEND TO SOLID LINE
Book BLACK HAMMER
Issue ANNUAL
Story Page # 30
Artist(s) ALLRED
INSTRUCTIONS FOR DOUBLE PAGE SPREAD: CUT AS SHOWN, ABUT PAGE EDGES, TAPE ON BACK. DO NOT OVERLAP.

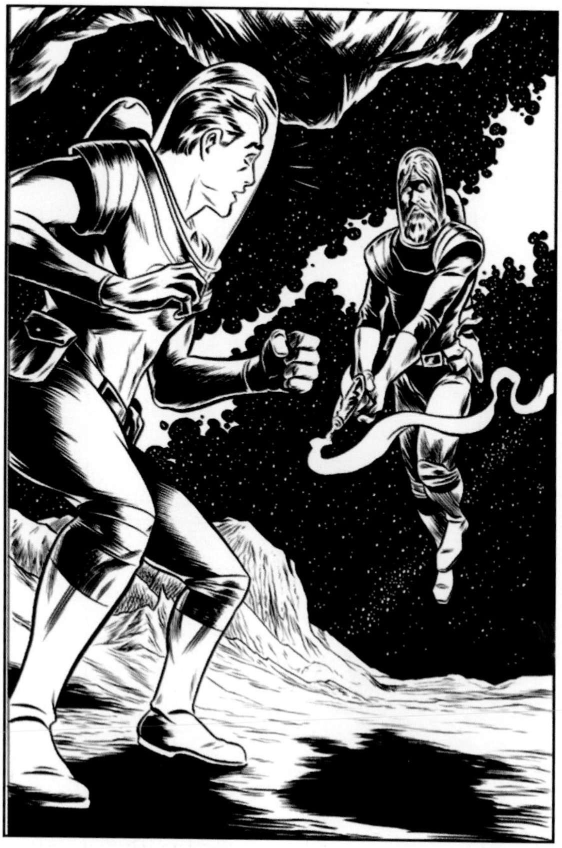

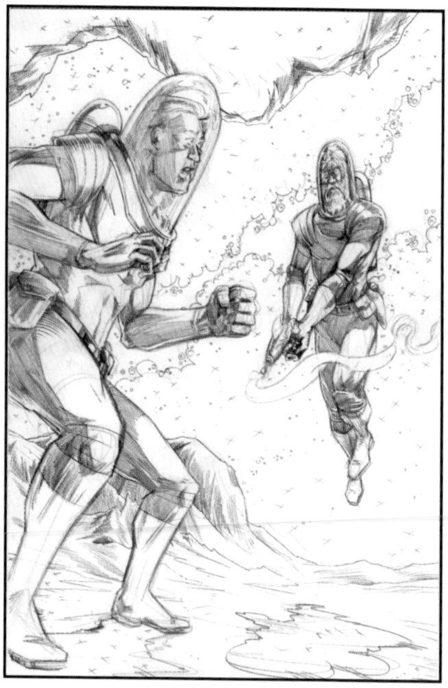

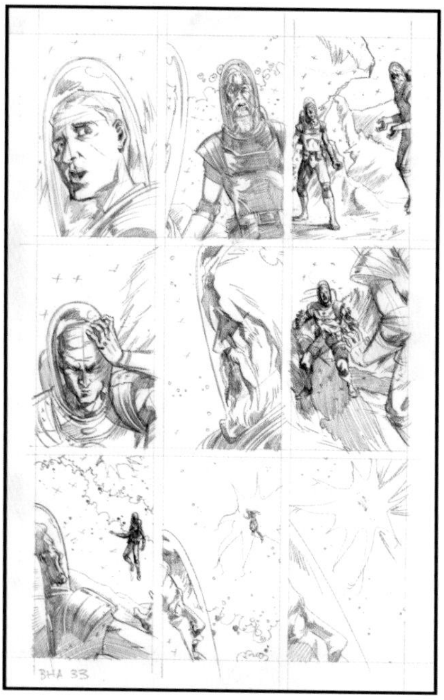
BHA 33

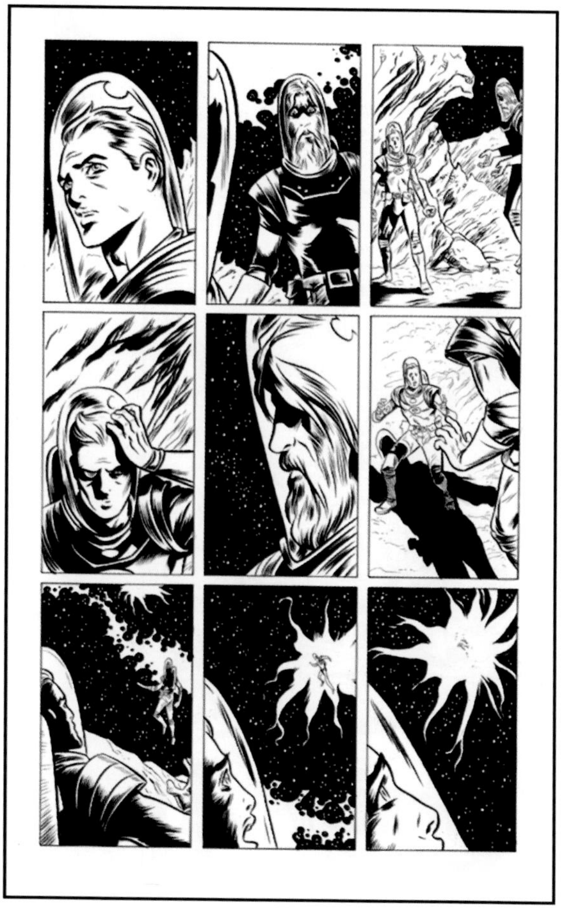

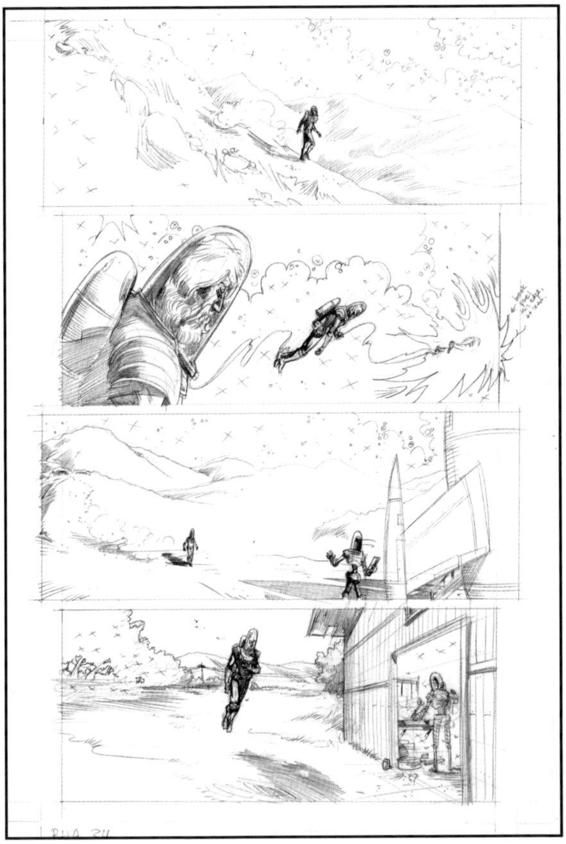
BHA 34

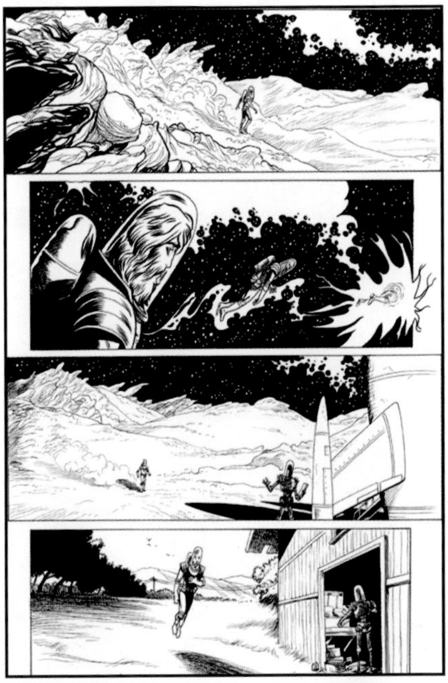

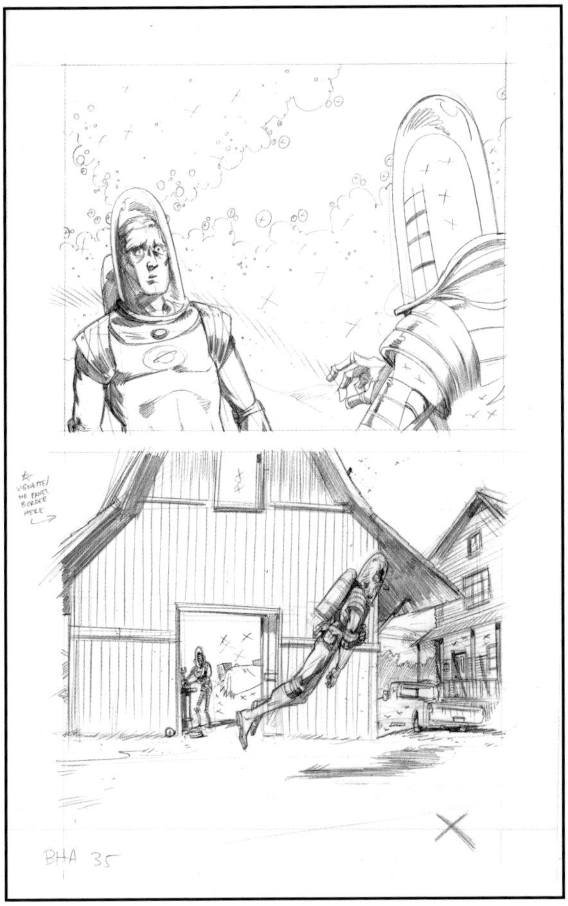
to
VIGNETTE/
NO PANEL
BORDER
HERE
BHA 35

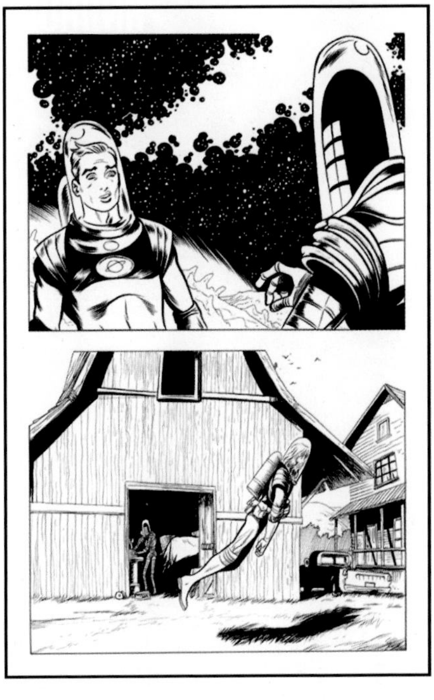

"If you think there's no room left in your life for another superhero comic, *Black Hammer* might just prove you wrong."—IGN

BLACK HAMMER™

ONCE THEY WERE HEROES, but the age of heroes has long since passed. Banished from existence by a multiversal crisis, the old champions of Spiral City—Abraham Slam, Golden Gail, Colonel Weird, Madame Dragonfly, and Barbalien—now lead simple lives in an idyllic, timeless farming village from which there is no escape! And yet, the universe isn't done with them—it's time for one last grand adventure.

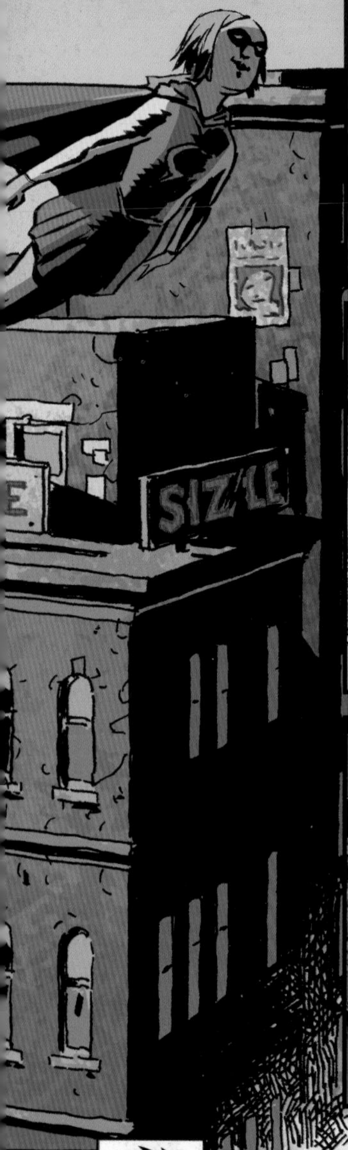

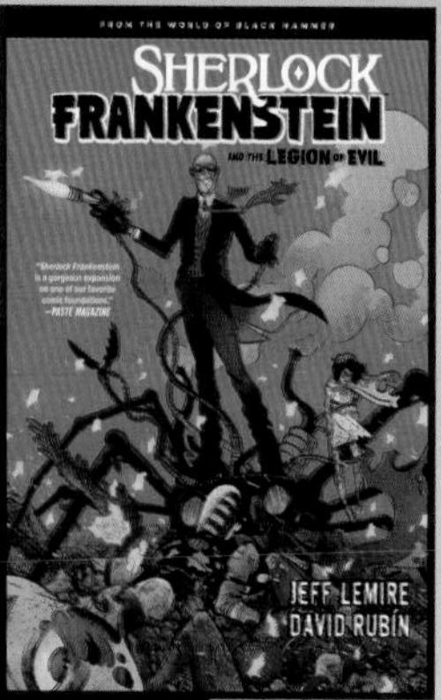
FROM THE WORLD OF BLACK HAMMER
SHERLOCK
FRANKENSTEIN
AND THE LEGION OF EVIL
JEFF LEMIRE
DAVID RUBIN

BLACK HAMMER
Written by Jeff Lemire
Art by Dean Ormston

VOLUME 1: SECRET ORIGINS
978-1-61655-786-7 • $14.99

VOLUME 2: THE EVENT
978-1-50670-198-1 • $19.99

VOLUME 3: AGE OF DOOM
978-1-50670-389-3 • $19.99

BLACK HAMMER LIBRARY EDITION VOLUME 1
978-1-50671-073-0 • $49.99

SHERLOCK FRANKENSTEIN & THE LEGION OF EVIL
Written by Jeff Lemire • Art by David Rubín

This mystery follows a reporter determined to find out what happened to her father, the Black Hammer. All answers seem to lie in Spiral City's infamous insane asylum, where some dangerous supervillain tenants reside, including Black Hammer's greatest foe—Sherlock Frankenstein!
978-1-50670-526-2 • $17.99

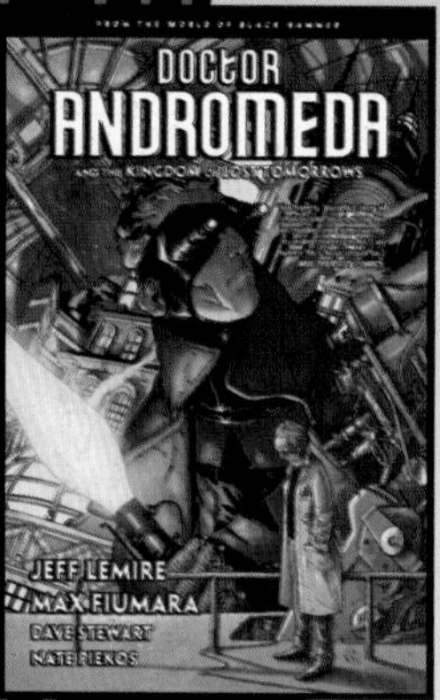
FROM THE WORLD OF BLACK HAMMER
DOCTOR
ANDROMEDA
AND THE KINGDOM OF LOST TOMORROWS
JEFF LEMIRE
MAX FIUMARA
DAVE STEWART
NATE PIEKOS

DOCTOR ANDROMEDA & THE KINGDOM OF LOST TOMORROWS
Written by Jeff Lemire • Art by Max Fiumara

This dual-narrative story set in the world of *Black Hammer* chronicles the legacy of a Golden-Age superhero wishing to reconnect with his estranged son, whom he hoped would one day take the mantle of Doctor Andromeda.
978-1-50670-659-7 • $17.99

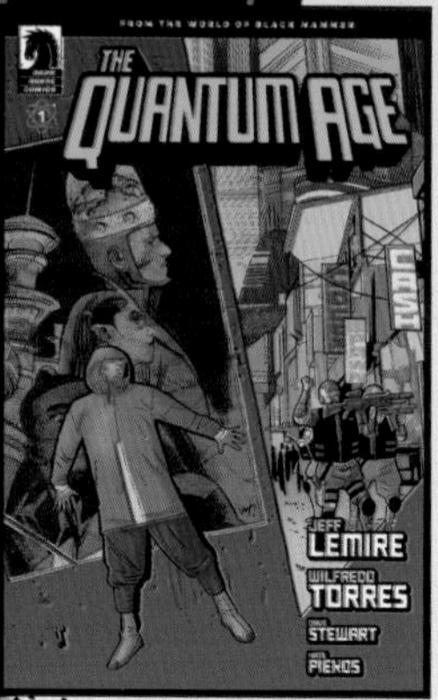
FROM THE WORLD OF BLACK HAMMER
THE
QUANTUM AGE
JEFF LEMIRE
WILFREDO TORRES
DAVE STEWART
NATE PIEKOS

THE QUANTUM AGE: FROM THE WORLD OF BLACK HAMMER
Written by Jeff Lemire • Art by Wilfredo Torres

A thousand years in the future, a collection of superheroes, inspired by the legendary heroes of Black Hammer Farm, must band together to save the planet from an authoritarian regime, while a young Martian struggles to solve the riddle of what happened to the great heroes of the twentieth century.

VOLUME 1
978-1-50670-841-6 • $19.99

BLACK HAMMER: STREETS OF SPIRAL
Jeff Lemire, Dean Ormston, Emi Lenox, and others

A Lovecraftian teen decides she will do anything to make herself "normal," a bizarre witch guides her guests through her house of horrors, and an all-star slate of guest artists illustrate a bizarre adventure with Colonial Weird on the farm. Also features a complete world guide to the *Black Hammer* universe and its characters!
978-1-50670-941-3 • $19.99

BLACK HAMMER '45: FROM THE WORLD OF BLACK HAMMER
With Jeff Lemire, Ray Fawkes, and Sharlene Kindt

During the Golden Age of superheroes, an elite Air Force crew called the Black Hammer Squadron bands together to combat the Nazis, a host of occult threats, and their ultimate aerial warrior the Ghost Hunter.
978-1-50670-850-8 • $17.99

DARK HORSE BOOKS

AVAILABLE AT YOUR LOCAL COMICS SHOP OR BOOKSTORE

TO FIND A COMICS SHOP IN YOUR AREA, VISIT COMICSHOPLOCATOR.COM. FOR MORE INFORMATION OR TO ORDER DIRECT:
On the web: darkhorse.com • E-mail: mailorder@darkhorse.com • Phone: 1-800-862-0052 Mon.–Fri. 9 a.m. to 5 p.m. Pacific Time.